P9-CCX-087

The Core Knowledge™ Series

Resource Books for Kindergarten Through Grade Six

DOUBLEDAY
New York London Toronto Sydney Auckland

THE · CORE · KNOWLEDGE · SERIES

What Your Second Grader Needs to Know

FUNDAMENTALS OF A GOOD SECOND-GRADE EDUCATION
(Revised Edition)

Edited by
E.D. HIRSCH, JR.

PUBLISHED BY DOUBLEDAY

a division of Bantam Doubleday Dell Publishing Group, Inc.

1540 Broadway, New York, New York 10036

DOUBLEDAY and the portrayal of an anchor with a dolphin are trademarks of Doubleday,
a division of Bantam Doubleday Dell Publishing Group, Inc.

BOOK DESIGN BY BONNI LEON-BERMAN

Library of Congress Cataloging-in-Publication Data

What your second grader needs to know: fundamentals of a good second-
    grade education / edited by E. D. Hirsch, Jr.
    Rev. ed.
        p.   cm. — (Core knowledge series)
    Includes bibliographical references and index.
    1. Second-grade (Education)—United States—Curricula.
2. Curriculum planning—United States.   I. Hirsch, E. D. (Eric
Donald), 1928–   .   II. Series.
LB1571 2nd.W477   1998
372.19—DC21   97-40772
                                                         CIP

ISBN: 0-385-48120-9

10 9 8 7 6 5 4 3 2 1

Editor-in-Chief of the Core Knowledge Series: E. D. Hirsch, Jr.

Editor, revised edition: John Holdren

Project Manager and Art Editor: Tricia Emlet

Writers: Diane Darst (Visual Arts); Tricia Emlet (Visual Arts); John Hirsch (Mathematics); Susan Tyler Hitchcock (Science); John Holdren (Language and Literature, History and Geography, Visual Arts, Music, Mathematics, Science); Mary Beth Klee (History and Geography); Janet Smith (Music)

Artists and Photographers: Jonathan Fuqua, Julie Grant, Steve Henry, Hannah Holdren, Sara Holdren, Phillip Jones, Bob Kirchman, Gail McIntosh, Jeanne Nicholson Siler, Nic Siler

Art and Photo Research, Art and Text Permissions: Jeanne Nicholson Siler

Research Assistant: Brandi Jordan Johnson

Computer Assistance: Barbara Fortsch

Acknowledgments

This series has depended on the help, advice, and encouragement of some two thousand people. Some of those singled out here already know the depth of our gratitude; others may be surprised to find themselves thanked publicly for help they gave quietly and freely for the sake of the enterprise alone. To helpers named and unnamed we are deeply grateful.

Advisors on Multiculturalism: Minerva Allen, Barbara Carey, Frank de Varona, Mick Fedullo, Dorothy Fields, Elizabeth Fox-Genovese, Marcia Galli, Dan Garner, Henry Louis Gates, Cheryl Kulas, Joseph C. Miller, Gerry Raining Bird, Connie Rocha, Dorothy Small, Sharon Stewart-Peregoy, Sterling Stuckey, Marlene Walking Bear, Lucille Watahomigie, Ramona Wilson

Advisors on Elementary Education: Joseph Adelson, Isobel Beck, Paul Bell, Carl Bereiter, David Bjorklund, Constance Jones, Elizabeth LaFuze, J. P. Lutz, Sandra Scarr, Nancy Stein, Phyllis Wilkin

Advisors on Technical Subject Matter: Marilyn Jager Adams, Karima-Diane Alavi, Richard Anderson, Judith Birsh, Cheryl Cannard, Barbara Foorman, Paul Gagnon, David Geary, Andrew Gleason, Ted Hirsch, Henry Holt, Blair Jones, Connie Juel, Eric Karell, Morton Keller, Joseph Kett, Charles Kimball, Mary Beth Klee, Barbara Lachman, Karen Lang, Michael Lynch, Diane McGuinness, Sheelagh McGurn, Joseph C. Miller, Jean Osborn, Vikas Pershad, Margaret Redd, Donna Rehorn, Gilbert Roy, Nancy Royal, Mark Rush, Janet Smith, Ralph Smith,

Keith Stanovich, Paula Stanovich, Nancy Strother, Nancy Summers, Marlene Thompson, James Trefil, Patricia Wattenmaker, Nancy Wayne, Christiana Whittington, Linda Williams, Lois Williams

Conferees, March 1990: Nola Bacci, Joan Baratz-Snowden, Thomasyne Beverley, Thomas Blackton, Angela Burkhalter, Monty Caldwell, Thomas M. Carroll, Laura Chapman, Carol Anne Collins, Lou Corsaro, Henry Cotton, Anne Coughlin, Arletta Dimberg, Debra P. Douglas, Patricia Edwards, Janet Elenbogen, Mick Fedullo, Michele Fomalont, Mamon Gibson, Jean Haines, Barbara Hayes, Stephen Herzog, Helen Kelley, Brenda King, John King, Elizabeth La-Fuze, Diana Lam, Nancy Lambert, Doris Langaster, Richard LaPointe, Lloyd Leverton, Madeline Long, Allen Luster, Joseph McGeehan, Janet McLin, Gloria McPhee, Marcia Mallard, William J. Maloney, Judith Matz, John Morabito, Robert Morrill, Roberta Morse, Karen Nathan, Dawn Nichols, Valeta Paige, Mary Perrin, Joseph Piazza, Jeanne Price, Marilyn Rauth, Judith Raybern, Mary Reese, Richard Rice, Wallace Saval, John Saxon, Jan Schwab, Ted Sharp, Diana Smith, Richard Smith, Trevanian Smith, Carol Stevens, Nancy Summers, Michael Terry, Robert Todd, Elois Veltman, Sharon Walker, Mary Ann Ward, Penny Williams, Charles Whiten, Clarke Worthington, Jane York

Schools: Special thanks to Three Oaks Elementary for piloting the original *Core Knowledge Sequence* in 1990. And thanks to the schools that have offered their advice and suggestions for improving the *Core Knowledge Sequence,* including (in alphabetical order): Academy Charter School (CO); Coleman Elementary (TX); Coral Reef Elementary (FL); Coronado Village Elementary (TX); Crooksville Elementary (OH); Crossroads Academy (NH); Gesher Jewish Day School (VA); Hawthorne Elementary (TX); Highland Heights Elementary (IN); Joella Good Elementary (FL); Mohegan School-CS 67 (NY); The Morse School (MA); Nichols Hills Elementary (OK); North East Elementary (MD); Ridge View Elementary (WA); R. N. Harris Elementary (NC); Southside Elementary (FL); Thomas Johnson Elementary (MD); Three Oaks Elementary (FL); Vienna Elementary (MD); Washington Core Knowledge School (CO). And to the many other schools teaching Core Knowledge—too many to name here, and some of whom we have yet to discover—our heartfelt thanks for "sharing the knowledge"!

Benefactors: The Brown Foundation, The Challenge Foundation, Mrs. E. D. Hirsch, Sr., The Walton Family Foundation.

Our grateful acknowledgment to these persons does not imply that we have taken their (sometimes conflicting) advice in every case, or that each of them endorses all aspects of this project. Responsibility for final decisions must rest with the editors alone. Suggestions for improvements are very welcome, and we wish to thank in advance those who send advice for revising and improving this series.

To Sofia,
who will enter second grade
in the year 2004.

A Note to Teachers

We hope you will find this book useful, especially those of you who are teaching in the growing network of Core Knowledge schools. Throughout the book, we have addressed the suggested activities and explanations to "Parents," since you as teachers know your students and will have ideas about how to use the content of this book in relation to the lessons and activities you plan. If you are interested in the ideas of teachers in Core Knowledge schools, please write or call the Core Knowledge Foundation (801 East High St., Charlottesville, VA 22902; 804-977-7550) for information on ordering collections of lessons created and shared by teachers in Core Knowledge schools. Many of these teacher-created lessons are available through the Core Knowledge Home Page on the Internet at the following address:

http://www.coreknowledge.org

Contents

II. History and Geography

Introduction 91

III. Visual Arts

Introduction 183

IV. Music

Introduction 205

V. Mathematics

Introduction 227

VI. Science

Introduction 295

Introduction
to the Revised Edition

This is a revision of the first edition of *What Your Second Grader Needs to Know*, first published in 1991. Almost nothing in that earlier book, which elicited wide praise and warm expressions of gratitude from teachers and parents, has become outdated. Why then revise the earlier book at all?

Because good things can be made better. In the intervening years since 1991, we at the Core Knowledge Foundation have had the benefit of a great deal of practical experience that can improve the contributions of these Core Knowledge books to early education. We have worked with and learned from an ever-growing network of Core Knowledge schools. At this writing, we can build on the experiences of hundreds of schools across the nation that are following the Core Knowledge curriculum guidelines. We have also received many suggestions from parents who are using the books. And, besides conducting our own research, we have continued to seek advice from subject-matter experts and multicultural advisors. All of these activities have enabled us to field test and refine the original *Core Knowledge Sequence*, the curriculum guidelines on which the Core Knowledge books are based.

What kind of knowledge and skills can your child be expected to learn in second grade at school? How can you help your child at home? These are questions that we try to answer in this book. It presents the sort of knowledge and skills—in literature, reading and writing, history and geography, visual arts, music, mathematics, and science— that should be at the core of a challenging second-grade education.

Because children and localities differ greatly across this big, diverse country, so do second-grade classrooms. But all communities, including classrooms, require some common ground for communication and learning. In this book we present the specific shared knowledge that hundreds of parents and teachers across the nation have agreed upon for American second graders. This core is not a comprehensive prescription for everything that every second grader needs to know. Such a complete prescription would be rigid and undesirable. But the book does offer a solid common ground that will enable young students to become active, successful learners in their classroom community and later in the larger communities we live in—town, state, nation, and world.

In this revised edition, we have retold some stories in more detail and placed a more engaging emphasis on the story in history. We have also included many color reproductions in the Visual Arts section. These improvements reflect contributions from many hands and minds. Our gratitude to all these advisors and contributors is great indeed.

A special and emphatic acknowledgment is owed to the director of the entire revision project, John Holdren of the Core Knowledge Foundation. He oversaw the research and consensus-building that led to the changes made in the underlying *Core Knowledge Sequence*. He sought and found excellent contributors to this revised edition. He devised ways to overcome what I and others had felt to be a shortcoming in the stories of the earlier edition—their too-great brevity and lack of narrative tension. He edited the contributions of our various writers, and himself wrote considerable portions of the book. For all of the improvements in this book, I owe a large debt of thanks to John Holdren. As is customary with a chief editor, however, I accept responsibility for any defects that may still be found in this book, and I invite readers to send criticisms and suggestions to the Core Knowledge Foundation.

We hope you and your child will enjoy this book, and that it will help lay the foundations upon which to build a lifetime of learning.

E. D. Hirsch, Jr.

General Introduction
to the Core Knowledge Series

I. WHAT IS YOUR CHILD LEARNING IN SCHOOL?

A parent of identical twins sent me a letter in which she expressed concern that her children, who are in the same grade in the same school, are being taught completely different things. How can this be? Because they are in different classrooms; because the teachers in these classrooms have only the vaguest guidelines to follow; in short, because the school, like many in the United States, lacks a definite, specific curriculum.

Many parents would be surprised if they were to examine the curriculum of their child's elementary school. Ask to see your school's curriculum. Does it spell out, in clear and concrete terms, a core of specific content and skills all children at a particular grade level are expected to learn by the end of the school year?

Many curricula speak in general terms of vaguely defined skills, processes, and attitudes, often in an abstract, pseudo-technical language that calls, for example, for children to "analyze patterns and data," or "investigate the structure and dynamics of living systems," or "work cooperatively in a group." Such vagueness evades the central question: what is your child learning in school? It places unreasonable demands upon teachers, and often results in years of schooling marred by repetitions and gaps. Yet another unit on dinosaurs or "pioneer days." *Charlotte's Web* for the third time. "You've never heard of the Bill of Rights?" "You've never been taught how to add two fractions with unlike denominators?"

When identical twins in two classrooms of the same school have few academic experiences in common, that is cause for concern. When teachers in that school do not know what children in other classrooms are learning on the same grade level, much less in earlier and later grades, they cannot reliably predict that children will come prepared with a shared core of knowledge and skills. For an elementary school to be successful, teachers need a common vision of what they want their students to know and be able to do. They need to have *clear, specific learning goals*, as well as the sense of mutual accountability that comes from shared commitment to helping all children achieve those goals. Lacking both specific goals and mutual accountability, too many schools exist in a state of curricular incoherence, one result of which is that they fall far short of developing the full potential of our children.

To address this problem, I started the nonprofit Core Knowledge Foundation in 1986. This book and its companion volumes in the Core Knowledge Series are designed to give parents, teachers—and through them, children—a guide to clearly defined learning goals in the form of a carefully sequenced body of knowledge based upon the specific content guidelines developed by the Core Knowledge Foundation (see below, "The Consensus Behind the *Core Knowledge Sequence*").

Core Knowledge is an attempt to define, in a coherent and sequential way, a body of widely used knowledge taken for granted by competent writers and speakers in the United States. Because this knowledge is taken for granted rather than explained when it is used, it forms a necessary foundation for the higher-order reading, writing, and thinking skills that children need for academic and vocational success. The universal attainment of such knowledge should be a central aim of curricula in our elementary schools, just as it is currently the aim in all world-class educational systems.

For reasons explained in the next section, making sure that all young children in the United States possess a core of shared knowledge is a necessary step in developing a first-rate educational system.

II. WHY CORE KNOWLEDGE IS NEEDED

Learning builds on learning: children (and adults) gain new knowledge only by building on what they already know. It is essential to begin building solid foundations of knowledge in the early grades when children are most receptive because, for the vast majority of children, academic deficiencies from the first six grades can *permanently* impair the success of later learning. Poor performance of American students in middle and high schools can be traced to shortcomings inherited from elementary schools that have not imparted to children the knowledge and skills they need for further learning.

All of the highest-achieving and most egalitarian elementary school systems in the world (such as those in Sweden, France, and Japan) teach their children a specific core of knowledge in each of the first six grades, thus enabling all children to enter each new grade with a secure foundation for further learning. It is time American schools did so as well, for the following reasons:

(1) Commonly shared knowledge makes schooling more effective.

We know that the one-on-one tutorial is the most effective form of schooling, in part because a parent or teacher can provide tailor-made instruction for the individual child. But in a nontutorial situation—in, for example, a typical classroom with twenty-five or more students—the instructor cannot effectively impart new knowledge to all the students unless each one shares the background knowledge that the lesson is being built upon.

Consider this scenario: in third grade, Ms. Franklin is about to begin a unit on early explorers: Columbus, Magellan, and others. In her class, she has some students who were in Mr. Washington's second-grade class last year and some students who were in Ms. Johnson's second-grade class. She also has a few students who moved in from other towns. As Ms. Franklin begins the unit on explorers, she asks the children to look at a globe and use their fingers to trace a route across the Atlantic Ocean from Europe to

North America. The students who had Mr. Washington look blankly at her: they didn't learn that last year. The students who had Ms. Johnson, however, eagerly point to the proper places on the globe. While two of the students who came from other towns pipe up and say, "Columbus and Magellan again? We did that last year."

When all the students in a class *do* share the relevant background knowledge, a classroom can begin to approach the effectiveness of a tutorial. Even when some children in a class do not have elements of the knowledge they were supposed to acquire in previous grades, the existence of a specifically defined core makes it possible for the teacher or parent to identify and fill the gaps, thus giving all students a chance to fulfill their potential in later grades.

(2) Commonly shared knowledge makes schooling fairer and more democratic.

When all the children who enter a grade can be assumed to share some of the same building blocks of knowledge, and when the teacher knows exactly what those building blocks are, then all the students are empowered to learn. In our current system, children from disadvantaged backgrounds too often suffer from unmerited low expectations that translate into watered-down curricula. But if we specify the core of knowledge that all children should share, then we can guarantee equal access to that knowledge and compensate for the academic advantages some students are offered at home. In a Core Knowledge school *all* children enjoy the benefits of important, challenging knowledge that will provide the foundation for successful later learning.

(3) Commonly shared knowledge helps create cooperation and solidarity in our schools and nation.

Diversity is a hallmark and strength of our nation. American classrooms are usually made up of students from a variety of cultural backgrounds, and those different cultures should be honored by all students. At the same time, education should create a *school-based* culture that is common and welcoming to all because it includes knowledge of many cultures, and gives all students, no matter what their background, a common foundation for understanding our cultural diversity.

In the next section, I will describe the steps taken by the Core Knowledge Foundation to develop a model of the commonly shared knowledge our children need (which forms the basis for this series of books).

III. THE CONSENSUS BEHIND THE Core Knowledge Sequence

The content in this and other volumes in the Core Knowledge Series is based on a document called the *Core Knowledge Sequence,* a grade-by-grade sequence of specific content guidelines in history, geography, mathematics, science, language arts, and the fine arts. The *Sequence* is not meant to outline the whole of the school curriculum;

rather, it offers specific guidelines to knowledge that can reasonably be expected to make up about *half* of any school's curriculum, thus leaving ample room for local requirements and emphases. Teaching a common core of knowledge, such as that articulated in the *Core Knowledge Sequence*, is compatible with a variety of instructional methods and additional subject matters.

The *Core Knowledge Sequence* is the result of a long process of research and consensus-building undertaken by the Core Knowledge Foundation. Here is how we achieved the consensus behind the *Core Knowledge Sequence*.

First we analyzed the many reports issued by state departments of education and by professional organizations—such as the National Council of Teachers of Mathematics and the American Association for the Advancement of Science—that recommend general outcomes for elementary and secondary education. We also tabulated the knowledge and skills through grade six specified in the successful educational systems of several other countries, including France, Japan, Sweden, and West Germany.

In addition, we formed an advisory board on multiculturalism that proposed a specific knowledge of diverse cultural traditions that American children should all share as part of their school-based common culture. We sent the resulting materials to three independent groups of teachers, scholars, and scientists around the country, asking them to create a master list of the knowledge children should have by the end of grade six. About 150 teachers (including college professors, scientists, and administrators) were involved in this initial step.

These items were amalgamated into a master plan, and further groups of teachers and specialists were asked to agree on a grade-by-grade sequence of the items. That sequence was then sent to some one hundred educators and specialists who participated in a national conference that was called to hammer out a working agreement on an appropriate core of knowledge for the first six grades.

This important meeting took place in March 1990. The conferees were elementary school teachers, curriculum specialists, scientists, science writers, officers of national organizations, representatives of ethnic groups, district superintendents, and school principals from across the country. A total of twenty-four working groups decided on revisions in the Core Knowledge Sequence. The resulting provisional *Sequence* was further fine-tuned during a year of implementation at a pioneering school, Three Oaks Elementary in Lee County, Florida.

In only a few years many more schools—urban and rural, rich and poor, public and private—joined in the effort to teach Core Knowledge. Based largely on suggestions from these schools, the *Core Knowledge Sequence* has since been revised. Revised editions of the books in the Core Knowledge Series reflect the revisions in the *Sequence*. Based on the principle of learning from experience, the Core Knowledge Foundation continues to work with schools and advisors to "fine-tune" the *Sequence*. Also, the foundation has now extended the *Sequence* to include grades 7 and 8, as well as preschool. (The *Core Knowledge Sequence* may be ordered from the Core Knowledge Foundation; see the end of this Introduction for the address.)

IV. *The Nature of This Series*

The books in this series are designed to give a convenient and engaging introduction to the knowledge specified in the *Core Knowledge Sequence*. These are resource books, addressed primarily to parents, but which we hope will be useful tools for both parents and teachers. These books are not intended to replace the local curriculum or school textbooks, but rather to serve as aids to help children gain some of the important knowledge they will need to make progress in school and to be effective in society.

Although we have made these books as accessible and useful as we can, parents and teachers should understand that they are not the only means by which the *Core Knowledge Sequence* can be imparted. The books represent a single version of the possibilities inherent in the *Sequence*, and a first step in the Core Knowledge reform effort. We hope that publishers will be stimulated to offer educational videos, computer software, games, alternative books, and other imaginative vehicles based on the *Core Knowledge Sequence*.

These books are not textbooks or workbooks, though when appropriate they do suggest a variety of activities you can do with your child. In these books, we address your child directly, and occasionally ask questions for him or her to think about. The earliest books in the series are intended to be read aloud to children. Even as children become able to read the books on their own, we encourage parents to help their children read more actively by reading along with them and talking about what they are reading.

You and your child can read the sections of this book in any order, depending on your child's interests or depending on the topics your child is studying in school, which this book may sometimes complement or reinforce. You can skip from section to section and reread as much as your child likes.

We encourage you to think of this book as a guidebook that opens the way to many paths you and your child can explore. These paths may lead to the library, to many other good books, and, if possible, to plays, museums, concerts, and other opportunities for knowledge and enrichment. In short, this guidebook recommends places to visit and describes what is important in those places, but only you and your child can make the actual visit, travel the streets, and climb the steps.

V. *What You Can Do to Help Improve American Education*

The first step for parents and teachers who are committed to reform is to be skeptical about oversimplified slogans like "critical thinking" and "learning to learn." Such slogans are everywhere, and unfortunately for our schools, their partial insights have been elevated to the level of universal truths. For example: "What students learn is not important; rather, we must teach students to learn *how* to learn." "The child, not the academic subject, is the true focus of education." "Do not impose knowledge on children before they are developmentally ready to receive it." "Do not bog children down in mere facts, but rather, teach critical-thinking skills."

Who has not heard these sentiments, so admirable and humane, and—up to a point—so true? But these positive sentiments in favor of "thinking skills" and "higher understanding" have been turned into negative sentiments against the teaching of important knowledge. Those who have entered the teaching profession over the past forty years have been taught to scorn important knowledge as "mere facts," and to see the imparting of this knowledge as somehow injurious to children. Thus it has come about that many educators, armed with partially true slogans, have seemingly taken leave of common sense.

Many parents and teachers have come to the conclusion that elementary education must strike a better balance between the development of the whole child and the more limited but fundamental duty of the school to ensure that all children master a core of knowledge and skills essential to their competence as learners in later grades. But these parents and teachers cannot act on their convictions without access to an agreed-upon, concrete sequence of knowledge. Our main motivation in developing the *Core Knowledge Sequence* and this book series has been to give parents and teachers something concrete to work with.

It has been encouraging to see how many teachers, since the first volume in this series was published, have responded to the Core Knowledge reform effort. If you would like more information about the growing network of Core Knowledge schools, please call or write the Director of School Programs at the Core Knowledge Foundation (see below for address).

Parents and teachers are urged to join in a grassroots effort to strengthen our elementary schools. The place to start is in your own school and district. Insist that your school clearly state the core of *specific* knowledge and skills that each child in a grade must learn. Whether your school's core corresponds exactly to the Core Knowledge model is less important than the existence of *some* core—which, we hope, will be as solid, coherent, and challenging as the *Core Knowledge Sequence* has proved to be. Inform members of your community about the need for such a specific curriculum, and help make sure that the people who are elected or appointed to your local school board are independent-minded people who will insist that our children have the benefit of a solid, specific, world-class curriculum in each grade.

You are invited to become a member of the Core Knowledge Network by writing the Core Knowledge Foundation, 801 East High Street, Charlottesville, VA 22902.

Share the knowledge!

E. D. Hirsch, Jr.
Charlottesville, Virginia

I.

Language and Literature

Reading, Writing, and Your Second Grader: A Note to Parents

In the Core Knowledge books for kindergarten and first grade, we described some features of an effective reading and writing program in schools. A good program, we said, is not only rich in literature but also presents varied opportunities for children to work and play with letters and sounds. An effective program presents important skills sequentially, with plenty of practice and review. It includes phonics and decoding (turning the written symbols into sounds), as well as practice in spelling, handwriting, punctuation, and grammar.

By the end of first grade, a reasonable goal is for children to become independent readers and writers. By this we don't mean that children should be able to read any book in the library or write a perfectly polished essay, but that they should be able to read books appropriate to beginning readers, and write legibly.

Nothing is more important in a child's schooling than learning to read and write by the end of first grade, or more important than extending that confident ability by the end of second grade.

Based on authoritative advice from mainstream scientific research, the Core Knowledge Foundation has compiled a description of reading and writing goals that a school should work to achieve with *all* students in second grade. Those goals are included in the *Core Knowledge Sequence,* the curriculum guidelines upon which this book is based. Parents who wish to have some benchmarks by which to gauge the adequacy and effectiveness of the reading and writing programs in their child's school should call or write the Foundation for information on ordering a copy of the *Core Knowledge Sequence.*

In addition, as parents you can do many things to help your children, such as:

- read aloud regularly and talk with your children about what they are reading
- take the children to the library
- help your children write thank-you notes and letters to relatives
- play word games like Hangman or Scrabble Junior
- check on homework
- be encouraging and supportive of your children's efforts to learn more about language

Suggested Resources for Parents and Children

The resources recommended here are meant to supplement at home the more thorough and systematic instruction that should take place in the classroom.

Ready . . . Set . . . Read: The Beginning Reader's Treasury and *Ready . . . Set . . . Read—and Laugh! A Funny Treasury for Beginning Readers*, compiled by Joanna Cole and Stephanie Calmenson (Doubleday, 1990 and 1995). Two nicely illustrated collections containing stories, poems, riddles, and word games by well-known writers like Arnold Lobel and Eve Merriam.

Spider. Colorful, attractive artwork illustrates each issue of this monthly magazine for children about six to eight years old, which features many stories, activities, and puzzles, with no advertising. Many libraries carry the magazine. For subscription information, write to The Cricket Magazine Group (315 Fifth Street, Peru, IL 61354) or call 800-827-0227.

Educators Publishing Service (EPS), 31 Smith Place, Cambridge, MA 02138-1000. This mail-order company has many good teacher-created resources, including programs on phonics, spelling, vocabulary-building, and more. Call 800-225-5750 for a catalogue.

Literature

INTRODUCTION

For your second grader, we offer a selection of poetry, stories, and myths. The poetry includes traditional rhymes as well as a few favorites by modern writers. We encourage you to read many more poems with your child, to delight in the play of language, and occasionally to encourage your child to memorize a favorite poem.

The stories presented here are mostly traditional tales that have stood the test of time. Some of the selections from other lands may not be familiar to American readers, but by including them here we hope to make them so. Parents and teachers may want to connect the folk tales we include from China, Japan, and India with the introductions to those lands in the World History section of this book. We also offer a selection of Greek myths, which you can tie in with the discussion of Ancient Greece in the World History section of this book.

The stories here are meant to complement, not replace, stories with controlled vocabularies and syntax that children may be given in school as part of their instruction in reading. While some second graders may be able to read the stories in this book on their own, those who find the language too complex can readily understand and enjoy these stories when the words are read aloud and talked about with an adult. You may also want to try some "shared reading," in which you read aloud parts of a story and your child reads aloud parts to you.

Many of these stories convey traditional values such as honesty, courage, generosity, and diligence. Those parents who hope that schooling will instill ethical values can feel somewhat reassured if their children are being taught good literature. For, next to human role models who exemplify the desired virtues, good literature is one of the best means of instilling ethical values. Plato said that stories are the most important part of early education, and advised parents and teachers to take great care in choosing the right stories: "Let them fashion the mind with such tales even more fondly than they mold the body."

We offer the stories in this book as a good starting point, and we encourage you and your child to explore further. Your local library has a treasury of good books, fiction and nonfiction. You might want to consult the lists of recommended works in such guides as:

Books That Build Character by William Kilpatrick et al. (Simon & Schuster/Touchstone, 1994)

Books to Build On: A Grade-by-Grade Resource Guide for Parents and Teachers edited by John Holdren and E. D. Hirsch, Jr. (Dell, 1996)

The New York Times Parent's Guide to the Best Books for Children by Eden Ross Lipson (Times Books, revised and updated 1991)

Poetry

Bed in Summer
by Robert Louis Stevenson

In winter I get up at night
And dress by yellow candle-light.
In summer, quite the other way,
I have to go to bed by day.

I have to go to bed and see
The birds still hopping on the tree,
Or hear the grown-up people's feet
Still going past me in the street.

And does it not seem hard to you,
When all the sky is clear and blue,
And I should like so much to play,
To have to go to bed by day?

Buffalo Dusk
by Carl Sandburg

The buffaloes are gone.
And those who saw the buffaloes are gone.
Those who saw the buffaloes by thousands and how they pawed the
   prairie sod into dust with their hoofs, their great heads down pawing
   on in a great pageant of dusk,
Those who saw the buffaloes are gone.
And the buffaloes are gone.

Caterpillars
by Aileen Fisher

What do caterpillars do?
Nothing much but chew and chew.

What do caterpillars know?
Nothing much but how to grow.

They just eat what by and by
will make them be a butterfly,

But that is more than I can do
however much I chew and chew.

Bee! I'm Expecting You!
by Emily Dickinson

Bee! I'm expecting you!
Was saying Yesterday
To Somebody you know
That you were due—

The Frogs got Home last Week—
Are settled, and at work—
Birds, mostly back—
The Clover warm and thick—

You'll get my Letter by
The seventeenth; Reply
Or better, be with me—
Yours, Fly.

Hurt No Living Thing
by Christina Rossetti

Hurt no living thing;
Ladybird, nor butterfly,
Nor moth with dusty wing,
Nor cricket chirping cheerily,
Nor grasshopper so light of leap,
Nor dancing gnat, nor beetle fat,
Nor harmless worms that creep.

Discovery
by Harry Behn

In a puddle left from last week's rain,
A friend of mine whose name is Joe
Caught a tadpole, and showed me where
Its froggy legs were beginning to grow.

Then we turned over a musty log,
With lichens on it in a row,
And found some fiddleheads of ferns
Uncoiling out of the moss below.

We hunted around, and saw the first
Jack-in-the-pulpits beginning to show,
And even discovered under a rock
Where spotted salamanders go.

I learned all this one morning from Joe,
But how much more there is to know!

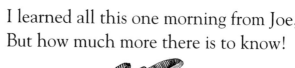

Harriet Tubman
by Eloise Greenfield

Harriet Tubman didn't take no stuff
Wasn't scared of nothing neither
Didn't come in this world to be no slave
And wasn't going to stay one either

"Farewell!" she sang to her friends one
    night
She was mighty sad to leave 'em
But she ran away that dark, hot night
Ran looking for her freedom

She ran to the woods and she ran
    through the woods
With the slave catchers right behind her
And she kept on going till she got to the North
Where those mean men couldn't find her

Nineteen times she went back South
To get three hundred others
She ran for her freedom nineteen times
To save Black sisters and brothers

Harriet Tubman didn't take no stuff
Wasn't scared of nothing neither
Didn't come in this world to be no slave
And didn't stay one either

And didn't stay one either

Lincoln
by Nancy Byrd Turner

There was a boy of other days,
A quiet, awkward, earnest lad,
Who trudged long weary miles to get
A book on which his heart was set—
And then no candle had!

He was too poor to buy a lamp
But very wise in woodmen's ways.
He gathered seasoned bough and stem,
And crisping leaf, and kindled them
Into a ruddy blaze.

Then as he lay full length and read,
The firelight flickered on his face,
And etched his shadow on the gloom,
And made a picture in the room,
In that most humble place.

The hard years came, the hard years went,
But, gentle, brave, and strong of will,
He met them all. And when today
We see his pictured face, we say,
"There's light upon it still."

The Night Before Christmas
(*Originally titled* A Visit from St. Nicholas)
by Clement C. Moore

'Twas the night before Christmas,
When all through the house
Not a creature was stirring, not even a mouse.
The stockings were hung by the chimney with care,
In hopes that St. Nicholas soon would be there.
The children were nestled all snug in their beds,
While visions of sugar plums danced in their heads.
And mama in her kerchief, and I in my cap
Had just settled our brains for a long winter's nap,
When out on the lawn there arose such a clatter,
I sprang from my bed to see what was the matter.
Away to the window I flew like a flash,
Tore open the shutters and threw up the sash.
The moon on the breast of the new fallen snow,
Gave the luster of midday to objects below.
When what to my wondering eyes should appear,
But a miniature sleigh and eight tiny reindeer
With a little old driver so lively and quick
I knew in a moment it must be St. Nick.
More rapid than eagles his coursers they came,
And he whistled, and shouted, and called them by name:
"Now, Dasher! Now, Dancer! Now, Prancer and Vixen!

On, Comet! On, Cupid! On Donder and Blitzen!
To the top of the porch! To the top of the wall!
Now dash away! Dash away! Dash away all!"
As dry leaves that before the wild hurricane fly,
When they meet with an obstacle, mount to the sky,
So up to the housetop the coursers they flew,
With a sleigh full of toys and St. Nicholas, too.
And then, in a twinkling, I heard on the roof
The prancing and pawing of each little hoof.
As I drew in my head and was turning around . . .
Down the chimney St. Nicholas came with a bound!
He was dressed all in fur from his head to his foot,
And his clothes were all tarnished with ashes and soot;
A bundle of toys he had flung on his back,
And he looked like a peddler just opening his pack.
His eyes—how they twinkled, his dimples how merry!
His cheeks were like roses, his nose like a cherry!
His droll little mouth was drawn up in a bow,
And the beard on his chin was as white as the snow.
The stump of a pipe he held tight in his teeth,
And the smoke it encircled his head like a wreath.
He had a broad face and a little round belly,
That shook when he laughed like a bowl full of jelly.
He was chubby and plump, a right jolly old elf,
And I laughed when I saw him in spite of myself!
A wink of his eye and a twist of his head
Soon gave me to know I had nothing to dread.
He spoke not a word, but went straight to his work,
And filled all the stockings—then turned with a jerk . . .
And laying his finger aside of his nose,
And giving a nod, up the chimney he rose!

He sprang to his sleigh, to his team gave a whistle,
And away they all flew like the down of a thistle.
But I heard him exclaim, 'ere he drove out of sight . . .
"Happy Christmas to all, and to all a good night!"

Seashell

by Federico García Lorca; translated by K. F. Pearson

They've brought me a seashell.

Inside it sings
a map of the sea.
My heart
fills up with water,
with smallish fish
of shade and silver.

They've brought me a seashell.

Something Told the Wild Geese
by Rachel Field

Something told the wild geese
It was time to go.
Though the fields lay golden
Something whispered,—"Snow."
Leaves were green and stirring,
Berries, luster-glossed,
But beneath warm feathers
Something cautioned,—"Frost."
All the sagging orchards
Steamed with amber spice,
But each wild breast stiffened
At remembered ice.
Something told the wild geese
It was time to fly,—
Summer sun was on their wings,
Winter in their cry.

Rudolph Is Tired of the City
by Gwendolyn Brooks

These buildings are too close to me.
I'd like to PUSH away.
I'd like to live in the country,
And spread my arms all day.

I'd like to spread my breath out, too—
As farmers' sons and daughters do.

I'd tend the cows and chickens.
I'd do the other chores.
Then, all the hours left I'd go
A-SPREADING out-of-doors.

Smart
by Shel Silverstein

My dad gave me one dollar bill
'Cause I'm his smartest son,
And I swapped it for two shiny quarters
'Cause two is more than one!

And then I took the quarters
And traded them to Lou
For three dimes—I guess he don't know
That three is more than two!

Just then, along came old blind Bates
And just 'cause he can't see
He gave me four nickels for my three dimes,
And four is more than three!

And I took the nickels to Hiram Coombs
Down at the seed-feed store,
And the fool gave me five pennies for them,
And five is more than four!

And then I went and showed my dad,
And he got red in the cheeks
And closed his eyes and shook his head—
Too proud of me to speak!

Who Has Seen the Wind?
by Christina Rossetti

Who has seen the wind?
Neither I nor you:
But when the leaves hang trembling,
The wind is passing through.

Who has seen the wind?
Neither you nor I:
But when the leaves bow down their heads,
The wind is passing by.

Windy Nights
by Robert Louis Stevenson

Whenever the moon and stars are set,
Whenever the wind is high,
All night long in the dark and wet,
A man goes riding by.
Late in the night when the fires are out,
Why does he gallop and gallop about?

Whenever the trees are crying aloud,
And ships are tossed at sea,
By, on the highway, low and loud,
By at the gallop goes he;
By at the gallop he goes, and then
By he comes back at the gallop again.

There Was an Old Man with a Beard
by Edward Lear

Edward Lear, an English artist and writer, was a master of the kind of humorous poem called a limerick. A limerick has five lines: the first two lines rhyme, then the next two lines rhyme, and the last line rhymes with the first two lines. The first line of a limerick often begins "There was a . . ." or "There once was a . . ." Limericks are fun to read aloud, and fun to make up: try it!

There was an Old Man with a beard,
Who said, "It is just as I feared!—
Two Owls and a Hen,
Four Larks and a Wren,
Have all built their nests in
      my beard!"

There Is a Young Lady, Whose Nose
by Edward Lear

There is a young lady, whose nose,
Continually prospers and grows;
When it grew out of sight,
She exclaimed in a fright,
"Oh! farewell to the end of my nose!"

Stories

The Blind Men and the Elephant

There were once six blind men who went to see an elephant. The first blind man stretched his hands in front of him and felt the animal's huge side. "This elephant is like a high, strong wall," he announced.

The second man, who was standing near the elephant's head, put his hand on its long, sharp tusk. "A wall? No! I would say that it is more like a spear."

The third man reached around the elephant's leg with both arms. "I hate to contradict you," he said, "but I am sure that the elephant is very like a tree."

The fourth man happened to reach up and touch the elephant's ear. "All of you are mistaken," he said. "The elephant is actually similar to a fan."

The fifth man was standing by himself at the elephant's other end. He happened to grab the animal's tail. "I don't understand the confusion," he said. "I am sure I am correct in saying that the elephant is much like a rope."

Now the elephant was a bit playful, so he tickled the sixth man with his trunk. The startled man pushed the trunk away and said with a shudder, "Please stay calm while I swear to you that the elephant is really a very large snake!"

"Nonsense!" said the others. Still, they quietly began to move away, and they never bothered to put their heads together to understand what the elephant was really like.

The Fisherman and His Wife
(A tale from the Brothers Grimm)

There was once a fisherman who lived with his wife in a little old run-down hut by the sea. Every day he went down to the sea to fish. One day, as he sat looking into the clear, shining water, he felt a strong tug on his line. He pulled and pulled with all his might, and out flopped a great big fish.

The fish spoke. "Please let me go," said the fish. "I am not an ordinary fish but an enchanted prince. Put me back in the water and let me live."

"Swim away!" said the fisherman. "I would not eat a fish that can talk!"

Then the fisherman went back to his wife in the little old run-down hut. He told her about the fish that could talk. She said, "You foolish man, that was a magic fish! Go back and ask him to change this hut into a pretty cottage."

The fisherman did not want to go, but his wife demanded it. So he walked slowly back to the sea. The water was no longer clear and shining but dull and green. The fisherman called:

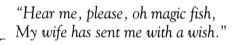

*"Hear me, please, oh magic fish,
My wife has sent me with a wish."*

The fish swam up and asked, "What do you want?"

"My wife wishes to live in a pretty cottage," said the fisherman.

"Go home," said the fish. "She has her cottage."

The fisherman went home. Sure enough, there was his wife standing in the yard of a pretty cottage.

"Now you shall be happy!" said the fisherman.

And she was—for about a week. Then the wife said, "Husband, I am tired of this tiny little cottage. I want to live in a big stone castle. Go ask the fish to give us a castle."

The fisherman walked slowly to the sea. The water had turned from dull green to dark purple and gray. The fisherman called:

*"Hear me, please, oh magic fish,
My wife has sent me with a wish."*

The fish swam up. The fisherman said, "My wife wishes to live in a big stone castle."

"Go home," said the fish. "You will find her in a castle."

When the fisherman got back, he could hardly believe his eyes. There stood a big stone castle. Inside, he saw servants, and golden chairs, and tables heaped with delicious foods.

"Now, indeed, you will be happy," said the fisherman to his wife.

And she was—until the next morning.

As the sun rose, the fisherman's wife poked him and said, "Husband, get up. Go to the fish at once and tell him that I wish to be queen of all the land."

"Alas!" cried the fisherman. "The fish cannot do that!"

"Go and ask him," said his wife.

So the sad fisherman walked to the sea. The water was black and the waves roared and crashed. The fisherman called:

> *"Hear me, please, oh magic fish,*
> *My wife has sent me with a wish."*

The fish swam up and asked, "Now what does she want?"

With his head hung low, the fisherman said, "My wife wishes to be queen of all the land."

"Go home," said the fish. "She is already queen."

The fisherman hurried home and found his wife sitting on a high throne of gold and diamonds. She wore a long silk dress and a golden crown. Servants and ladies hurried here and there to do whatever she wished.

"Now," said the fisherman, "you must be truly happy."

And she was—until that evening. As the moon began to rise in the sky, the wife said, "Husband, I order you to go to the fish and tell him to give me the power to make the sun and the moon rise and set whenever I choose."

The fisherman walked back to the sea. Thunder roared and lightning flashed. Huge dark waves crashed around him. The fisherman had to shout,

> *"Hear me, please, oh magic fish,*
> *My wife has sent me with a wish."*

The fish swam up and asked, "What does she want?"

The fisherman replied, "My wife wants the power to make the sun and the moon rise and set whenever she chooses."

The fish only said, "Go home."

And so he did. And there he found his wife sitting in the little old run-down hut. And there they live, to this very day.

Talk
(Retold by Harold Courlander and George Herzog)

"Talk" is a folk tale from the Ashanti people (also called Asante), who live in West Africa, in what is now the country of Ghana. Many Ashanti are farmers, and their major crops include cacao (a main ingredient in chocolate) and, as you'll see in the story, yams. To better appreciate a detail near the end of this story, it may help to know about an Ashanti tradition: almost every Ashanti man and woman once owned a carved wooden stool. Besides being useful, the stool, according to tradition, embodied the owner's spirit.

Once, not far from the city of Accra on the Gulf of Guinea, a country man went out to his garden to dig up some yams to take to market. While he was digging, one of the yams said to him:

"Well, at last you're here. You never weeded me, but now you come around with your digging stick. Go away and leave me alone!"

The farmer turned around and looked at his cow in amazement. The cow was chewing her cud and looking at him.

"Did you say something?" he asked.

The cow kept on chewing and said nothing, but the man's dog spoke up.

"It wasn't the cow who spoke to you," the dog said. "It was the yam. The yam says leave him alone."

The man became angry because his dog had never talked before, and he didn't like his tone besides. So he took his knife and cut a branch from a palm tree to whip his dog. Just then the palm tree said:

"Put that branch down!"

The man was getting very upset about the way things were going, and he started to throw the palm branch away, but the palm branch said:

"Man, put me down softly!"

He put the branch down gently on a stone, and the stone said:

"Hey, take that thing off me!"

This was enough and the frightened farmer started to run for his village. On the way he met a fisherman going the other way with a fish trap on his head.

"What's the hurry?" the fisherman asked.

"My yam said, 'Leave me alone!' Then the dog said, 'Listen to what the yam says!' When I went to whip the dog with a palm branch the tree said, 'Put that branch down!' Then the palm branch said, 'Do it softly!' Then the stone said, 'Take that thing off me!' "

"Is that all?" the man with the fish trap asked. "Is that so frightening?"

"Well," the man's fish trap said, "did he take it off the stone?"

"Wah!" the fisherman shouted. He threw the fish trap on the ground and began to run with the farmer, and on the trail they met a weaver with a bundle of cloth on his head.

"Where are you going in such a rush?" he asked them.

"My yam said 'Leave me alone!' " the farmer said. "The dog said, 'Listen to what the yam says!' The tree said, 'Put that branch down!' The branch said, 'Do it softly!' And the stone said, 'Take that thing off me!' "

"And then," the fisherman continued, "the fish trap said, 'Did he take it off?' "

"That's nothing to get excited about," the weaver said, "no reason at all."

"Oh yes it is," his bundle of cloth said. "If it happened to you, you'd run too!"

"Wah!" the weaver shouted. He threw his bundle on the trail and started running with the other men.

They came panting to the ford in the river and found a man bathing.

"Are you chasing a gazelle?" he asked them.

The first man said breathlessly:

"My yam talked at me and it said, 'Leave me alone!' And my dog said, 'Listen to your yam!' And when I cut myself a branch the tree said, 'Put that branch down!' And the branch said, 'Do it softly!' And the stone said, 'Take that thing off me!' "

The fisherman panted, "And my trap said, 'Did he?' "

The weaver wheezed, "My cloth spoke too!"

"Is that why you're running?" the man in the river asked.

"Well, wouldn't you run if you were in their position?" the river said.

The man jumped out of the water and began to run with the others. They ran down the main street of the village to the house of the chief. The chief's servants brought his stool out, and he came and sat on it to listen to their complaints. The men began to recite their troubles.

"I went out to my garden to dig yams," the farmer said, waving his arms. "Then everything began to talk! My yam said, 'Leave me alone!' My dog said, 'Pay attention to your yam!' The tree said, 'Put that branch down!' The branch said, 'Do it softly!' And the stone said, 'Take it off me!' "

"And my fish trap said, 'Well, did he take it off?' " the fisherman said.

"And my cloth said, 'You'd run too!' " the weaver said.

"And the river said the same," the bather said hoarsely.

The chief listened to them patiently, but he couldn't refrain from scowling.

"Now this is really a wild story," he said at last. "You'd better all go back to your work before I punish you for disturbing the peace."

So the men went away, and the chief shook his head and mumbled to himself, "Nonsense like that upsets the community."

"Fantastic, isn't it?" his stool said. "Imagine, a talking yam!"

The Emperor's New Clothes
(Based on the story by Hans Christian Andersen)

There was once an emperor who loved fine clothes. He had a different coat for every hour of the day. He loved to walk about and show off his fancy outfits.

One day two strangers arrived in town. They were thieves but they said they were weavers. They told the emperor they could weave the most beautiful cloth in the world. They told him it was a magic cloth, because only smart and able people could see it.

The emperor gave them a lot of money and told them to begin weaving the magic cloth right away. Day and night the two men pretended to be weaving. But they had nothing at all on their looms.

The emperor grew curious to see the cloth. But then he remembered that only smart and able people could see it. What if he could not see it? Just to be safe, he sent his chief advisor instead.

The advisor found the two men hard at work. "Do you like the cloth?" they asked. "Isn't it beautiful?" The advisor did not dare to admit that he could not see any cloth. That would mean he was stupid! So he pretended to see the cloth. He said it was very fine and lovely.

Now the emperor went to look for himself. After all, if his advisor had seen the cloth, surely he could see it, too. But the emperor saw nothing on the looms. "This is terrible!" he thought. "Am I stupid?" But out loud he said, "It is magnificent!" He told the weavers to make him a new suit out of the cloth as soon as possible.

For days, the dishonest weavers pretended to cut and sew their invisible cloth. All those who saw them pretended to admire their work, for they did not wish to appear stupid.

At last the day came for the emperor to wear his new clothes in public. In his dressing room, the emperor took off his clothes, and the weavers pretended to help him put on the make-believe clothes. The emperor looked at himself in the mirror.

"How handsome you look, your majesty!" said the tricky weavers.

The emperor stepped out of the palace, followed by many advisors and servants. The streets were lined with great crowds. Everyone said, "The emperor's new clothes are lovely! How well they fit!" No one would admit he could see nothing, for no one wanted to appear stupid.

But then a little child cried out, "He hasn't got anything on!"

A hush fell over the crowd. Then everyone began to whisper, "The child is right. The emperor isn't wearing a thing!" Then people began to giggle and laugh as they cried out, "He hasn't got anything on!"

At last the emperor knew he had been tricked. He tried to march back into the palace as proudly as ever. But he was blushing from head to toe, as everyone could plainly see.

How Iktomi Lost His Eyes
(A story from the Assiniboine tribe)

Iktomi was walking through the woods one afternoon when he heard a strange noise: a bird was singing in his language, Assiniboine! Each time the bird sang the song, its eyes flew from its head and perched in the top of a tall tree, and when it sang another song, its eyes fluttered back again.

Iktomi wanted to learn this trick because he thought everyone would admire his power so much that he could be a great chief someday. He asked, "Little brother, would you please show me how to do that?"

After the bird taught Iktomi how to do the trick, he warned him, "You must use this trick no more than four times."

Iktomi tried it once to make sure it worked. Sure enough, his eyes flew up to the treetop and then fluttered down again. He was so excited that he tried it a second time and a third time. And when he ran into Brother Gopher, he did it again, just to show off. Gopher was very impressed. But Iktomi forgot that he had now used the trick four times.

When he returned to camp, he gathered everyone around to watch his powerful trick. Iktomi sang the bird's song, and up flew his eyes to a treetop. Iktomi was very proud, and the people gasped. He sang again, and waited for the people to praise him. But his eyes refused to come back. Iktomi pleaded with his eyes, and the people began to laugh.

Iktomi was frightened because he had not listened to the bird's warning, and he stumbled from the camp to find the bird. He couldn't see a thing! Suddenly, he heard a little field mouse ask, "Why are you crying?" When Iktomi explained, the little field mouse felt sorry for him. "Take one of my eyes," he said, "And then you won't be afraid." Iktomi thanked the little mouse, and set out again.

Soon, he ran into a buffalo calf. "Why are you blinded in one eye?" the calf asked. When Iktomi told him, the calf said, "Take one of my eyes, and then you can find the bird." And Iktomi took one of the calf's eyes and thanked it.

Blessed with the kindness and the sight of the animals, it wasn't long before Iktomi found the bird. "Please help me," he said. "I will never again be so vain or try to be more powerful than anyone else." With this promise, the bird taught him a new song, and when Iktomi sang it, his eyes flew down from the tree and returned to his head. Happy, Iktomi set out to give the animals their own eyes back.

Check your library for funny Iktomi stories by Paul Goble, including *Iktomi and the Berries, Iktomi and the Boulder,* and *Iktomi and the Buffalo Skull* (Orchard Books).

The Magic Paintbrush
(A folk tale from China)

Once upon a time, long ago in the land of China, there lived a poor orphan named Ma Liang. He had no one to care for him or protect him. So, to make a living, he gathered bundles of firewood to sell. But what he really wanted to do, more than anything else in the world, was paint. Ma Liang was so poor, however, that he could not buy even a single paintbrush.

One day, as Ma Liang passed by the village school, he saw the children busily painting pictures. "Please, sir," said Ma Liang to the teacher, "I would like to paint, but I have no brush. Will you loan me one?"

"What!" cried the teacher. "You are only a little beggar boy. Go away!"

"I may be poor," said Ma Liang, "but I *will* learn to paint!"

The next time he went to gather firewood, Ma Liang used a twig to draw birds on the ground. When he came to a stream, he dipped his hand in the water and used his wet finger to draw a fish on the rocks. That night, he used a piece of burned wood to draw animals and flowers.

Every day Ma Liang found time to make more pictures. People began to notice. "How lifelike the boy's pictures look!" they said. "That bird he has drawn looks as though it's ready to fly away. You can almost hear it sing!"

Ma Liang enjoyed hearing the people's praise, but still he thought, "If only I had a paintbrush!"

One night, after Ma Liang had worked hard all day, he fell into a deep sleep. In a dream, he saw an old man with a long white beard and a kind face. The old man held something in his hand. "Take this," he said to Ma Liang. "It is a magic paintbrush. Use it with care."

When Ma Liang awoke, he found his fingers wrapped around a paintbrush. "Am I still dreaming?" he wondered. Quickly he got up and painted a bird. The picture flapped its wings and flew away!

He painted a deer. As soon as he had put the last spot on the animal's coat, it brushed its nose against Ma Liang then ran into the woods.

"It *is* a magic brush!" said Ma Liang. He ran to where his poor friends lived. He painted toys for the children. He painted cows and tools for the farmers. He painted bowls full of food for the hungry.

No good thing can remain a secret forever. Soon, news of Ma Liang and the magic paintbrush reached the ears of the greedy emperor.

"Bring me that boy and his brush!" the emperor commanded. His soldiers found Ma Liang and brought him back to the palace.

With a scowl, the emperor looked at Ma Liang. "Paint me a dragon!" he yelled. Ma Liang began to paint. But instead of painting a lucky dragon, he painted a slimy toad that hopped right on the emperor's head!

"Stupid boy!" said the emperor. "You will regret that!" He grabbed the magic paintbrush and ordered his soldiers to throw Ma Liang in jail.

Then the emperor called for his royal painter. "Take this brush and paint me a mountain of gold," he commanded. But when the royal painter finished the picture, all the gold turned into rocks.

"So," said the emperor, "this brush will only work for the boy. Bring him to me!"

Ma Liang was brought to the emperor. "If you will paint for me," said the emperor, "I will give you gold and silver, fine clothes, a new house, and all the food and drink you want."

Ma Liang pretended to agree. "What do you want me to paint?" he asked.

"Paint me a tree that has gold coins for leaves!" said the emperor with greed in his eyes.

Ma Liang took the magic paintbrush and began to paint. He painted many blue waves, and soon the emperor saw an ocean before him.

"That is not what I told you to paint!" he barked.

But Ma Liang just kept painting. In the ocean he painted an island. And on that island he painted a tree with gold coins for leaves.

"Yes, yes, that's more like it," said the emperor. "Now, quickly, paint me a boat so that I can get to the island."

Ma Liang painted a big sailboat. The emperor went on board with many of his highest officials. Ma Liang painted a few lines and a gentle breeze began to blow. The sailboat moved slowly toward the island.

"Faster! Faster!" shouted the emperor. Ma Liang painted a big curving stroke, and a strong wind began to blow. "That's enough wind!" shouted the emperor. But Ma Liang kept painting. He painted a storm, and the waves got higher and higher, tossing the sailboat like a little cork on the water. Then the waves broke the boat to pieces. The emperor and his officials were washed up on the shore of the island, with no way to get back to the palace.

And as for Ma Liang, people say that for many years, he went from village to village, using his magic paintbrush to help the poor wherever he went.

A Christmas Carol
(Based on the story by Charles Dickens)

Once there was a tight-fisted, grasping, greedy man named Ebenezer Scrooge. On a cold, bleak, biting Christmas eve, old Scrooge sat in his office. His poor clerk, Bob Cratchit, shivered in the next room, for Scrooge gave him only one coal for his fire.

Scrooge frowned at Bob Cratchit and growled, "I suppose you'll be wanting the whole day off tomorrow."

"Yes sir," the clerk replied meekly. "If it's convenient."

"It's not convenient," said Scrooge. "Be here even earlier the next morning!"

"Thank you sir," said Bob Cratchit. "And a merry Christmas to you, sir."

"Christmas! Bah, humbug!" grumbled Scrooge as he left the office. Through the frost and fog, he made his way home. As he approached his front door, he stopped and stared. Where he expected to see the door knocker, he saw a face! It was the face of his old business partner, Jacob Marley. But Marley had been dead now for seven years. Scrooge blinked his eyes, and the face vanished.

"Bah, humbug!" said Scrooge as he walked in. He changed into his robe and slippers. He was about to fix his dinner when he heard a noise. It sounded like someone dragging heavy chains over the floor. Then, right through the closed door walked the ghost of Jacob Marley. Around his waist was wrapped a large chain.

"Hear me!" said the ghost. "I wear the chain I forged in life. I cared only about money. And you are making your own chain now, Ebenezer. You care too much for money, and too little for your fellow man. You must change, before it is too late! There is still a chance for you to escape my fate. You will be visited by three spirits." Then, with a fearful groan, the ghost vanished.

When the clock struck one, a pale hand drew back the curtain that hung around Scrooge's bed. It was the first spirit. It looked like a child but at the same time like an old man. "I am the Ghost of Christmas Past," said the spirit. Then the spirit took Scrooge's hand. Suddenly Scrooge found himself in an old school room. All the children were gone home for the holidays—all but one. One neglected child sat at his desk. "Why, that's me," said Scrooge. And he sobbed as he recalled his sad, lonely childhood.

Scrooge had a dim sense of being back in his bed again. He heard the clock striking and saw a bright light. He got out of bed and saw a large, bearded man wearing a loose robe and a crown of holly. This jolly giant was seated on a great heap of roast turkeys, pies, apples, oranges, cakes, and puddings.

"Come in and know me better, man!" laughed the spirit. "I am the Ghost of Christmas Present. Touch my robe!"

When Scrooge touched the robe, he found himself moving through the busy city streets on a Christmas morning. He saw smiling faces and heard people wishing each other a merry Christmas. As the spirit took him from house to house, they could see people making their Christmas dinners. Then they came to the home of Bob Cratchit. The family was sitting down to a meager dinner, but they seemed as happy as if they had a great feast before them. The happiest of all was the youngest child, a small, frail boy called Tiny Tim, who walked with a crutch.

Scrooge saw Bob Cratchit lift his glass and say, "A merry Christmas to us all, my dears!"

"And God bless us, every one," said Tiny Tim. Scrooge saw how Bob held his little son close by his side, as if he feared he might lose him.

"Spirit," said Scrooge, "tell me if Tiny Tim will live."

"I see an empty seat," said the spirit, "and a crutch without an owner. If things remain as they are, the child will die."

"Oh, no, kind Spirit!" said Scrooge. "Say he will be spared."

But the Ghost of Christmas Present was disappearing before Scrooge's eyes. And in his place, Scrooge saw a dark, hooded phantom. "Am I in the presence of the Ghost of Christmas Yet to Come?" asked Scrooge.

The spirit did not answer but pointed onward with its hand. Scrooge found himself in a dark house. On the bed, beneath a sheet, lay something cold, still, and lifeless. Scrooge heard people talking outside.

"When did he die?" asked a man.

"Last night," said another.

"It's likely to be a very cheap funeral," said a third, and they all laughed.

The silent spirit spread its dark robe like a wing, and suddenly Scrooge was at Bob Cratchit's house. It was quiet. Very quiet. The noisy Cratchit children now sat still as statues in a corner. Near the wall a crutch leaned against an empty chair. Then Scrooge heard Bob Cratchit's voice. "I am sure that we shall never forget poor Tiny Tim," he said. "Oh, my little, little child!"

Again the spirit waved its dark robe, and now Scrooge found himself in a graveyard choked with weeds. The spirit stood among the graves and pointed to one.

Scrooge crept toward the grave. And there he read upon the stone his own name, EBENEZER SCROOGE.

"No, Spirit!" cried Scrooge. He clutched at the spirit's robe. "I am not the man I was. Please tell me I may yet change what you have shown me." The spirit began to pull away but Scrooge held on tight. "Good Spirit," he cried, "I will honor Christmas in my heart, and try to keep it all the year!"

Scrooge tried to grasp the spirit's hand, but suddenly the phantom was gone. Scrooge found himself sitting in his own bed with his arms around the bedpost.

Yes, the bed was his own, and the room was his own. Best of all, his life was still his own, and there was still time to make himself a better man. Scrooge ran to the window and called to a boy passing in the street, "What's today, my fine fellow?"

"It's Christmas day, of course!" said the boy.

"I haven't missed it!" said Scrooge. Then he said to the boy, "Do you know that big prize turkey they're selling in the store in the next street?"

"You mean the one as big as me?" said the boy.

"A remarkable boy!" cried Scrooge. "Yes, that's the one. Run to the store and tell them to take it to Bob Cratchit's house. If you're back in half an hour, I'll give you a nice reward."

Scrooge dressed quickly and hurried into the street. "Merry Christmas!" he cried to everyone he met. He patted children on the head, and found that everything gave him happiness.

The next morning, Scrooge arrived early at his office, before Bob Cratchit. When Bob entered, Scrooge tried very hard to put on his old voice and growled, "Well, what do you mean by coming in eighteen and a half minutes late?"

"I am very sorry, sir," said Bob Cratchit.

"I am not going to stand for that sort of thing any longer!" barked Scrooge. "And therefore," he said, as he leaped down from his stool, "I am going to raise your salary! A merry Christmas to you, Bob Cratchit!"

From then on, Scrooge helped Bob Cratchit's family, and he shared his wealth with other people in need. To Tiny Tim, who did *not* die, Scrooge became like a second father. He became as good a friend, as good a master, and as good a man as the good old city knew. And it was always said of him, that he knew how to keep Christmas well. May that be truly said of all of us. And, as Tiny Tim observed, "God bless us, every one!"

"Before Breakfast" (from *Charlotte's Web*)
by E. B. White

PARENTS: *Here we present the first chapter of a book that has become a beloved classic even in the short time since it was published in 1952.* Charlotte's Web *tells the story of a young girl named Fern, her pig, Wilbur, and Wilbur's dear friend, the wise spider named Charlotte. We hope you'll take this first chapter as an invitation to read aloud the whole book with your child. (The pictures here are by Garth Williams, from the original edition.)*

"Where's Papa going with that ax?" said Fern to her mother as they were setting the table for breakfast.

"Out to the hoghouse," replied Mrs. Arable. "Some pigs were born last night."

"I don't see why he needs an ax," continued Fern, who was only eight.

"Well," said her mother, "one of the pigs is a runt. It's very small and weak, and it will never amount to anything. So your father has decided to do away with it."

"Do *away* with it?" shrieked Fern. "You mean *kill* it? Just because it's smaller than the others?"

Mrs. Arable put a pitcher of cream on the table. "Don't yell, Fern!" she said. "Your father is right. The pig would probably die anyway."

Fern pushed a chair out of the way and ran outdoors. The grass was wet and the earth smelled of springtime. Fern's sneakers were sopping by the time she caught up with her father.

"Please don't kill it!" she sobbed. "It's unfair."

Mr. Arable stopped walking.

"Fern," he said gently, "you will have to learn to control yourself."

"Control myself?" yelled Fern. "This is a matter of life and death, and you talk about *controlling* myself." Tears ran down her cheeks and she took hold of the ax and tried to pull it out of her father's hand.

"Fern," said Mr. Arable, "I know more about raising a litter of pigs than you do. A weakling makes trouble. Now run along!"

"But it's unfair," cried Fern. "The pig couldn't help being born small, could it? If *I* had been very small at birth, would you have killed *me?*"

Mr. Arable smiled. "Certainly not," he said, looking down at his daughter with love. "But this is different. A little girl is one thing, a little runty pig is another."

"I see no difference," replied Fern, still hanging on to the ax. "This is the most terrible case of injustice I ever heard of."

A queer look came over John Arable's face. He seemed almost ready to cry himself.

"All right," he said. "You go back to the house and I will bring the runt when I come in. I'll let you start it on a bottle, like a baby. Then you'll see what trouble a pig can be."

When Mr. Arable returned to the house half an hour later, he carried a carton under his arm. Fern was upstairs changing her sneakers. The kitchen table was set for breakfast, and the room smelled of coffee, bacon, damp plaster, and wood smoke from the stove.

"Put it on her chair!" said Mrs. Arable. Mr. Arable set the carton down at Fern's place. Then he walked to the sink and washed his hands and dried them on the roller towel.

Fern came slowly down the stairs. Her eyes were red from crying. As she approached her chair, the carton wobbled, and there was a scratching noise. Fern looked at her father. Then she lifted the lid of the carton. There, inside, looking up at her, was the newborn pig. It was a white one. The morning light shone through its ears, turning them pink.

"He's yours," said Mr. Arable. "Saved from an untimely death. And may the good Lord forgive me for this foolishness."

Fern couldn't take her eyes off the tiny pig. "Oh," she whispered. "Oh, *look* at him! He's absolutely perfect."

She closed the carton carefully. First she kissed her father, then she kissed her mother. Then she opened the lid again, lifted the pig out, and held it against her cheek. At this moment her brother Avery came into the room. Avery was ten. He was heavily armed—an air rifle in one hand, a wooden dagger in the other.

"What's that?" he demanded. "What's Fern got?"

"She's got a guest for breakfast," said Mrs. Arable. "Wash your hands and face, Avery!"

"Let's see it!" said Avery, setting his gun down. "You call that miserable thing a pig? That's a *fine* specimen of a pig—it's no bigger than a white rat."

"Wash up and eat your breakfast, Avery!" said his mother. "The school bus will be along in half an hour."

"Can I have a pig, too, Pop?" asked Avery.

"No, I only distribute pigs to early risers," said Mr. Arable. "Fern was up at daylight, trying to rid the world of injustice. As a result, she now has a pig. A small one, to be sure, but nevertheless a pig. It just shows what can happen if a person gets out of bed promptly. Let's eat!"

But Fern couldn't eat until her pig had had a drink of milk. Mrs. Arable found a baby's nursing bottle and a rubber nipple. She poured warm milk into the bottle, fitted the nipple over the top, and handed it to Fern. "Give him his breakfast!" she said.

A minute later, Fern was seated on the floor in the corner of the kitchen with her infant between her knees, teaching it to suck from the bottle. The pig, although tiny, had a good appetite and caught on quickly.

The school bus honked from the road.

"Run!" commanded Mrs. Arable, taking the pig from Fern and slipping a doughnut into her hand. Avery grabbed his gun and another doughnut.

The children ran out to the road and climbed into the bus. Fern took no notice of the others in the bus. She just sat and stared out of the window, thinking what a blissful world it was and how lucky she was to have entire charge of a pig. By the time the bus reached school, Fern had named her pet, selecting the most beautiful name she could think of.

"Its name is Wilbur," she whispered to herself.

She was still thinking about the pig when the teacher said: "Fern, what is the capital of Pennsylvania?"

"Wilbur," replied Fern, dreamily. The pupils giggled. Fern blushed.

How the Camel Got His Hump
by Rudyard Kipling

PARENTS: *Like all of Kipling's humorous* Just So Stories, *this tale comes alive when read aloud.*

In the beginning of years, when the world was so new and all, and the Animals were just beginning to work for Man, there was a Camel, and he lived in the middle of a Howling Desert because he did not want to work; and besides, he was a Howler himself. So he ate sticks and thorns and tamarisks and milkweed and prickles, most 'scruciating idle; and when anybody spoke to him he said "Humph!" Just "Humph!" and no more.

Presently the Horse came to him on Monday morning, with a saddle on his back and a bit in his mouth, and said, "Camel, O Camel, come out and trot like the rest of us."

"Humph!" said the Camel and the Horse went away and told the Man.

Presently the Dog came to him, with a stick in his mouth, and said, "Camel, O Camel, come and fetch and carry like the rest of us."

"Humph!" said the Camel; and the Dog went away and told the Man.

Presently the Ox came to him with the yoke on his neck and said, "Camel, O Camel, come and plow like the rest of us."

"Humph!" said the Camel; and the Ox went away and told the Man.

At the end of the day the Man called the Horse and the Dog and the Ox together, and said "Three, O Three, I'm very sorry for you (with the world so new-and-all); but that Humph-thing in the Desert can't work, or he would be here by now, so I am going to leave him alone, and you must work double-time to make up for it."

That made the Three very angry (with the world so new-and-all), and they held a palaver and an *indaba,* and a *punchayet,* and a powwow on the edge of the Desert; and the Camel came chewing milkweed *most* 'scruciating idle, and laughed at them. Then he said "Humph!" and went away again.

Presently there came along the Djinn* [jin] in charge of All Deserts, rolling in a cloud of dust (Djinns always travel that way because it is Magic), and he stopped to palaver and powwow with the Three.

"Djinn of All Deserts," said the Horse, "is it right for any one to be idle, with the world so new-and-all?"

"Certainly not," said the Djinn.

"Well," said the Horse, "there's a thing in the middle of your Howling Desert (and he's a Howler himself) with a long neck and long legs, and he hasn't done a stroke of work since Monday morning. He won't trot."

"Whew!" said the Djinn, whistling, "that's my Camel, for all the gold in Arabia! What does he say about it?"

"He says 'Humph!' " said the Dog, "and he won't fetch and carry."

"Does he say anything else?"

"Only 'Humph!' and he won't plow," said the Ox.

"Very good," said the Djinn. "I'll 'humph' him if you will kindly wait a minute."

The Djinn rolled himself up in his dust cloak, and took a bearing across the desert, and found the Camel most 'scruciatingly idle, looking at his own reflection in a pool of water.

*A djinn is a genie, a magical spirit.

"My long and bubbling friend," said the Djinn, "what's this I hear of your doing no work, with the world so new-and-all?"

"Humph!" said the Camel.

The Djinn sat down, with his chin in his hand, and began to think a Great Magic, while the Camel looked at his own reflection in the pool of water.

"You've given the Three extra work ever since Monday morning, all on account of your 'scruciating idleness," said the Djinn; and he went on thinking Magics, with his chin in his hand.

"Humph!" said the Camel.

"I shouldn't say that again if I were you," said the Djinn; "you might say it once too often."

And the Camel said "Humph!" again; but no sooner had he said it than he saw his back, that he was so proud of, being covered with a great big lolloping humph.

"Do you see that?" said the Djinn. "That's your own humph that you've brought upon yourself by not working. Today is Thursday, and you've done no work since Monday, when the work began. Now you are going to work."

"How can I," said the Camel, "with this humph on my back?"

"That's made a-purpose," said the Djinn, "all because you missed those three days. You will be able to work now for three days without eating, because you can live on your humph; and don't you ever say I never did anything for you. Come out of the Desert and go to the Three, and behave. Humph yourself!"

And the Camel humphed himself, humph and all, and went away to join the Three. And from that day to this the Camel always wears a humph (we call it "hump" now, not to hurt his feelings); but he has never yet caught up with the three days that he missed at the beginning of the world, and he has never yet learned how to behave.

El Pajaro Cu
(A folk tale from Mexico)

When God made the world, He took great care in forming the birds. He made their bodies and then feathered them, creating Owl and Dove and Peacock, each different from the other. And then He ran out of feathers. The last bird, Pajaro Cu [PA-ha-row COO], received no feathers whatsoever. Pajaro Cu didn't seem to care. He went anywhere he wished, never caring that he was as naked as the palm of your hand.

But the other birds worried.

"What can we do for him?" asked Owl.

"Pity on the little thing," said Dove.

"He looks awful," said Peacock. "All of the other animals talk about him."

The birds agreed that something must be done.

Then Owl said, "If we each give him one of our feathers, he'll be completely covered, and we'll never feel the difference."

All of the birds thought this was a splendid idea. Parrot gave a green feather; Canary's was yellow; Guinea Bird offered silver; Crow gave black; Swan's was white; and Redbird gave a bright red feather. Just as Pajaro Cu was about to receive his new coat, Peacock suddenly screeched, "No! With these feathers, Pajaro Cu will be the most beautiful bird around, and before long, he will be strutting about with pride."

"But we can't leave him naked," said Dove. "He is a disgrace to the entire community of birds!"

Everyone, including Pajaro Cu, wondered what to do.

"I know," said Owl. "If you each give him your feather, I will watch over him and protect us all from his vanity."

In no time at all, Pajaro Cu was the best-dressed bird around. Even Peacock was awed into silence. Lifting his glistening wings, Pajaro Cu flew straight to the pond, where he took one look at his marvelous self, and darted high up toward heaven.

Owl, old and heavy, tried to follow him, but his short wings weren't meant for such flying. Slowly, he spiraled back down to earth, where he found the others waiting in the branches.

Parrot said, "None of us has ever flown to heaven. This can only bring trouble. We're all going to pay for his vanity."

"It's Owl's fault," said Peacock. "I warned you all."

Whereupon they drove Owl from his tree and chased him. Owl found safety in a cave. Many days passed while he pondered: how can we lure Pajaro Cu from heaven? One day, he received a visitor.

"Oh, do come in, Roadrunner," cried Owl. "I am ever so glad to see you."

"I have brought you some dinner," Roadrunner said.

"Thank you. But whatever am I to do?" said Owl.

"You must stay here," Roadrunner warned. "Crow has sworn to kill you unless you get back his feather."

Owl said, "Then I will hunt by night, when Crow is asleep. And I will call for Pajaro Cu until he comes."

"And I will search for him on the road," said Roadrunner.

Even today they are looking. This is why Roadrunner streaks from one place to another, searching the road for Pajaro Cu. And when you listen at night, you can hear Owl calling "Cu, Cu, Cu, Cu, Cu."

Beauty and the Beast

Once upon a time there lived a very rich merchant with his three daughters. But all at once the merchant lost his fortune, and nothing remained but a little cottage in the woods, far from town. He told his daughters they would have to move there and work hard and live simply. The older daughters complained bitterly, but the youngest daughter, who was called Beauty, tried to make the best of things.

One day, many months later, the merchant heard that one of his ships, which he had thought lost, had landed and was full of many valuable things. As he prepared to make the long trip to claim his goods, he asked his daughters what he might bring them. The older two asked for fancy gowns and jewels. But Beauty said, "Dear father, please bring me a rose, for I have not seen one since we came here, and I love them so much."

When the merchant finally reached his ship, he found that all his goods had been stolen. So he turned toward home, as poor as when he started his journey.

Not far from home, the snow began to fall and the wind blew so hard it almost knocked the merchant off his horse. Suddenly he came upon a palace with lights blazing. He found the door open, so he entered. "Hello!" he called out, but no one answered. He came to a large dining hall, where there was a warm fire and a little table with a delicious meal just right for one person. After he had eaten, he looked for someone to thank, but no one appeared. He came upon a garden, blooming even in the middle of winter. He saw a beautiful rose bush and remembered Beauty's wish. He

reached out to pluck a single rose. But just as the stem broke, he heard a loud *roar* behind him.

The startled merchant turned around to see a terrible creature, half man and half beast. "How dare you!" snarled the Beast.

"Please forgive me," said the frightened man, "I only wanted a rose for my daughter, Beauty."

"I will forgive you, on one condition," said the Beast. "You must give me one of your daughters. Go and see if any of them loves you enough to save your life!"

When the sad father returned home and told what had happened, Beauty did not hesitate. "I will go," she said quietly.

"No, Beauty," said her father. "I am old, and have only a few years to live. I shall go back to the Beast."

"You shall not return to that castle without me," said Beauty. Her father tried to change her mind, but Beauty was determined.

Beauty and her father returned to the castle. When she first saw the Beast, she could not help shuddering but she tried to hide her fear. The Beast loaded a trunk filled with treasure onto Beauty's father's horse. As Beauty watched her father ride away, she began to cry.

"Beauty," said the Beast, "things are not as bad as you think. You have given yourself for your father's sake, and your goodness will be rewarded. Only listen to me and take this advice: Do not be deceived by appearances. Trust your heart, not your eyes."

As the days passed, Beauty walked in the lovely gardens, where the birds sang to her. She found a huge library filled with books she wanted to read.

At first the Beast's looks scared Beauty, but she soon grew used to them. The Beast treated her with great kindness. Every evening as she sat down to supper, the Beast appeared to talk with her as she ate. Soon she looked forward to their conversations. But when the meal was over and it was time to say good night, the Beast always turned to her and asked, "Beauty, will you marry me?" And though she cared for him more every day, Beauty always answered, "No."

One night, the Beast noticed a worried look on Beauty's face. "Beauty," he said, "I cannot bear to see you unhappy. What is the matter?" She told him that she missed her family, and that she especially longed to see her father. "But Beauty," said the Beast, "if you leave me, I fear that I will die of sadness."

"Dear Beast," said Beauty softly, "I do not want to leave you. But I long to see my father. Only let me go for one month, and I promise to come back and stay for the rest of my life."

"Very well," sighed the Beast. "But remember your promise. And take this magic ring. When you want to come back, turn the ring round upon your finger and say, 'I wish to go back to my Beast.' "

When Beauty awoke the next morning, she found herself back in her father's house—not the old country cottage, but a fine new house in town bought with the riches the Beast had given them. Her father hugged her and wept for joy. Soon her sisters came to visit with their new husbands. They pretended to be happy, but they were not. One sister had married a very handsome man who was so in love with his own face that he thought of nothing else. The other sister had married a clever man who liked to make fun of people, especially his wife.

Day after day, Beauty enjoyed being with her father and doing whatever she could to help him. When the time came for her to return to the Beast, she found that she could

not bring herself to say good-bye to her father. Every day she told herself, "Today I will go back." But every night she put it off again.

Then one night, she dreamed that she was wandering in the garden around the Beast's castle, when suddenly she heard painful groans. She looked down and saw the Beast lying on the ground. He seemed to be dying.

Beauty awoke with a start. "Oh, how could I do this to my poor Beast?" she cried. "Is it his fault he is ugly? Why did I refuse to marry him? I would be happier with him than my sisters are with their husbands. The Beast is honest and good, and that matters more than anything else."

She turned the ring round on her finger and said firmly, "I wish to go back to my Beast." In an instant, she found herself at the cas-

tle. She ran through the rooms, calling aloud for the Beast. There was no answer. Then she remembered her dream. She ran to the garden, and there she found the Beast stretched on the ground.

"Oh, he is dead, and it is all my fault!" she cried. She fell to the ground and took him in her arms. As the Beast slowly opened his eyes, Beauty cried, "Oh, Beast, how you frightened me! I never knew how much I loved you until now, when I feared it was too late."

In a faint voice the Beast said, "Beauty, I was dying because I thought you had forgotten your promise. But you have come back. Can you really love such an ugly creature as I am?"

"Yes," said Beauty.

Then once again the Beast asked, "Beauty, will you marry me?"

She answered, "Yes, dear Beast."

As she spoke, a blaze of light flashed around her. Beauty gasped and covered her eyes. When she opened them again, she no longer saw the Beast. But there, lying at her feet, was a handsome prince.

"What has happened to my Beast?" she asked.

"I was the Beast," said the prince. "A wicked fairy put a spell on me and changed me into a monster until a maiden would agree to marry me. You are the only one who has been good enough to see past my appearance and into my heart."

Beauty gave the young prince her hand to help him rise. Side by side they walked into the castle. And the very next day, with Beauty's father looking on, they were married. And they lived happily ever after.

The Tongue-Cut Sparrow
(A folk tale from Japan)

Long, long ago in Japan, there lived an old man and his wife. The old man was good, kind, and hardworking, but his wife was cross, mean, and bad-tempered. They had no children, so the old man kept a tiny sparrow as a pet. Every day when he came home from working in the woods, he loved to pet the little bird, talk to her, and feed her food from his own plate. The sparrow's sweet singing brought happiness into the old man's life. But his wife did not like the sparrow. She complained that her husband paid too much attention to a silly bird.

One morning, the old man went away to cut wood,

and his wife prepared to wash clothes. On this day, she had made some starch, which she set out in a wooden bowl. While her back was turned, the sparrow hopped down on the edge of the bowl and pecked at some of the starch. When the old woman saw the sparrow, she got so mad that she grabbed a pair of scissors and cut off the sparrow's tongue. "Go away, you greedy thing!" she shrieked, and the poor bird flew away to the woods.

When the old man returned home and heard what had happened, he felt very sad for his pet. The next morning, he went to the woods to look for the sparrow. Everywhere he went he cried, "Oh sparrow, little sparrow! Where are you, my friend?"

The woods grew thick and dark, and the old man began to worry that he might never see the sparrow again. With little hope he called out, "Little sparrow, please come home!" And just then he heard the fluttering of the sparrow's wings. And, to his great surprise, he heard the sparrow speak.

"Old man," said the sparrow, "you have been very kind to me. Now I wish to show you kindness in return." She led the old man to a pretty little house with a bamboo garden and a tiny waterfall. "Come in and meet my family," said the sparrow.

The old man bowed, removed his shoes, and entered the sparrow's house. Inside, many sparrows were singing sweet songs. They served the old man a delicious meal, with rice cakes, sweet candies, and plenty of hot tea. Then they did a wonderful dance that brought joy to his heart.

"This has been a magical day for me," said the old man, "and I thank you for your kindness. But I see that the sun is setting. Forgive me, but I must return home before my wife starts to worry."

"Before you go," said the sparrow, "please accept a gift." She placed two baskets before the old man. One was big and heavy, while the other was small and light. "Please choose one of these," said the sparrow, "and do not open the basket until you reach home."

The old man was not greedy, so he chose the small basket. With many thanks and good-byes, he left the sparrow's house and returned home.

When the old man arrived at his home, he told his wife all that had happened. Then they opened the small basket. It spilled over with jewels, gold and silver coins, and other treasures.

The old man was delighted, but his wife cried, "You fool! Why didn't you take the big basket?" Then, without another word, she hurried into the woods to find the sparrow's home.

When she at last arrived at the sparrow's house, she called out, "Sparrow! Let me in!" Of course the polite sparrow invited her into the house, and served her some hot tea. She took one sip and then said, "Enough of this. I am ready to leave." The sparrow again brought out two baskets, one big and one small. "Please choose one," said the sparrow, "and do not open it until you return home." The old woman grabbed the big basket and ran out the door.

"Oof!" she cried, "this basket is so heavy!" She sat down to rest. She looked at the basket. "Why should I wait to get home?" she said. "One little peek won't hurt."

She opened the basket. Instead of gold and silver, it was filled with toads that leaped into her hair, snakes that slithered around her arms and legs, and wasps that stung her all over.

The old woman screamed and ran as fast as she could. When she reached home, she fell into the old man's arms. He took care of her, and when she got better, she said to him, "I was too greedy, and I am sorry that I hurt the sparrow."

From that day forward, the old woman helped the old man feed any birds that came to their house, and their home was always filled with sweet songs.

The Tiger, the Brahman, and the Jackal
(A folk tale from India, retold by Virginia Haviland)

You can read about India in the World History section of this book. A Brahman is a member of a respected social group in India that includes such people as scholars and priests.

nce upon a time, a tiger was caught in a trap. He tried in vain to get out through the bars, and rolled and bit with rage and grief when he failed.

By chance a poor Brahman came by.

"Let me out of this cage, O pious one!" cried the tiger.

"Nay, my friend," replied the Brahman mildly, "you would probably eat me if I did."

"Not at all!" swore the tiger with many oaths. "On the contrary, I should be forever grateful, and serve you as a slave."

When the tiger sobbed and sighed and wept and swore, the pious Brahman's heart softened, and at last he consented to open the door of the cage. Out popped the tiger and, seizing the poor man, cried, "What a fool you are! What is to prevent my eating you now? After being cooped up so long I am terribly hungry!"

The Brahman pleaded loudly for his life. At first the tiger ignored his pleas, but then the beast promised to let the Brahman go if the man could find three things that thought the tiger's action unjust.

So the Brahman set out to find something to ask. He first asked a pipal tree what it thought of the matter, but the pipal tree replied coldly, "What have you to complain about? Don't I give shade and shelter to everyone who passes by, and don't they in return tear down my branches to feed their cattle? Don't whimper—be a man!"

Then the Brahman, sad at heart, went farther afield till he saw a buffalo turning a well-wheel. But he fared no better from it, for it answered, "You are a fool to expect gratitude! Look at me! While I gave milk they fed me on cottonseed and oil cake, but now I am dry they yoke me here, and give me refuse as fodder!"

The Brahman sadly asked the road to give him its opinion.

"My dear sir," said the road, "how foolish you are to expect anything else! Here I am, useful to everybody, yet all, rich and poor, great and small, trample on me as they go past, giving me nothing but the ashes of their pipe and the husks of their grain!"

At this the Brahman turned back sorrowfully. On the way he met a jackal who called out, "Why, what's the matter, Mr. Brahman? You look as miserable as a fish out of water!"

The Brahman told him all that occurred. "How very confusing!" said the jackal when the recital was ended. "Would you mind telling me over again, for everything has got so mixed up?"

The Brahman told it all over again, but the jackal shook his head in a distracted sort of way and still could not understand.

"It's very odd," said he, sadly, "but it all seems to go in at one ear and out at the other! I will go to the place where it all happened, and then perhaps I shall be able to give a judgment." So they returned to the cage, where the tiger was waiting for the Brahman, sharpening his teeth and claws.

"You've been away a long time!" growled the savage beast. "But now let us begin our dinner."

"*Our* dinner!" thought the wretched Brahman, his knees knocking together with fright. "What a remarkably delicate way of putting it!"

"Give me five minutes, my lord!" he pleaded, "in order that I may explain matters to the jackal here, who is somewhat slow in his wits."

The tiger consented, and the Brahman began the whole story over again, not missing a single detail, and spinning as long a yarn as possible.

"Oh, my poor brain! Oh, my poor brain!" cried the jackal, wringing his paws. "Let me see! How did it all begin? You were in a cage, and the tiger came walking by—"

"Pooh!" interrupted the tiger. "What a fool you are! *I* was in the cage."

"Of course!" cried the jackal, pretending to tremble with fright. "Yes! I was in the cage—no I wasn't—dear! dear! where are my wits? Let me see—the tiger was in the Brahman, and the cage came walking by—no, that's not it, either! Well, don't mind me, but begin your dinner, for I shall never understand!"

"Yes, you shall!" returned the tiger, in a rage at the jackal's stupidity. "I'll *make* you understand! Look here—I am the tiger—"

"Yes, my lord!"

"And that is the Brahman—"

"Yes, my lord!"

"And that is the cage—"

"Yes, my lord!"

"And I was in the cage—do you understand?"

"Yes—no—please, my lord—"

"Well?" cried the tiger impatiently.

"Please, my lord! How did you get in?"

"How! Why in the usual way, of course!"

"Oh, dear me! My head is beginning to whirl again! Please don't be angry, my lord, but what is the usual way?"

At this the tiger lost patience and, jumping into the cage, cried, "This way! Now do you understand how it was?"

"Perfectly!" grinned the jackal, as he dexterously shut the door. "And if you will permit me to say so, I think matters will remain as they were!"

How Wendy Met Peter Pan

PARENTS: *The Peter Pan stories were written by writer James M. Barrie in the early 1900s. Some children today may know the story of the boy who refuses to grow up from the Disney animated movie or the Broadway musical with Mary Martin. Here we present the opening episodes, in which we meet the Darling family children and Peter Pan. We encourage you to check your library for more adventures of Peter Pan to share with your children.*

Once upon a time there were three children, named Wendy, John, and Michael Darling, who lived in a lovely house with lots of toys and picture books. They had a most unusual nurse to look after them, called Nana, and she was really a large dog. She bathed and dressed the children, and saw that they got up and went to bed at the proper time.

One night, when the children had been bathed and put to bed, the bedroom window flew open and a boy dropped in. He was dressed in a ragged shirt of leafy green and brown, and he had wild, uncombed hair. When Nana saw him, she growled and jumped at him. She did not catch him, for he leaped back out the window. But she did catch his shadow. When Mrs. Darling found it on the floor the next morning, she rolled it up carefully and put it away in a drawer.

Nothing more happened until about a week later. Mr. and Mrs. Darling were dressing to go to a party, and Nana was busy getting the children ready for bed. Now, the only person at Number 14 (which was the Darlings' house) who did not much care for Nana was Mr. Darling. And on this night, when Nana happened to rub up by accident against Mr. Darling, and a lot of her long hairs came off on his nice new pants, Mr. Darling shouted, "I won't have a dog in the house! I shall tie her up in the back yard!" And he did.

Poor Nana whined, for it was starting to snow. Then she barked, for she could smell danger in the air.

It was all dark and quiet in the room where Wendy, Michael, and John lay sleeping. But it was only dark for a moment. For as soon as Mr. and Mrs. Darling had left for the party, a bright light flew in at the window and darted to and fro around the room. It was Tinker Bell, a lovely little-girl fairy, come to search for the shadow that belonged to Peter Pan.

In a moment, through the window came Peter Pan himself. "Oh, Tink," he called softly, "have you found my shadow?"

She answered in a voice like a tiny bell with a silvery tinkle, which is the fairy language. She said that his shadow was in the big box—she meant the chest of drawers—but it was too big for her to open. Peter had his shadow out in a second, and he was so excited at getting it back that he did not notice that he closed Tinker Bell in the drawer!

"Bother!" said Peter, because his shadow wouldn't join to him again. He tried to stick it back on with some soap, but that didn't work. He was so disappointed that he sat on the floor and cried.

His sobs woke Wendy, and she sat up in bed. She had seen Peter before in dreams, so she was not surprised to see him now. She asked politely, "Boy, why are you crying?"

Peter got up, and they bowed to each other. "What's your name?" he asked.

"Wendy Moira Angela Darling," she replied. "What is your name?"

"Peter Pan."

"And where do you live?" asked Wendy.

Peter answered, "Second to the right, and then straight on till morning."

"Does your mother know you are here?" asked Wendy.

"Don't have a mother," said Peter.

"Oh!" exclaimed Wendy. "No wonder you were crying."

"I wasn't crying about mothers," Peter snapped. "I was crying because I can't get my shadow to stick on. Besides, I wasn't crying."

Wendy fetched her needle and thread, and she sewed the shadow on to Peter's foot. Peter danced about and crowed with joy. And instead of saying, "Thank you, Wendy, how kind you are," he crowed, "Oh, how clever I am!" For, to tell the truth, Peter was very conceited.

"Peter," said Wendy, "how old are you?"

"Don't know," said Peter.

"If you did have a mother," said Wendy, "she could tell you how old you are."

"Oh, she *might*," said Peter, "but I ran away the day I was born! It was because I heard my father and mother talking about what I would be as a grown-up man. And I don't ever want to grow up! I want to stay a little boy and have fun for ever and ever and ever! That's why I ran away to live with the fairies."

"Fairies!" exclaimed Wendy. "Really and truly? Oh, Peter, where do they come from?"

"Well," said Peter, "when the first baby that ever was laughed for the first time that ever was—"

"What was the baby's name?" asked Wendy.

"Don't interrupt," said Peter. "Anyhow, its laugh broke up into a thousand little tiny pieces, and they all went skipping about and turned into fairies. But there are only a few fairies now, because children don't believe in them. They can't live unless they're believed in. And every time a child says, 'I don't believe in fairies,' then another fairy falls down dead." Then Peter got a surprised look on his face. "Oh!" he said. "I wonder where—Tink! Tink! Where are you? Listen, Wendy. Do you hear anything?"

"I hear a sound like tiny bells," said Wendy. "It seems to be coming from the chest of drawers."

"That's Tink!" said Peter. He opened a drawer and Tinker Bell flew out. And she was in a rage!

"Tink," said Peter, "watch your language! You shouldn't say such things. Yes, of course I'm sorry, but how could I know you were in the drawer?" Tink settled for a moment on top of a clock. She glared at Wendy and made a sharp jangling sound.

"What did she say?" asked Wendy.

"She says you are a big ugly girl," said Peter. "But you mustn't mind her."

Wendy did not like this, so she decided to talk about something else. "Tell me about where you live, Peter," she said.

"Mostly I live in the Never-Land with the Lost Boys," he said.

"Are they fairies?" said Wendy.

"No," said Peter. "They are the children who fall out of their carriages when their nurses aren't watching them. Then the fairies pick them up, and if nobody comes for them in seven days, they are brought to the Never-Land. And I am their captain."

"But why are they all boys?" asked Wendy.

"Because girls are too clever to fall out of their carriages," said Peter.

Then he asked, "Wendy, do you know any stories? I don't know any," he said, "so I come here to hear them. But sometimes I have to leave before I hear the end. Oh, Wendy, your mother was telling such a lovely story the last time I came, all about a prince who couldn't find the lady who wore a glass slipper."

"That was the story of Cinderella!" exclaimed Wendy. "And the prince *did* find her in the end, and they lived happily ever after. Oh, Peter, I could tell you so many wonderful stories!"

Peter got a greedy look in his eyes. "Wendy," he said, "come back with me and tell us stories. You could be a mother for us."

"Oh, but I can't," said Wendy. "What would my mother say? And besides, I can't fly."

"I'll teach you," said Peter. "We just jump on the back of the wind, and away we go. And when we get to the Never-Land, there are mermaids, and fairies, and Indians, and—" Peter was going to say "pirates," but he thought it better not to mention them.

"Oooh, it would be splendid!" cried Wendy. "But would you teach Michael and John to fly, so that they could come too?"

"If you like," said Peter. So Wendy shook her brothers and woke them up. "Peter Pan is here," she cried, "and he's going to teach us to fly!"

Peter blew some fairy dust on each of them and said, "All you have to do is think lovely, wonderful thoughts, and wriggle your shoulders, and let go."

In half a minute the three little Darlings were flying around the room, their heads bumping against the ceiling. "Come on!" cried Peter. And out the window they flew.

This is just the beginning of the story. To read about the children's adventures in the Never-Land, check your library for a book about Peter Pan.

American Tall Tales

America is a big country with a big appetite for stories about big deeds and larger-than-life heroes. These stories, called *tall tales*, may have a bit of truth, but they mostly serve up a heaping portion of humorous exaggeration. You may already know some tall tale heroes, such as Johnny Appleseed and Casey Jones (which we introduced in stories in the Kindergarten book in this series). Now you can meet three more favorite American tall tale characters.

Paul Bunyan

As a baby, Paul Bunyan was mighty big. How big? Well, when he sneezed, he blew the birds from Maine to California. When he got a bad case of the hiccups, people for miles around ran out of their houses screaming, "Earthquake! Earthquake!"

When Paul Bunyan grew up, he became a logger. There was no one who could match Paul at cutting down trees. In those days, as Americans were moving West and building the country, they had to cut down a lot of trees to make their homes, not to mention their schools, churches, boats, and furniture.

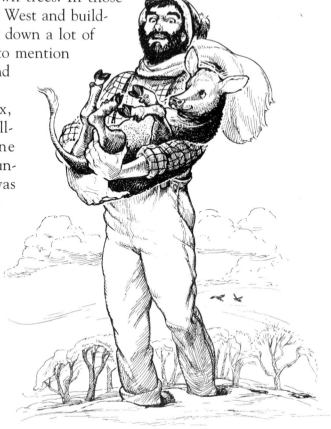

Paul made himself a giant ax, with a handle carved out of a full-grown hickory tree. With one swing, he could bring down a hundred trees. Once, when Paul was tired after a hard day of logging, he let his ax drag behind him as he walked back to the logging camp. It dug a ditch that people today call the Grand Canyon.

Sometimes, being so big and all, Paul got to feeling lonely with no one his size around. But then came the Winter of the Blue Snow. It was called that because it was so cold that even the snow shivered and turned blue. One day, as Paul made his way through the blue snowdrifts, he saw two big, blue, furry things sticking up out of the snow. He reached down and gave a pull. They turned out to be two big blue ears. And connected to them was a giant blue baby ox!

Paul carried the half-frozen creature home, wrapped him in blankets and fed him. And when the baby ox looked up and gave Paul a big friendly lick on the face, Paul laughed and said, "Babe, we're goin' to be great friends!"

And they were. Babe grew up to be so big that, if you were standing at his front legs, you had to use a telescope to see all the way to his back legs. Everywhere Paul went, from Maine to Minnesota to Oregon and back, Babe went too. Paul chopped down the trees and Babe hauled them to the rivers, where he would dump in the logs so they could float to the sawmills.

One day, Paul said to Babe, "What this here country needs is a canal runnin' down the middle of it to float logs in." So Paul started digging. He threw great mounds of dirt and rocks to the right and the left. On one side he made the Rocky Mountains, and on the other side he made the Appalachians. And when Babe kicked over a huge bucket of water to fill the canal, well, that there became the Mississippi River.

Wherever there was logging to be done, Paul and Babe were ready to work. The last place they were seen, people say, was up in Alaska, where you can still hear the echoes when Paul shouts, *"T-i-m-b-e-r!"*

Pecos Bill

This is the story of the greatest cowboy who ever was, named Pecos Bill.

One day when Bill was just a baby, his Pa came running up to his Ma shouting, "Pack up everything we got, Ma! There's neighbors moved in near about fifty miles away, and it's gettin' too crowded here."

So Ma and Pa loaded a covered wagon with everything they owned and headed West. It was a long, hard, hot journey. The children in the back of the wagon, all eighteen of them, got to fussing and hollering so loud that Ma said you couldn't hear the thunder over their noise.

One day, the wagon bumped over a big rock, and out the back fell baby Bill. With all the fussing and fighting, nobody noticed. The wagon just kept on going. So Bill found himself sitting in the dirt somewhere near the Pecos River in Texas, and that's how he came to be named Pecos Bill. But that was later.

Little Bill was tough. He didn't cry. He just crawled along on the dusty plain, keeping his eyes peeled for whatever came along. And the first thing to come along was a coyote.

When the coyote saw this dirty, naked little creature crawling around on all fours, she thought he was a cute little animal, even if his ears were mighty small. Little Bill reached up and patted the coyote's head and said, "Doggie."

The doggie, I mean coyote, liked Bill so much that she took him home to her den, and Bill grew up with the coyotes. The coyotes taught him to roam the prairies and howl at the moon. They taught him the secrets of hunting, and how to leap like an antelope and run like the wind. They taught him how to be so still that he was almost invisible. They showed him how to steer clear of the rattlesnake.

The years went by, about eighteen of them to be exact, and Bill grew up strong and healthy. One day as Bill was playing tag with some prairie dogs, he saw a most unusual sight. It seemed to be a big animal with four legs, or was it six legs? And why did it have one head up front and another on top?

Well, it turned out to be a horse with a man riding it. Bill ran around the horse a bit, then he slowly crept forward and took a sniff of the man's boot. "Get up!" the man cried. "You're a man, not a coyote!" But Bill shook his head, *no*. So the man tried to make Bill understand, but no matter what he said, Bill kept shaking his head, *no*. Then the man said, "Well, Mr. Birthday Suit, if you're a coyote, then where's your long bushy tail?" Bill looked around and, sure enough, he had no tail. So, seeing the sad truth that he wasn't a coyote but a human instead, Bill went back with the man, who turned out to be a cowboy named Bowlegs.

At first Bill thought he would rather stay a coyote. He couldn't stand the way clothes scratched and pulled at his skin, or the way boots came between his bare feet and the good old dirt. And he couldn't see the need for a knife or fork when it was just as easy to use your fingers to pick up your meat and tear it with your teeth.

One day, Bowlegs said to Bill, "If you're goin' to be a cowboy, you need a horse. Let's go to town and buy one." On the way to town, they saw a herd of wild mustangs running across the open range. One was prancing and bucking and kicking like all get-out. "That's the horse for me!" said Bill.

"Wait!" cried Bowlegs. "He's too wild. He'll kick your head in." But Bill leaped on the horse's back and held on tight. That horse bucked so hard it started doing somersaults, but it couldn't throw Bill off. And so Bill and his horse, which he named Widow-Maker, became the best of friends. But don't you get the idea that Widow-Maker was tamed, no sir! There wasn't a cowboy around besides Bill who could ride him.

Pretty soon Bill taught the cowboys some new ways to do things. He showed them how to take a rope with a loop at the end of it, called a lariat, and how to ride a horse and spin the rope and toss it over the head of a running cow and pull the cow down all at once. "That there," said Bill, "is the way you *lasso* a cow." He taught them how to keep a big herd of cows together instead of letting the cows run any which way all over the range. He even taught them how to sing cowboy songs around the campfire at night, in a voice that sounded like a lonesome coyote's howl.

Then came a terrible drought. No rain fell, the sun beat down, and Texas turned drier than a dead leaf in a fire. The horses and cows started to shrivel up like raisins. So

Bill jumped on Widow-Maker and rode up near Oklahoma. There, the skies were purple-black, the thunder roared, the lightning crashed, and coming straight at Bill was the giant, whirling funnel cloud of an angry cyclone. Bill took out an extra long lariat, gave it a good hard toss, and bingo! he lassoed that cyclone. Then he jumped on the cyclone's back, pulled his rope tight, and headed it down across Texas, all the while squeezing the rain out of it as he went.

So the cows and horses got the water they needed, and Bill thought he hadn't had so much fun since the day he first rode Widow-Maker.

John Henry

There are many stories, as well as many songs, about John Henry. A song that tells a story is called a ballad. Here is one familiar version of the ballad of John Henry, and it shows how, as America expanded westward, our country came to rely more and more on new machines, including the railroad. While the railroad helped the country grow, not everybody felt good about it or the other new machines. As you'll see, the story of John Henry tells about a showdown between a man—John Henry, who hammered in railroad spikes—and a machine, the steam drill.

When John Henry was a little baby
Sittin' on his daddy's knee,
He picked up a hammer and a little piece of steel,
Said, "This hammer's gonna be the death of me, Lord, Lord,
This hammer's gonna be the death of me."

Well, the captain said to John Henry,
"Gonna bring that steam drill 'round.
Gonna take that steam drill out on the job,
Gonna whop that steel on down, Lord, Lord,
Gonna whop that steel on down."

John Henry said to the captain,
"Well, a man ain't nothin' but a man.
But before I let a steam drill beat me down
I'd die with a hammer in my hand,
     Lord, Lord,
I'd die with a hammer in my hand."

Now the man that invented the steam
     drill,
He thought he was mighty fine.
But John Henry drove his fifteen feet
And the steam drill only made nine,
     Lord, Lord,
The steam drill only made nine.

John Henry hammered in the mountains
And his hammer was strikin' fire.
Well, he hammered so hard that it broke
     his poor heart,
And he laid down his hammer and he died,
     Lord, Lord,
He laid down his hammer and he died.

They took John Henry to the graveyard,
And they buried him in the sand.
And every locomotive comes a-roarin' by
Says, "There lies a steel-drivin' man,"
     Lord, Lord,
"There lies a steel-drivin' man."

Myths from Ancient Greece

Heroes and Monsters, Gods and Goddesses

Here are some stories that have been around for two thousand years or more. These stories come to us from ancient Greece. (In the World History section of this book, you can read about the great civilization in ancient Greece.) We call these stories "myths." Many myths tell about brave heroes, great battles, terrible monsters, or gods and goddesses. Some myths explain why we have seasons, or why there are volcanoes, or how constellations got in the sky. Of course today we know the real reasons that all these things happen. But long, long ago, many people believed the myths were true. Even though we no longer believe the old myths, we like to tell them because they're such wonderful stories.

Like the people in other ancient civilizations you've learned about, the ancient Greeks believed in many gods and goddesses. The Greeks built beautiful temples, like the Parthenon, to honor their gods. In the Greek myths, the gods and goddesses sometimes act like normal people—like you and me. They need to eat, drink, and sleep. They can be happy one moment and angry the next. They fall in love and get married. They play tricks on each other. They argue and fight with each other.

Unlike people, however, the Greek gods had magical powers. Some gods could change into an animal, or hurl lightning bolts from the sky! Also, the Greeks believed the gods were immortal—which means that they never died, but lived forever.

The ancient Greeks believed the gods and goddesses lived on a mountain that rose high above the clouds, called Mount Olympus. From there, they looked down on the earth, and they used their powers to help the people they liked or hurt the people they didn't like.

Let's meet some of the main Greek gods and goddesses.

Zeus [ZOOCE], the king of the gods, controlled the heavens and decided arguments among the gods. He could change his shape in an instant. If he wanted, he could come to earth as a swan, or as a fierce bull. When he was angry, he had the power to throw lightning bolts down from the heavens!

Hera [HAIR-uh], the wife of Zeus, was queen of the gods and the goddess of marriage. She could be a very jealous person. But her husband, Zeus, had a habit of falling in love with many other goddesses and women, so Hera usually had a good reason to be jealous.

Poseidon [poe-SIDE-un], the god of the sea, was an especially important god to the Greeks. Can you think of why? (Look at a map and see what's around Greece.) Poseidon could make the oceans as calm as a sleeping baby, or he could stir up high waves to crush a ship to pieces. In pictures, Poseidon often has a long beard and holds a trident, a kind of long pitchfork with three prongs.

Apollo [uh-PAUL-oh], a son of Zeus, was the god of light. He is sometimes called Phoebus [FEE-bus] Apollo. "Phoebus" means "brilliant" or "shining." He was also the god of poetry and music. No one could sing so beautifully or play so sweetly on the lyre (an instrument like a small harp). He was also the god of healing, as well as the god of archery.

Artemis [AR-tuh-miss], the twin sister of Apollo, was the goddess of the moon and the goddess of hunting. She loved the woods and the wild creatures who lived there. She loved to be free and on her own. So she asked her father, Zeus, to promise that he would never make her get married—which is a promise Zeus kept.

Aphrodite [af-roe-DIE-tee] was the goddess of love and beauty. When she was born, she rose out of the sea from the gentle waves on a cushion of soft foam. She had a son called **Eros** [AIR-oss], though you may know him by a more familiar name, Cupid. Maybe you've seen a picture of him on Valentine's Day cards. The Greeks said that when Aphrodite wanted someone to fall in love, she ordered Eros to shoot that person with one of his magic arrows. If he hit you with an arrow, then you would fall in love with the first person you saw! No one could resist the power of his magic arrows, not even Zeus.

Ares [AIR-eez] was the cruel and merciless god of war. Wherever he went, death and destruction followed. No one liked him, not even his parents, Zeus and Hera!

Hermes [HER-meez], the messenger god, carried commands from the gods to humans on earth. In pictures, he often has wings on his hat or sandals to show how fast he traveled.

Hephaestus [hih-FES-tus] was the god of fire and the forge. He could cause volcanoes, making the earth spit up hot flames and lava. (The word, "volcano," comes from the Roman name for this god, Vulcan.) But most of all he used fire to make things. He used it to heat metal and make armor, swords, and spears, or beautiful cups and shining jewelry. Hephaestus was lame, and spent his time working at his fiery forge.

Athena [uh-THEE-nah; "TH" as in "thin"] was the goddess of wisdom. For the people of the Greek city called Athens, she was a special goddess, for they believed she protected their city. She had a most unusual birth. One day Zeus had a terrible headache. He complained to Hephaestus, who took his hammer and struck Zeus on the head! Out of Zeus's head jumped Athena, already grown-up and fully dressed in a suit of armor.

Hades [HAY-deez] was the grim god of the underworld, the dark and shadowy underground place that the Greeks believed people went to when they died. The Greeks often called this place Hades, the same name as the god who ruled there over the dead.

Same Gods, Different Names

The gods and goddesses of the ancient Greeks were later worshipped by the people of ancient Rome. (You'll learn more about the Romans in the third-grade book in this series.) If you look in your library for books of myths, you may find that some books use the Greek names for the gods while others use the Roman names. Here's a chart to help you keep track of who's who. Are you familiar with some of the Roman names?

Greek name	Roman name	Greek name	Roman name
Zeus	Jupiter (or Jove)	Ares	Mars
Hera	Juno	Hermes	Mercury
Poseidon	Neptune	Hephaestus	Vulcan
Apollo	Apollo	Athena	Minerva
Artemis	Diana	Hades	Pluto
Aphrodite	Venus		

Gods of Nature and Mythical Creatures

The Greeks believed in other gods and goddesses connected to the earth and nature.

Dionysus [die-uh-NIE-sus] was the god of wine. Everywhere he went he taught people how to grow grapes and make wine. But sometimes Dionysus and his helpers made people act wild or do crazy things.

Demeter [dih-MEE-ter] was the goddess of grain and of the harvest. The Greeks believed that, because of her, corn and other grains grew in the fields, and trees grew tall, and flowers bloomed. By the way, the Roman name for Demeter was Ceres [SEER-eez]. From that name we get our word for a food that you might often eat for breakfast—cereal!

In Greek myths you might meet some curious creatures. Some are beautiful, like the winged horse called **Pegasus.**

Some are scary, like Cerberus [SIR-bur-us], a dog that belonged to Hades, the god of the underworld.

This dog was not man's best friend! He had three snarling heads. He guarded the gate to the underworld. He let in the spirits of the dead and then made sure they didn't get out.

Some mythical creatures are part human and part animal. The centaur [SEN-tar] was part human and part horse.

An odd-looking fellow named **Pan** had goat horns on his head and his feet were goat hooves.

He was a wild and frisky creature who loved to dance through the forests and mountains. He played lively music on a set of pipes that we now call "panpipes."

Prometheus Brings Fire, Pandora Brings Woe

Here is a myth about how a good thing happened, followed by a very bad thing.

Once, only the gods on Mount Olympus had fire. On earth, the people had nothing to give them light in the darkness, or warm them on a cold night, or cook their food.

A brave and powerful giant named Prometheus [pruh-MEE-thee-us] felt sorry for mankind. He stole fire from the gods and took it to the people on earth.

When Zeus, king of the gods, found out what Prometheus had done, he was furious. To punish him, he had Prometheus tied to a rock with un-

breakable chains. Day after day, a fierce eagle flew down and ripped and clawed at the body of poor Prometheus. (Much later, Prometheus was finally set free by a hero named Hercules—but that's another story.)

Now, Zeus looked down on the earth and said, "Let the people keep their fire. I will make them a hundred times more miserable than they were before they had it." And so he told Hephaestus to use his skills to make a woman at his forge. Zeus called this woman Pandora, and when he breathed life into her, she was as sweet and lovely as the flowers in spring. He sent Pandora to earth, and he gave her a closed box and told her never to open it.

But Pandora was very, very curious. Every time she looked at the box she wanted to know what was in it. She knew very well that Zeus had told her not to open it. But, she said to herself, what harm could it do to take just one little peek inside? And so she lifted the lid. Out from the box flew all the bad things in the world—pain, disease, disaster, sorrow, jealousy, and hatred.

But some people say there was one more thing in Pandora's box—Hope. Hope is what keeps people going despite all the bad things in the world.

Oedipus and the Sphinx

Long ago, near the Greek city of Thebes [theebs], there lived a terrible creature called the Sphinx [sfinks]. She had the face of a woman but the body of a lion with wings. When travelers came to the city, she would swoop down upon them. Then she would ask them a riddle. If they could answer the riddle, she would let them go. But if they couldn't, she would eat them! So far, no one could answer the riddle. Everyone in Thebes lived in fear of the monster.

Then one day a very smart and brave young man named Oedipus [ED-ih-pus] was on his way to Thebes. When the Sphinx saw him, she smiled, for she thought she would soon have a tasty lunch.

"Answer this riddle," she said to Oedipus, "or meet your doom. What creature goes on four feet in the morning, on two feet at noon, and on three feet in the evening?"

Oedipus looked up at the Sphinx and said, "Man. In childhood he crawls on his hands and knees, which is like four feet. In the middle of his life, when he is grown up, he walks on two feet. And in the evening of his life, when he is old, he uses a cane, which is like walking on three feet."

Oedipus had solved the riddle! The Sphinx was so angry that she threw herself in the ocean and drowned. And the people of Thebes were so grateful to Oedipus that they made him their new king.

Theseus and the Minotaur

Once upon a time, not far from Greece on the island of Crete, there lived a king named Minos [MY-noce]. King Minos led a war against the Greek city of Athens. He burned the ships of the Athenians, and destroyed their fields and gardens. Then he sent a cruel message to the ruler of Athens, King Aegeus [EE-joos]. "Every nine years," said King Minos, "when the springtime comes, you shall choose seven of your youths and seven of your maidens and send them to me in a ship. If you fail to do this, my soldiers will burn your city to the ground."

"But," the Athenians asked, "what shall happen to the youths and maidens?"

"In Crete," said King Minos, "there is giant maze called the Labyrinth, designed by the master inventor, Daedalus [DED-ah-lus]. Whoever goes in the Labyrinth can never find his way out. Deep inside there lives a monster, half-man and half-bull, called the Minotaur [MIN-oh-tar]. I will put your youths and maidens into the Labyrinth, and there they will be eaten by the Minotaur."

And so, when nine years had passed, and the flowers began to bloom in the spring, there was no joy in Athens, but only tears and sadness. Seven youths and maidens were put on board a black-sailed ship and sent to their terrible fate in the Labyrinth.

Now, another nine years had almost passed, when a young man arrived in Athens. His name was Theseus [THEE-see-us; "TH" as in "thin"], and he was a prince. In fact, he was the son of King Aegeus. He had been raised by his mother in a faraway town. Now that he was grown he had come to Athens to meet his father, the King. King Aegeus embraced his son with great happiness.

Theseus arrived in Athens just a few days before seven youths and seven maidens were to be sent to the Minotaur. When Theseus learned of this, he said, "I will take the place of one of the youths. I will kill the Minotaur and all of us shall return safely." King Aegeus begged his son not to go. But Theseus promised his father, "When I return, I will change the sail of the ship from black to white, so you will know that I have succeeded."

The ship sailed to the island of Crete. When they arrived, the young victims were marched through the streets on their way to the Labyrinth. And that is when Ariadne [ar-ee-ADD-nee], the lovely daughter of King Minos, saw Theseus. She could not bear the thought of sending this young, handsome prince to his death. And so she went to Daedalus, the inventor of the Labyrinth. She asked him how anyone who entered the great maze could get out again. Daedalus gave her a clever idea, and she rushed to the prison where Theseus was locked up.

Ariadne whispered, "Listen, Theseus. If you will promise to marry me and take me with you to Athens, I will help you." Theseus gladly agreed. Then Ariadne gave him a ball of string and told him to tie one end to the gate of the Labyrinth and unwind the ball as he went along. That way, he could follow the string to find his way back out.

Theseus soon found himself deep in the dark, winding halls of the Labyrinth. He heard a rumbling, growling sound. It was the Minotaur, snoring in his sleep. Theseus leaped on the beast. He had never wrestled so strong or savage an opponent. With fierce roars, the Minotaur fought back. But Theseus had taken the beast by surprise, and in the end the Minotaur lay dead.

Theseus followed the string back out of the Labyrinth. With Ariadne's help, he freed the other Greek youths and maidens. Then they all boarded the ship and set sail for Athens.

But oh, what a sad mistake followed! In his rush, Theseus forgot to replace the ship's black sail with a white one. His father, who had been sitting for days on a cliff looking out over the sea, awaited the return of his son. Now, when King Aegeus saw the black-sailed ship, he fainted and fell forward into the sea. And ever since then the sea where he drowned has been called the Aegean Sea.

Daedalus and Icarus

As you know, the master inventor Daedalus designed the Labyrinth for King Minos. Daedalus also showed Ariadne how Theseus could escape from the Labyrinth. When King Minos found this out, he was so angry that he threw Daedalus in the Labyrinth, along with his young son, Icarus [IK-er-us].

Not even the man who invented the Labyrinth could find his way out of it. Would the father and son die there? No—for when Daedalus saw the seagulls flying overhead, he got an idea.

Little by little, he gathered many feathers. He fastened them together with wax, and so made two pairs of wings like those of a bird. He put one pair on himself and the other pair on Icarus. He showed his son how to move his arms and catch the wind with his wings.

"Now, son," he said, "let us fly away from here. But listen carefully. Do not fly too high, or you will get too close to the sun, and the wax on your wings will melt."

Daedalus and Icarus flew up out of the Labyrinth, over the sea, away from the island of Crete. "Oh," cried Icarus, "it's wonderful to be free and flying through the air!"

"Yes," said Daedalus, "but do not fly too close to the sun."

A puff of wind lifted Icarus up. He was so excited that he forgot what his father told him. Higher and higher he flew, toward the highest heavens.

The warm sun began to melt the wax, and one by one the feathers fell from his wings. Then down, down, down fell Icarus into the sea. Daedalus cried out in grief as he saw the waters close over his son far below.

Arachne the Weaver

In all of Athens, no one could spin such fine thread or weave such wonderful cloth as the young woman named Arachne [uh-RAK-nee]. People from miles around came to admire her cloth. Arachne grew so proud of her weaving that she began to boast, "I am the most wonderful weaver in the world!"

"Yes, of course," said her friends, "next to the great goddess Athena."

"Athena? Ha!" said Arachne. "Can she spin thread so fine, or weave it into cloth as beautiful as mine? Why, I could teach her a thing or two!"

An old woman in a dark cloak spoke to Arachne. "Be careful, my dear," she said. "You must show respect for the gods. Your boasting may anger Athena."

"I'm not afraid of Athena," snapped Arachne. "Let her come here and we'll see who is the better weaver."

Then the old woman threw back her cloak. There was a flash of light, and there stood the gray-eyed goddess, Athena. "I am ready," said Athena quietly. "Take me to a loom, and let us begin. When we are finished, if your work is best, then I will weave no more. But if my work is best, then you will never weave again. Do you agree?"

"I agree," said Arachne. "Let us begin." She went to one loom and Athena to another. The people looked on in wonder as the goddess and the young woman wove brilliant designs into their cloth.

With threads of many colors, Arachne wove cloth as fine and light as a silken web. "How beautiful!" said the people. "It almost seems as if she could weave sunlight and rainbows into her cloth."

Arachne stepped back from her loom and turned to look at Athena's work. Into her cloth the goddess had woven flowers that seemed to bloom, and a stream that seemed to ripple by, and clouds that seemed to float peacefully in a blue sky, and above them the dazzling figures of the immortal gods themselves. When the people looked at it, they were so filled with wonder that they gasped. Arachne herself had to admit that Athena's work was more beautiful than her own. She hid her face in her hands and wept. "Oh, how can I live if I must never spin or weave again?" she cried.

When Athena saw that Arachne would never have any joy unless she could spin and weave, she said, "I cannot break the agreement we had, but I will change you so that you spin and weave forever." And with a touch, she turned Arachne into a spider, which ran to a corner and quickly began to spin and weave a beautiful, shining web.

And that is why some people say that all spiders in the world are the children of Arachne.

Today, scientists use a special name for the class of animals that spiders belong to. Spiders are not insects but *arachnids*.

Swift-Footed Atalanta

Atalanta [at-uh-LAN-tuh] was a beautiful Greek maiden who could run faster than the winds. She loved nothing better than to run freely across the fields, through the woods, and up and down the hills.

Atalanta's father thought that she should get married and settle down. But she cared nothing for the many young men who came daily to ask to marry her. So many men came, in fact, that one day she announced, "If you wish to marry me, then hear this. I will marry the man who can beat me in a race."

"Fine!" the men cried. "Let's start now."

"But there is one more thing," said Atalanta. "Whoever runs this race and loses to me shall also lose his life."

"That should scare them away," thought Atalanta, "for they know that I can outrun the wind."

And indeed, many of the men began to cough and feel a cold coming on, or suddenly remembered that they had forgotten some important business that they simply *had* to attend to at once.

But a few men stayed. Yes, they had heard about Atalanta's swiftness, but after all, could they be beaten by a *girl?* Nonsense!

And so these men raced Atalanta. She even gave them a head start of a hundred paces. But for each, it was a race to his doom.

Then one day there arrived a young man named Hippomenes [hip-POM-eh-neez]. Atalanta liked his fair features, his gentle eyes, and his brave spirit, and she felt pity for him. "Do not run against me," she said, "for I shall surely beat you, and that will be your end."

"Let me try anyway," said Hippomenes. Of course he knew that he did not have a chance to outrun her. But he had prayed to Aphrodite, the goddess of love, and asked for her help to win Atalanta as his wife. And Aphrodite had answered his prayers by giving him three golden apples and telling him what to do with them.

The race began. Even though Atalanta started a hundred paces behind Hippomenes, she quickly caught up to him. When he heard her breath close beside him, he took one of the golden apples and threw it over his shoulder.

When Atalanta saw the glittering apple, she left the path to pick it up. Hippomenes pulled ahead a little. But Atalanta easily caught up with him again. As she did, he threw the second golden apple even farther from the path. Again Atalanta left the path to get the apple, for she knew that she could still win. Again she caught up with Hippomenes, who was puffing and gasping. He took the third apple and threw it as far as he could. With an invisible nudge from Aphrodite, the apple rolled down a hill.

Atalanta could see that if she chased this apple, she might fall too far behind to win. But she dashed aside and grabbed the apple. Then she strained every muscle to catch up with Hippomenes. They were coming closer and closer to the finish line. She could see his face and hear his hard breathing. With one last burst of speed, she could pass him.

Suddenly, however, Atalanta felt something for Hippomenes that was not pity, but something warmer and more generous. And so she did not speed up, and the young man crossed the finish line first. With a laugh, Atalanta took his hand and led him to her father's house, where they were married that very day. And from above, Aphrodite looked down and smiled on the happy couple.

Demeter and Persephone

Demeter [dih-MEE-ter] was the goddess of all that grows from the ground. She made the corn and grain ripen, the orchards bear fruit, and the flowers bloom.

More than anything else, Demeter loved her daughter, Persephone [per-SEF-uh-nee]. Once, when Demeter was away looking after the crops in the fields, Persephone was playing in a field of flowers. As she stopped to pick a flower, she happened to pull the plant up by its roots, leaving a little hole in the ground. Then suddenly the hole grew wider and deeper, and Persephone heard a rumbling like thunder below her.

From the dark hole, four coal-black horses burst forth, pulling a golden chariot with a tall, sad-eyed driver wearing a golden crown. "I am Hades, king of the underworld," he said. "Come with me and be my queen." Then he snatched Persephone in his arms and carried her to his kingdom below.

When Demeter returned home, she could not find her daughter. She asked everyone, but no one had seen her. Then she asked the Sun, who sees all. And he told her that he had seen Hades take Persephone to the underworld to be his queen.

When Demeter heard this, she wept. She was so sad

that the golden corn and waving wheat died, the trees dropped their leaves, and the grass turned brown. All the earth was cold and bare. And Demeter cried out, "Nothing shall grow upon the earth until my daughter is returned to me."

Then Zeus, king of the gods, saw that the people and animals were hungry, for they had no grain or fruit to eat. And so he sent Hermes, the messenger god, to tell Hades to let Persephone go back to her mother. "You know the law, Hermes," said Zeus. "As long as the girl has not eaten any food of the underworld, she may leave. But anyone who eats down there must stay there forever."

Hermes flew from the heights of Olympus to the depths of the underworld. "King of this dark place," said Hermes to Hades, "even you must obey the will of mighty Zeus. Bid farewell to your queen."

Then Hermes turned to Persephone. "Take my hand and let us go," he said. "But first, tell me, have you eaten anything while you were down here?"

"No," said the girl, "nothing but a few seeds from that bright red fruit, the pomegranate, which I plucked from a tree."

Hades smiled. "Then you must stay with me," he said. But Zeus gave a command. He said that for each seed Persephone had eaten, she must spend one month of every year in the underworld with Hades. But she would be allowed to spend the other months with her mother.

And that is why every year, when Persephone must leave her mother and return to Hades, we have winter on earth. But while Demeter has Persephone with her, then she is happy, and brings forth the flowers and trees and crops from the warm earth.

The Labors of Hercules

Most people know the Greek hero Heracles by the familiar Roman name Hercules, which we use here.

Hercules was the strongest man on earth. But he did not always use his strength wisely. Once, in a fit of anger, he struck and killed someone, though he did not mean to. He went to the temple of Apollo to ask what he could do to make up for his terrible mistake. He was told to go to the home of his cousin, a king named Eurystheus [yur-ISS-thoos], and do whatever the king asked him to do.

King Eurystheus was a weak, mean man, and he was jealous of his big, strong cousin.

So when Hercules came to serve him, he tried to think of the most difficult and dangerous tasks he could.

"Hercules," said the king, "for your first labor, go to the land of Nemea [neh-ME-ah]. A terrible lion has been killing both cattle and people there. He is so strong that he can kill a man with one blow of his huge paw. His hide is so tough that no sword, spear, or arrow can pierce it. You are to kill the Nemean lion, and bring its skin back to me."

"Well," thought the king to himself, "that should be the end of Hercules." But he did not know his cousin's strength. When Hercules found the lion, he jumped on the beast and grabbed him. Then he squeezed with all his might until at last the lion was dead. But how could he take off the lion's skin? When he tried to use his knife, the blade broke into pieces. Then Hercules got an idea: he used one of the lion's own sharp claws, and sure enough it cut the skin. After he had cleaned the skin, he wrapped it around him like a coat, with the head as a hood.

When Hercules returned, looking like a lion walking on two legs, the king was frightened. "Stay outside the palace," he said, "and I will call out my orders to you."

The king ordered Hercules to kill a fire-breathing, nine-headed monster called the Hydra. Hercules used his huge club to knock off one of the monster's heads, but then two heads grew back in its place! So he grabbed a large stick and set one end on fire. Then, as he swung his club to knock off each head, he held the fire to the neck to keep any other heads from growing back.

When King Eurystheus heard that Hercules had killed the Hydra, he thought, "He kills beasts and monsters so easily that I must think of another kind of labor. Ah, I know! I will send him across the mountains to clean the stables of King Augeas [aw-GEE-us]. They are the biggest and dirtiest stables in the world, filled with the waste of thousands of oxen and cattle."

When Hercules reached the Augean stables, he saw that it would take many years for a single man to clean them, even a man as strong as himself. But as he looked around he saw a river that ran nearby. "Why not use that?" he thought. So he asked

King Augeas to have all the animals taken out of the stable for a day. Then he dug a ditch from the river to the stable, and let the water run through the building. The water washed away all the filth in no time. Hercules filled the ditch and set the river back on its normal course.

"Very clever, Hercules," said King Eurystheus. "But now it's time for a real challenge. For your next labor, I order you to bring me the golden apples guarded by those three magical maidens, the Hesperides" [heh-SPARE-ih-deez]. The king chuckled because he knew that these apples belonged to Hera, queen of the gods, and were kept in a secret garden that no one had ever found. Hercules knew that he could not find the Hesperides. But he could find their father, Atlas, the great giant who carried the heavens and earth upon his shoulders.

"Mighty Atlas," said Hercules, "will you tell me where to find the golden apples of the Hesperides?"

"I cannot tell you such a secret," said Atlas. "But I could get the apples for you myself, if only I did not have to hold the heavens and earth on my shoulders."

"Go and get the apples," said Hercules, "and I will hold the heavens and earth for you."

"I would be glad to have someone else carry this load for a while," said Atlas. So Hercules took the heavens and earth upon his own shoulders. His knees shook and he gasped, "Hurry, Atlas, for I do not know how long I can hold this."

In a short while Atlas came back with the golden apples, but he did not hand them over. "Hercules," he said, "I will take these apples to King Eurystheus myself." Hercules could see that Atlas did not plan to come back. So he said, "Thank you, Atlas, that is kind of you. But before you go, would you please hold the heavens and earth for just a moment? I'm not as strong as you so I need to put a pad on my shoulders to ease the pain."

"All right," said Atlas. He put down the apples and took the load from Hercules's shoulders.

"Thanks for the apples," said Hercules, and he hurried off.

After Hercules completed these and other labors, the gods allowed him to leave King Eurystheus. He traveled all over Greece, doing many great deeds wherever he went.

In your school classroom or library you may have a book full of maps called an *atlas*. The word "atlas" comes from the name of the mythical character who held the heavens and earth on his shoulders.

Learning About Language

PARENTS: *Written language has special characteristics that children need to learn in order to be able to talk about language and make progress in their writing. The section that follows introduces a number of terms and rules of written language, but children will need practice in school for these terms and conventions to sink in. In this book we introduce some terms and concepts that will be built on in later books. For example, in this book we introduce some parts of speech, and later books will introduce other parts of speech, as well as explain more about the parts introduced here.*

Sentences

When you read this, you are reading a sentence. Now you are reading another sentence. What is a sentence? It's a group of words that expresses a complete thought.

Here are three groups of words. Are they all sentences?

(1) Jennifer walks to the beach.
(2) She takes her dog with her.
(3) In the water.

Both (1) and (2) are sentences, but not (3)—it does not express a complete thought. It leaves you wondering, "Who is in the water? Doing what?" But let's change (3) "In the water" by adding some words.

Jennifer and her dog swim in the water.

Now, is that a sentence? Yes it is. It expresses a complete thought.

Every sentence has a *subject* and a *predicate*. Here are some examples.

subject	predicate
Jennifer	walks to the beach.
She	takes her dog with her.
Jennifer and her dog	swim in the water.

Can you tell me which words make up the
subject and which words make up the predicate in these sentences?

Our teacher baked cupcakes for a class party.

The alien spaceship landed in our yard.

Peter Piper picked a peck of pickled peppers.

Two Rules for Writing Sentences

Rule 1. Every sentence must begin with a capital letter. Look at the sentences on
this page. Notice that every sentence begins with a capital letter.

Rule 2. You must end a sentence with a punctuation mark. You use a different
mark for different kinds of sentences.

Most often you use the little dot called a period. You use a period to end sentences
that tell something. The sentence you are reading here ends with a period.

Some sentences ask a question. If you write a sentence that asks a question, you end
it with a question mark. Is it raining today?

To show excitement, you use an exclamation point. We won! What an amazing
shot!

Nouns Name a Person, Place, or Thing

Look around you. What do you see? A book? A chair? A window? A yard or a street?
Book, chair, window, yard, street—all those words are *nouns.*

A noun names a person, place, or thing. In the sentences below, the nouns are
printed in blue:

The new boy from Texas brought his rabbit in a cage to school.
The rabbit got out. It ran to the cafeteria and ate a big salad.

Can you pick out the nouns in these sentences?

My sister likes slimy frogs.
The basketball swished through the net.
We saw amazing paintings and statues in the museum.

All these are nouns, too:

Elm Street   Johnson Elementary School
Fido   George Washington

Did you notice that all those nouns just named begin with a *capital letter?* That's because they don't name just any person, place, or thing, like "school," but a certain place, like Johnson Elementary School, or a certain person, like George Washington.

We call nouns that name a certain person, place, or thing *proper nouns.* You begin a proper noun with a capital letter. Your own name is a proper noun, too, so you begin each word in it with a capital letter.

Singular and Plural Nouns

A noun can name one thing, or it can name more than one. Another name for just one of something is *singular.* All of these are singular nouns:

car   pencil   pig

Another name for more than one is *plural.* All of these are plural nouns:

cars   pencils   pigs

You can see that to change most singular nouns to plural, all you have to do is add the letter *s.* But for nouns that end in *s, ss, ch, sh,* or *x,* you need to add *es* to show more than one, like this:

singular	plural
bus	bus**es**
dress	dress**es**
lunch	lunch**es**
wish	wish**es**
fox	fox**es**

For some plural nouns, you don't use *s* or *es*, but instead you spell the word in a new way, like this:

singular	plural
foot	feet
tooth	teeth
child	children
woman	women
man	men

Verbs: Action Words

sing dance eat laugh jump shout imagine throw

All of those words are *verbs*. Verbs usually show actions. They show what someone or something does.

Jake eats a pizza.   Hannah opens a present.

Can you tell me which word is the verb in each of these sentences?

Lisa eats a banana.
The monkey slips on a banana peel.
The monkey chases Lisa.

Verbs: Past and Present

Verbs can tell about actions that happen now, or actions that happened before. We say that an action that happens now is in the *present*. We say that an action that happened before is in the *past*.

These verbs are in the present. (Notice how some end in *s* and some don't.)

Today I dance.   Ben dances with Alice.
Sherry dances with me.   We all dance together.

These verbs are in the past:

Yesterday I danced.   Ben danced with Alice.
Sherry danced with me.   We all danced together.

You can change many verbs from present to past by adding *ed*, like this:

present   **past**
Today I laugh.   Yesterday I laugh*ed*.
Juanita walks to town.   Last week she walk*ed* to school.
Today we watch a movie.   Yesterday we watch*ed* a movie.

But some verbs are different. Here are some verbs to watch out for. Try making up some sentences using these verbs in the past and in the present.

verb in the present   **verb in the past**
I see, you see   I saw, you saw
he sees   he saw
I do, they do   I did, they did
she does   she did
I come, you come   I came, you came
he comes   he came
I run, we run   I ran, we ran

verb in the present   **verb in the past**
he runs   he ran
I go, you go   I went, you went
she goes   she went

verb in the present   **verb in the past**
we give, you give   we gave, you gave
he gives   he gave
you sing, they sing   you sang, they sang
she sings   she sang

You need to pay special attention to make sure you use two verbs correctly. These verbs are **be** and **have**.

	be		have
present	**past**	**present**	**past**
I am	I was	I have	I had
he, she, it is	he, she, it was	he, she, it has	he, she, it had
we are	we were	we have	we had
you are	you were	you have	you had
they are	they were	they have	they had

Adjectives Describe Things

You know two kinds of words, nouns and verbs. Now let's find out about another kind, adjectives.

Adjectives are the words we use to *describe* nouns (people, places, or things). Adjectives can tell how something looks or tastes or feels or sounds.

a slippery fish   a loud noise   a cute puppy with black and white fur

Can you pick out the adjectives in these sentences?

Sara loves her old, soft, fuzzy blanket.
The brown cow ate a large pizza.
Let's tell scary stories.

Sometimes adjectives tell how many. The words in blue in these sentences are adjectives that tell how many:

I have many pets.
I have two cats, one hamster, and some goldfish.
I take good care of every pet.

You can use adjectives to compare. Often all you have to do is add *er* or *est,* like this:

Batman is strong.   Hercules is stronger.   Superman is the strongest.

My cat is small.   Jane's cat is smaller.   Allie's cat is the smallest.

More About Words: Antonyms and Synonyms

Let's play a word game. I'm going to tell you a word, then you tell me an *antonym.* Antonyms are words that mean the opposite of each other. What is the opposite of cold? Hot. So, cold and hot are antonyms. Tall and short are antonyms. Now, can you tell me an antonym for each of these words?

happy   tall
fast   win

Okay, let's change the game a little. This time I'm going to tell you a word and I want you to tell me a *synonym*. Synonyms are words that mean the same or almost the same thing. Pretty and beautiful are synonyms. Big and large are synonyms. Can you tell me a synonym for each of these words?

fast   angry   powerful   leap

Now, look at these pairs of words. Are they synonyms or antonyms?

love   hate

thin   skinny

begin   start

shout   whisper

loud   quiet

shiny   dull

calm   peaceful

wild   tame

loud   quiet

Contractions

When you write, sometimes you combine two words into one short word called a *contraction*. To show that letters have been left out in a contraction, you use the punctuation mark called an *apostrophe*, like this:

I am = I'm   do not = don't   can not = can't

you are = you're   is not = isn't   are not = aren't

Abbreviations

Have you ever looked at the address on a letter? You might see something like this:

The address uses many *abbreviations*. Abbreviations save time by making words shorter. Here are the words that go with the abbreviations in that address:

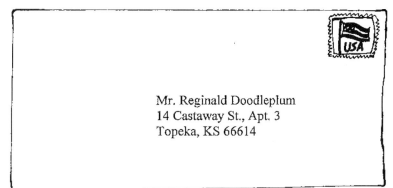

Mr. Reginald Doodleplum
14 Castaway St., Apt. 3
Topeka, KS 66614

Mr.   Mister
St.   Street
Apt.   Apartment
KS   Kansas

In addresses you may see other common abbreviations, such as Rd. (Road), Ave. (Avenue), or Ct. (Court). Every state, including your own, has a two-letter abbreviation, which is written in addresses before the zip code as two capital letters without a period. What is the postal abbreviation for your state?

Many abbreviations begin with a capital letter and end with a period. When you write to someone and you want to be polite, you might use an abbreviation like this:

Dear Mrs. Grundy,
Dear Ms. Greer,
Dear Mr. Chips,
Dear Dr. Frankenstein,   (Dr. stands for Doctor)

The word "Miss" is not an abbreviation, and does not end with a period.

Using Capital Letters

You already know that you always use a capital letter when you start a sentence. When else do you use a capital letter? You use a capital letter when you write names of particular people, places, or things, such as:

Cindy G. Smith
Lassie
Alberto's Restaurant

When you use an initial in a name, you write it as a capital letter followed by a period. For example, in Cindy G. Smith, the "G." stands for Gail. How do you write your middle initial?

Here are some other rules for using capital letters when you write.

- When you refer to yourself, use a capital "I."
- Capitalize the months of the year and the days of the week.

> January
> February
> Monday
> Tuesday

- Capitalize the names of holidays.

> Thanksgiving
> Independence Day
> Mother's Day

- Capitalize the names of countries, cities, states, and landmarks.

> Canada
> Los Angeles, California
> Statue of Liberty

- Capitalize the name of a sports team.

> Chicago Bulls
> Green Bay Packers
> Middletown Patriots

> Notice that when you write the name of a city and a state together, you put a comma between them, like this:
> > Orlando, Florida
> > Denver, Colorado
> > Seattle, Washington
>
> Also, when you write a date, you put a comma between the day and the year, like this:
> > May 31, 1998
> > July 4, 1776
>
> **Try writing today's date.**

- Capitalize all the important words when you write the title of a book. You don't capitalize little words like *a*, *an*, *the*, *in*, or *of*, unless it's the first word of the title, because you always capitalize the first word. Also, when you write the title of a book, underline it, like this:

Little House in the Big Woods

The Velveteen Rabbit

Familiar Sayings

PARENTS: *Every culture has phrases and proverbs that make no sense when carried over literally into another culture. To say, for example, that someone has "let the cat out of the bag" has nothing to do with setting free a trapped kitty. Nor—thank goodness—does it ever literally "rain cats and dogs"!*

The sayings and phrases in this section may be familiar to many children, who hear them at home. But the inclusion of these sayings and phrases in the Core Knowledge Sequence has been singled out for gratitude by many parents and teachers who work with children from home cultures that are different from the culture of literate American English.

Back to the drawing board.

People use this saying when something they're doing doesn't work out, and they feel as though they need to start over from the beginning.

"Ahmad, what are you doing?" asked his mother.
"I'm trying to write a poem for Kim's birthday. But it doesn't sound right. I think I need to go back to the drawing board."

Better late than never.

People use this saying to mean that it's better that something happens late than not at all.

"Mario, I'm sorry I'm so late getting to your birthday party. I had a flat tire!"
"That's okay, Dad. Better late than never!" said Mario.

Cold feet.

People say that someone gets "cold feet" when that person decides not to do something because he or she is afraid.

"I want to jump off the diving board, but every time I try I get cold feet."

Don't cry over spilled milk.

People use this saying to mean that once something is done or something is lost, you shouldn't keep feeling sorry or worrying about it.

"Hey, Greg, why so sad? You aren't still disappointed about losing the spelling bee, are you? Come on, don't cry over spilled milk."

Don't (or can't) judge a book by its cover.

People use this saying to mean that the way something looks may not tell you much about what it's really like. They also use it to mean that the way a person looks may not tell you much about what that person is really like.

"Bill, pick Margaret for our baseball team," said Johnny.

"Margaret? Are you kidding?" said Bill. "She's so quiet and shy. What does she know about baseball?"

"Bill, you can't judge a book by its cover," said Johnny. "She may be quiet and shy, but I've seen her play. She can really hit!"

Easier said than done.

People use this saying to mean that it's sometimes easy to say what should be done, but it's harder to do it.

Rachel and Tom found an old, bent bicycle frame in a trash pile. "Let's take it home and fix it," said Rachel.

"Easier said than done," said Tom. "Where are we going to get two wheels and a chain to fit this bike? And how are we going to straighten the frame?"

Eaten out of house and home.

People use this phrase, often humorously, to mean that a huge amount of food gets eaten, so much, in fact, that someone may have to sell a home to pay for all the food!

"Are you excited that your sister is getting married?" Marie asked Mary Jo.

"I am. My grandpa and grandma are coming to the wedding, and my aunts and uncles and cousins, too. But my dad seems a little worried. He says all Mom's relatives are going to eat us out of house and home."

Get a taste of your own medicine.

People use this expression to mean that someone who has been bothering or mistreating others gets treated in the same way.

"So, did Sakir play any tricks on you guys at school today, Rosa?" asked her sister.

"Nope," replied Rosa. "And I don't think he will for a while. He finally got a taste of his own medicine. During the school assembly we presented him with a medal for playing mean tricks. And he was *really* embarrassed."

Two heads are better than one.

People use this saying to mean that when one person is having trouble with a task or problem, a second person can often help out.

Pete was playing a geography game on the computer. "Rosie," he asked his friend, "what goes next to California?"

"Well," said Rosie, "Nevada and Utah? Or maybe Arizona?"

"Nevada and Arizona both fit. Hey, thanks."

"Anytime," Rosie replied. "After all, two heads are better than one."

In hot water.

People use this phrase to mean in bad trouble.

"What was your favorite part of the movie?" Ryan asked Rita.

"I liked the part when they fell into the snake pit and the snakes were slithering all over them, and then the bad guys found them and sealed the pit," Rita said.

"Yeah," Ryan agreed, "they were really in hot water."

Keep your fingers crossed.

People use this expression in several ways. They say it to keep off danger. And they say it to try to help make a wish come true.

"What do you want for Christmas, Carmen?" asked José.

"Well, I'd like to have a bicycle, but I'm really keeping my fingers crossed that my grandmother will be out of the hospital by Christmas Day."

Practice what you preach.

People use this saying to mean that you should act the way you tell others to act.

"Mom. Mom! *Help!* Ben took my train. He shouldn't grab my toys," Chris wailed. Then Chris yanked the train out of his little brother's hands.

"That's enough, boys," said their mother. "Ben, you shouldn't take the toy Chris is playing with. And, Chris, if you grab things back from him, he will think it's okay to grab things from you. Please try to practice what you preach."

Get up on the wrong side of the bed.

People use this phrase to mean someone is in a bad mood.

"Boy was my mom a grouch this morning. I think she got up on the wrong side of the bed."

Turn over a new leaf.

To turn over a new leaf is to make a big change in the way you act.

"I've been late to school nine times already this year. But starting today I'm going to turn over a new leaf. No matter what happens, I'm going to be on time."

Where there's a will there's a way.

This saying means if you're determined to do something, you'll find a way to do it.

"I can't believe our Girl Scout troop needs to sell six hundred boxes of cookies to top last year's record," said Hilary. "That's impossible."
"Oh no, it's not," said Tina. "Where there's a will there's a way!"

You can't teach an old dog new tricks.

People use this saying to mean that as you get older you get more set in your ways. Once you get used to doing something in a certain way, it becomes very hard to learn a different way to do it.

"Grandfather, why are you going this way to the market? Why don't you take the new road?" asked Mei Jing.
"Oh," laughed her grandfather, "I always forget that new road because I've gone this way all my life. I guess you can't teach an old dog new tricks."

II.

History and Geography

INTRODUCTION

For many years American elementary schools, especially in kindergarten through third grade, have taught "Social Studies" rather than history. Social Studies have typically been made up of lessons about the family, neighborhood, and community. This focus on the personal and the local can be of value, but it is only a beginning.

As anyone knows who has witnessed children's fascination with dinosaurs, knights in armor, or pioneers on the prairie, young children are interested not just in themselves and their immediate surroundings but also in other people, places, and times. In second grade, we can take advantage of children's natural curiosity and broaden their horizons by introducing them to knowledge of other times and places. An early introduction to history and geography can foster an understanding of that broad world beyond the child's locality, and make him or her aware of varied people and ways of life. Such historical study can also begin to develop our children's sense of our nation's past and its significance.

For parents and schools following the *Core Knowledge Sequence,* we can also build on the knowledge children have gained in kindergarten and first grade—knowledge about the world and how it is represented on maps and globes, knowledge of ancient Egypt, the American Revolution, and much more. (See *What Your Kindergartner Needs to Know* and the revised edition of *What Your First Grader Needs to Know.*)

In the following pages, we introduce—let us emphasize *introduce*—a variety of people and events, most of which will be treated more fully in the Core Knowledge books for the later grades. The idea in second grade is to plant seeds of knowledge that can grow later. The purpose is not for the child to achieve deep historical knowledge but rather to become familiar with people, terms, and ideas in such a way that, in later years, when the child hears them mentioned or reads about them, she enjoys the satisfying sense that "I know something about that."

Learning history is not simply a matter of being able to recall names and dates, though the value of getting a firm mental grip on *a few* names and dates—such as 1607 and 1776—should not be discounted. While second graders have not developed a sophisticated sense of chronology, the development of a chronological sense is aided by having at least a few dates fixed in mind and associated with specific events, so that later, as children grow, they can begin to place these dates and events into a more fully developed sense of what happened when.

While it's good to help children grasp a few important facts, for young children the best history teaching emphasizes the "story" in history. In some cases, it is hard—but not entirely necessary—to separate history from legend, such as, for example, the story of how a young Alexander the Great tamed the wild horse Bucephalus. While we have made every effort to respect historical accuracy, we have also tried to put the facts, when possible, into the form of a good story. We encourage parents and teachers to go beyond these pages to help children learn about history through art projects, drama, music, and discussions.

A Note on the History of World Religions: In the World History and Geography section, we introduce children not only to ancient civilizations but also to topics in the history of world religions. As the many people who contributed to the development of the *Core Knowledge Sequence* agreed (see pages xix–xxi), religion is a shaping force in the history of civilization, and thus should be part of what our children know about. The pages on religion have benefitted from the critiques of religious scholars and representatives of various faiths, whom we wish to thank for their advice and suggestions. In introducing children to the history of world religions, we focus on major symbols, figures, and stories. Our goal is to be descriptive, not prescriptive, and to maintain a sense of respect and balance.

A Note on Geography: We encourage teachers and parents to place special emphasis on the geographical topics in the following pages. The elementary years are the best years to gain a lasting familiarity with the main features of world geography, such as the continents, the larger countries, the major rivers and mountains, and the major cities of the world. These spatial forms and relationships, when connected with interesting stories, are not likely to be forgotten. Such knowledge may be reinforced by regular work with maps, which should include a lot of active drawing, coloring, and identification of place names. Drawing maps, as well as associating shapes with names of places, can be fun. Not only fun, but also important parts of what children need to know if they are to have the geographical knowledge they will need to understand the modern world.

Suggested Resources

World History and Geography
India, Hinduism, and Buddhism
Buddha by Susan Roth (Delacorte, 1994)
The Cat Who Went to Heaven by Elizabeth Jane Coatsworth (Macmillan, 1958)
Living in India by Anne Singh (Young Discovery Library, 1988)
Sacred River by Ted Lewin (Clarion Books, 1995)

Ancient China
The Great Wall of China by Leonard Everett Fisher (Macmillan, 1986)
Growing Up in Ancient China by Ken Teague (Troll, 1994)

Japan
How My Parents Learned to Eat by Ina R. Friedman (Houghton Mifflin, 1984)
Japan by Karen Jacobsen (Childrens Press, 1982)

Ancient Greece
A Coloring Book of Ancient Greece (Bellerophon Books, 1994)
D'Aulaire's Book of Greek Myths by Ingri and Edgar Parin d'Aulaire (Doubleday, 1962)
Growing Up in Ancient Greece by Chris Chelepi (Troll, 1993)

American History and Geography

Introduction to the Constitution
The Constitution by Warren Colman (Childrens Press, 1987)

The War of 1812
By the Dawn's Early Light: The Story of the Star-Spangled Banner by Steven Kroll
    (Scholastic, 1993)

Westward Expansion
The Amazing Impossible Erie Canal by Cheryl Harness (Macmillan, 1995)
The Cherokee by Emilie Uttag Lepthien (Childrens Press, rev. ed. 1992)
The Girl Who Loved Wild Horses by Paul Goble (Bradbury / Aladdin, 1978)
Wagon Wheels by Barbara Brenner (HarperCollins, 1993)

Introduction to the Civil War
Journey to Freedom by Courtni Wright (Holiday House, 1997)
Just a Few Words, Mr. Lincoln: The Story of the Gettysburg Address by Jean Fritz (Grosset
    & Dunlap, 1993)
Thunder at Gettysburg by Patricia Lee Gauch (Dell Yearling, 1975)

Immigration
Coming to America: The Story of Immigration by Betsy Maestro (Scholastic, 1996)

Civil Rights
Martin Luther King, Jr. by Carol Greene (Childrens Press, 1989)
A Picture Book of Rosa Parks by David A. Adler (Holiday House, 1993)
The Story of Ruby Bridges by Robert Coles (Scholastic, 1993)

Geography of the Americas
The Great Kapok Tree by Lynne Cherry (Harcourt Brace, 1990)
North America and *South America* by D. V. Georges (Childrens Press, 1986)

For more good resources, see *Books to Build On: A Grade-by-Grade Resource Guide for Parents and Teachers* edited by John Holdren and E. D. Hirsch, Jr. (Dell, 1996).

World History and Geography

A Quick Geography Review

Can you name the seven continents?* Trace the map below. Then locate each continent and write its name on the map.

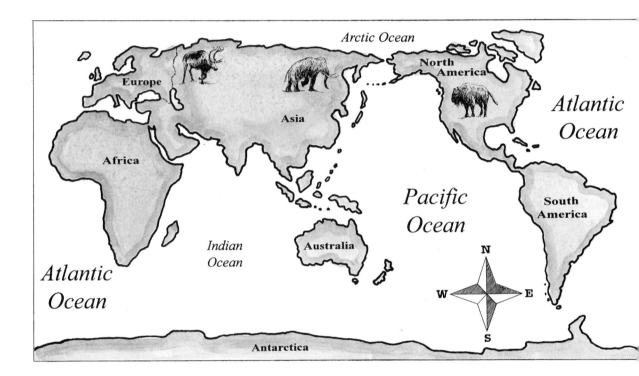

*They are, from biggest to smallest, Asia, Africa, North America, South America, Antarctica, Europe, Australia.

Check your library for two books by Jack Knowlton and Harriet Barton: *Maps and Globes* (HarperCollins, 1985) and *Geography from A to Z: A Picture Glossary* (Harper-Collins, 1988).

The next time you have a globe available try this:

- Locate and name the seven continents.
- Find these important oceans: the Atlantic, the Pacific, the Indian, and the Arctic oceans.
- Locate the North Pole and the South Pole.
- Locate the imaginary line called the equator. The equator divides the globe into two equal parts. We call the part of the globe above the equator the Northern Hemisphere. The part of the globe below the equator is the Southern Hemisphere. ("Hemi" means half, so a hemisphere is half a sphere.) Is Australia in the Northern or Southern Hemisphere? Which hemisphere is Europe in—Northern or Southern?

Settle Down!

Let's think back to some of the history you learned in first grade.

Let's start by going *way, way* back to the times that are called "prehistoric." Do you remember learning that long, long ago, before there were any towns or cities, people lived by moving around to find food? They looked for plants they could eat, and they followed herds of animals they could hunt.

But then a big change happened: people learned to grow large amounts of food. And when they could grow enough food to eat, they didn't have to keep moving around. So the people settled down. As more and more people settled in one place, cities began.

The first cities were built along the banks of some famous flooding rivers. Do you remember the important river in Africa that's the world's longest river? (It's the Nile River.) And do you remember the two big rivers in the part of Asia with that really long name, Mesopotamia? (They are the Tigris and Euphrates rivers.) In these places the water and rich soil helped people grow large amounts food, so they could stay in one place and build the first cities.

The first cities were the beginning of civilization. What does "civilization" mean? To answer that, let's look at what happened in the first cities.

In the first cities, people started to do many different kinds of jobs besides the old work of getting food, taking

Here is part of an ancient city. What jobs mentioned in this book are the people doing?

care of children, and fighting in wars. In a city, you need places to live. So, some people took on the job of building houses. They didn't have time to grow food. But other people grew food, and they began to sell their food to the people who didn't have time to grow it themselves.

As the cities grew, different people did more and more different jobs. Some made clothes, or cooked, or cleaned. Some sold things, such as cloth, tools, or jewelry. Others became artists, musicians, teachers, or scholars.

When large numbers of people live together, they need rules to get along. They need laws. Long ago, who made the laws? Usually the laws were made by a powerful ruler, like a pharaoh or king. Sometimes these rulers made fair laws. But sometimes they made unfair laws that took away the people's freedom and made their lives very hard.

Do you remember the strong ruler named Hammurabi? In a great city called Babylon, Hammurabi made many laws. One reason we

This worker is using a stone to pound a metal bowl into shape.

know about these laws is that they were written down—in fact, they were carved in stone. Writing is one of the most important developments in human history. Writing allows us to save and pass on knowledge. Do you remember what we call the writing of the ancient Egyptians? (It's called "hieroglyphics.")

SUN

OX

RIVER

This writing from ancient Mesopotamia is called cuneiform, which means "wedge-shaped."

So, civilization means many things, including
- learning how to farm
- building cities
- making laws
- living in one place
- different people doing different jobs
- and, in some places, learning to write.

CIVILIZATIONS IN ASIA

Long Ago in Asia: Civilization in the Indus Valley

In the first-grade book in this series, you learned about King Tut and the civilization of ancient Egypt. Thousands of years ago, while the pharaohs in Egypt built pyramids along the banks of the Nile, another civilization was growing in another part of the world. Let's go there now.

Look at the map on page 98 and find India. Can you find the Indus River? The Indus River, like the Nile in Africa, overflowed its banks every year. These yearly floods made the land around the river very fertile ("fertile" land is land that's good for growing many big, healthy plants). So, like the people in ancient Egypt and Mesopotamia, the people in the Indus Valley could grow lots of food because of the flooding river, fertile soil, and warm weather.

After they learned how to farm, what do you think the people in the Indus Valley did next? If you said, "Settle down and build cities," you're right.

Not long ago, archaeologists discovered the ancient cities of the Indus Valley. (Do you remember what archaeologists do?) The archaeologists were amazed to see how the old cities, like Mohenjo-Daro, were laid out in a very neat and organized way. The

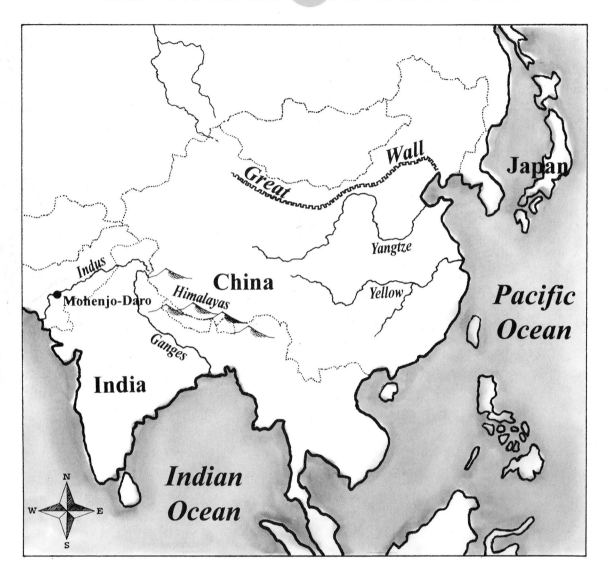

streets were as straight as a ruler. The houses were like boxes with flat roofs made of sun-baked brick. If you had lived back then, you might have taken a woven mat up to the roof and spread it out for a nap in the warm breeze and sunshine.

Civilization Along the Ganges

Historians—the people who study history—know that long, long ago, the people of ancient India began to leave their cities along the Indus River. But why did they leave? Was there some great disaster, such as a terrible flood or earthquakes? That is something we just don't know.

But we do know that after the people left the cities along the Indus River, a new civ-

These high mountains north of the Ganges River are called the Himalayas [him-uh-LAY-uz].

ilization developed in another part of India. This civilization grew along the banks of yet another flooding river, called the Ganges [GAN-jeez]. Can you find the Ganges River on the map on page 98?

The Ganges is the longest river in India. In ancient India, many people made their home near the Ganges. But then new people came to this region, and they did not come as friends. These new people, who came from the northwest, were called Aryans (AIR-ee-uns). The Aryans had large and powerful armies. They conquered and ruled over the Indian people living along the Ganges. They changed the way the Indian people lived. Let's look at some of the biggest changes, starting with their religion.

Hinduism

The Aryans changed the religion of the Indian people. Over many years, the gods of the Aryans combined with the gods worshipped by the Indian people. This was the beginning of Hinduism.

Hinduism is the oldest religion still practiced in the world today. Before we learn more about Hinduism, think back to the religions you've already learned about (in the first-grade book in this series). Do you remember learning that Judaism, Christianity,

This is a statue of the Hindu god called Shiva.

and Islam all teach about one God?

Well, Hinduism is different, and may seem a little confusing at first. That's because most Hindus believe in one God *and* in many gods. For Hindus, the one God is called Brahman. Hindus believe Brahman is a spirit in everything in the universe—in people, animals, trees, water, the ground, the stars, *everything*.

So, Brahman is the one God of Hinduism. But in Hinduism there are also thousands and thousands of different gods. For Hindus, these thousands of gods are like different faces or names of Brahman.

Among the many thousands of gods in Hinduism, there are three main gods. Most Hindus believe that these three main gods are sort of in charge of all the others. They are called Brahma, Vishnu [VISH-noo], and Shiva [SHE-vah].

Hindus believe Brahma is the creator god, the god who made everything. Vishnu is the god who preserves and defends life. Shiva is the god of destruction and new life. In pictures, Shiva is often shown dancing in a ring of fire. Why fire? Because fire can destroy, but it can also help make new things.

Besides having many gods, Hinduism is different from Judaism, Christianity, and Islam in other ways. Hinduism has no single leader or teacher. You remember that be-

Some animals are sacred to Hindus. For Hindus, the cow is the most sacred animal. Hindus are strictly forbidden to kill a cow or eat its meat. Many Hindus are vegetarians—they do not eat any meat.

For Hindus, the Ganges is a holy river. Many Hindus try to make a trip to the Ganges and wash themselves in the water.

lievers in Christianity follow the teachings of Jesus. And Muslims follow Muhammad. But Hinduism has no one leader or teacher that every Hindu is expected to follow.

A Story from the Holy Books of Hinduism

You've learned about religions that have a book of sacred writings. For Jews, the holy book is the Hebrew Bible, the first part of which is called the Torah. The holy book of Christians is the Bible. And the holy book of Muslims is the Qu'ran. Hinduism does not have one holy book—instead, it has several sacred books.

One of the oldest sacred books of Hinduism is the Rig Veda [RIG VAY-da]. It is filled with beautiful poems, and it tells Hindus how to celebrate weddings, funerals, and holy days. If you lived in India today, you could still hear many people saying hymns from the Rig Veda at important times in their lives.

Another important holy book for Hindus is the Ramayana [RAHM-ah-YAHN-ah]. It is full of stories of great deeds and adventures. Many stories in the Ramayana tell about the hero, Prince Rama [RAHM-ah]. In some of these stories, the Hindu god Vishnu takes the form of the human hero, Rama. Here is a story about Rama and Sita [SEE-tah]. It shows the importance of being courageous, and reminds people that evil can be very tricky, but good can win in the end.

Rama and Sita: A Tale from the Ramayana

Once long ago in India, in the kingdom of Ayodha [ah-YOD-ha], there lived a king called Dasaratha [DAHS-ah-RAH-tha]. He was growing old and tired, and he decided that it was time to pass on the kingdom to his favorite son, Prince Rama. But King Dasaratha's wife, who was Rama's stepmother, wanted her own son, Prince Bharat [bah-RAHT], to be king. She knew that Dasaratha loved her so much that he would give her anything she desired. So she went to him and asked him to send Rama to the forest of Dandak for fourteen years and make Bharat king. Dasaratha was both angry and upset, but he did exactly as she asked.

The next day, Rama left his father's palace with his wife, Sita, and his brother, Lakshman, and went into the dark forest of Dandak. On their journey they met an old wise priest who warned them that demons hid within the shadows of the trees. He gave Rama a quiver of magic arrows to protect himself from the evil in the forest.

After many days traveling, Rama, Sita, and Lakshman came to a place where the old man had told them they would be safe. They built themselves a house from hardened earth and bamboo. And so they lived happily for many years.

Then one day a little fawn came running out of the forest. It was the most beautiful animal Sita had ever seen and she begged Rama to catch it for her. Leaving Lakshman to look after his wife, Rama chased the little fawn deeper and deeper into the forest. It led him down winding paths, through tangles of branches, into darkened thickets, until he

was completely lost. No matter how fast he ran, he could never quite catch it.

Suddenly Sita thought she heard Rama's voice crying from the forest: "Help me, Lakshman, help me!"

Lakshman ran off into the forest to try to find his brother. No sooner was he out of sight than an ugly little old man appeared as if from nowhere. As Sita watched, the little old man grew, his face changed, and there stood Ravana [ra-VAH-na], the king of the demons!

Sita screamed but there was no one to hear her. Rama and Lakshman were now both lost in the heart of the forest. Ravana had sent the little deer to draw Rama away and then tricked Lakshman with false cries for help. Now, with a wave of his hand, Ravana summoned his magic chariot and he swept Sita up and away into the sky, over the forest and across the plains and mountains beyond, until at last they crossed the sea and landed on the demon island of Lanka.

Rama and Lakshman finally found their way home. They realized that they had been tricked and that Sita had been taken away by demons. Picking up his quiver of magic arrows and his bow, Rama set out with Lakshman in search of his wife. They traveled for many miles through the forests and across the plains and mountains, but they found no sign of her.

Then one day, as they were crossing a wooded mountain pass, an enormous ape jumped down from a rock onto the path in front of them. "I am Hanuman," he said, "the captain of the Vanar tribe of monkeys." He told them how he had seen Ravana's chariot flying through the sky with Sita aboard, and he promised Rama that he and his army would help in the search for Sita. He clapped his paws together and suddenly, down from the rocks, came hundreds and hundreds of monkeys.

Rama and his new army traveled on across the mountains until they reached the seashore, where the angry waves grew higher and higher, beating wildly against the rocks. Rama could not see how he would ever reach the demon island of Lanka. Then Hanuman said, "We must build a bridge to the island from trees and rocks and anything else we can find."

All the monkeys set to work. They broke off boulders from the cliffs and hurled them into the sea. When the bridge was finally finished, Rama led his army across the sea.

With a roar, Ravana and his hordes of demons came to meet them. Rama took a magic arrow from his quiver and let it fly. The arrow struck Ravana and the demon sank to the ground. A great cheer went up—Ravana was dead and Rama had won.

Rama and Sita were together again at last, and the streets of Lanka were filled with the sounds of laughter and singing as the celebrations began.

Fourteen years had passed since Rama had left his father's palace and now it was time for him to return to Ayodha. In a magic chariot drawn by swans, Rama and Sita flew up into the clouds to begin their last journey home.

In the late fall in India, many Hindus celebrate Rama's victory over Ravana, and the homecoming of Rama and Sita, in a festival called Diwali [dih-VAH-lee]. As part of the festival, the people light many lamps and candles, and sometimes they put on plays telling the story of Rama and Sita.

Buddha: The Enlightened One

You've just learned about one great religion that began in India—Hinduism. Now let's learn about another, called Buddhism [BOO-dhiz-um].

Buddhism began in India. Today Buddhism is the religion of millions of people, but most of them are *not* in India. Today many of these people live in Southeast Asia, China, and Japan. But Buddhism began in India, and it grew out of Hinduism. It began a long time ago, with a young prince named Siddhartha Gautama [sid-DART-tuh GOW-tuh-muh].

Siddhartha was born the son of a very rich king and queen. His father ruled a kingdom in the foothills of the high Himalayan mountains. Siddhartha wore soft, beautiful clothes made of the finest silk. Colorful flowers, soft music, and sweet smells surrounded him. When he walked, servants held umbrellas over him to keep off the sun or rain. When he grew to be sixteen years old, he married a beautiful princess.

What a life! All pleasure, and no pain. Siddhartha's father, the king, tried to make sure that his son was always happy. He even ordered that no one who was sick, old, or poor should ever come near the prince. That way, thought the king, the prince would live in a world without suffering, a world filled with beautiful things and happy people.

But one day, when Siddhartha was riding in his chariot outside the palace walls, he saw an old, gray-haired man, bent over and wrinkled, leaning on a stick. Soon after, he saw a sick man lying along the side of the road, and heard his painful cries for help. Later, for the first time in his life, he saw a dead person. Finally, he saw a holy man with a shaved head and a peaceful expression on his face.

This statue of Buddha was made over a thousand years ago in India.

Now Siddhartha knew what his father had tried so hard to hide from him. He saw that there is pain in the world, and that people grow old and die. He was troubled by what he had seen, and he thought for a long time. Was it right that just because he was born rich, he should be comfortable and happy while other people were unhappy and miserable?

Then he made a hard decision. He made up his mind to leave his family, his home, and his easy, comfortable life. He set off to try to understand why there was suffering and what to do about it. He cut off his long hair. He gave his soft silk gowns to a poor man and put on the poor man's old, ragged clothes. He wandered for years and years, looking for answers to his questions.

Then one night he sat down under a tree to be quiet and think. He sat and thought for a long time, and in the morning when the sun rose, he felt that now he understood. He had become "enlightened," which means wise and aware. And so he was called Buddha, which means "the enlightened one, the one who knows."

What did Buddha know? He said that he now understood that suffering and death are part of life. He said that life is like a great wheel in which birth, suffering, and death come round and round again. And he said that the most important thing is to live a life of goodness. Buddha taught people how to be good, and many people, including his wife and his father, began to follow his teachings. He said, for example, that people should harm no living thing. He told his followers to be kind and merciful to humans and animals alike.

King Asoka: From War to Peace

About two hundred years after Buddha died, a king helped spread Buddha's teachings. King Asoka didn't believe in Buddha's teachings at first. You remember that Buddha said people should harm no living thing. But King Asoka was a warrior. He led his soldiers in fierce battles, in which many men were hurt or killed. Through these wars he brought the northern and southern parts of India together under his rule.

But after one fierce and bloody battle, King Asoka looked around and saw the death and hardship caused by war. He remembered that Buddha had said, "Harm no living thing," and he felt ashamed. He decided to stop making war and instead to devote himself to spreading Buddha's teachings throughout his kingdom. All over India he built hospitals for both people and animals. He told his workers to plant trees and dig wells for fresh water. He even set up houses along the road for travelers who were tired from walking great distances.

King Asoka wanted the people of India to learn more about Buddha's teachings, so he had Buddha's words carved on tall pillars and put them in places where many people would see them. Even though Asoka strongly believed in Buddha's teachings, he also believed that kings should let their people worship as they wanted to. So, many

Many people still visit this giant statue of Buddha in Japan.

Indian people felt they could worship their different gods and also listen to Buddha's words.

King Asoka sent Buddhist priests across Asia to tell people in other lands about Buddha's teachings. So Buddha's ideas spread all over Asia, and Buddhism remains one of the largest religions in the world today.

Asoka had this statue of lions (called a capital) put up at the place where Buddha first explained his beliefs about peace. This capital has become a symbol for India in the same way the bald eagle has become a symbol for the United States.

A Wise Teacher in China: Confucius

Look at the map on page 98. You know where India is. Now look north and east of India and find the big country called China.

Long, long ago, about the same time that Buddha lived in India, another wise man was teaching in China. His name was Confucius. Confucius was a very peaceful man. But during his life, China was not a peaceful country. Instead, many groups were fighting each other. They rode around the countryside and robbed and hurt the people in the villages.

Confucius, who was wise, gentle, and thoughtful, grew tired of all this fighting. He said that the fighting should stop and that all the people should come together under a single wise ruler. The people, he said, should obey a good ruler, while a good ruler should take care of the people. He said to the rulers, "You are there to rule, not to kill. If you desire what is good, the people will be good."

Confucius said many other things about how people should live and treat each other.

Confucius

For example, he said that you should respect your parents and teachers, and honor your ancestors.

You know the Golden Rule, don't you? It says, "Do unto others as you would have them do unto you." Confucius was the first person we know of to teach the Golden Rule, although he put it this way: "What you do not wish for yourself, do not do to others."

Many people in China began to listen to his teachings, which became known as "Confucianism." Confucianism is not a religion, like Islam or Christianity, because Confucius did not have anything to say about God or the gods. Confucianism is a way of thinking about how to live a good life and how to treat others.

China: Great Rivers and a Great Wall

If you look at the map on page 98, you can see that China is separated from India by the high Himalaya Mountains. Where did civilization begin in China? You can probably guess—yes, by a river! Just as in ancient India, Egypt, and Mesopotamia, the first cities in China were built near rivers that regularly flooded and left rich soil, good for growing grains like millet and rice. Look at the map on page 98 and find these two important rivers in China: the Yellow River and the Yangtze River. (In China, the Yellow River is called the Huang He, and the Yangtze is called the Chang Jiang.)

Between these rivers, the people in China long ago built their first cities. Some of the people built large houses, created art, made fine clothes, and sent their children to schools. But many of the people were poor, because their rulers kept fighting one another to try to become the one all-powerful ruler.

Finally, one strong and very strict ruler brought China together under his leadership. He was China's first emperor, and he was called Qin Shihuangdi [CHIN shih-hwahng-DEE]. The name "China" comes from his family name, "Qin" (which you pronounce "chin").

Not long ago, archaeologists discovered the tomb of Qin Shihuangdi, the first emperor of China. This is one of thousands of life-sized soldiers made of clay they found in the tomb.

This is only a small part of the Great Wall of China.

Qin stopped the rulers from fighting among themselves. But he still had to worry about fighting against people who were attacking China from the north. These people were rough warriors called Mongols.

Qin decided that one way he could protect the Chinese people would be to build a wall big enough and strong enough to keep out the Mongols. There were already some big walls made of packed dirt, and Qin ordered many people to do the hard work of connecting these walls, as well as building new walls.

But this was too big a job to finish in one lifetime. Many years after Qin, later emperors of China ordered many workmen to keep making the wall longer and longer. The work was very hard, since the wall went on for more than a thousand miles, up mountains, down valleys, and along the curving paths of rivers. The workmen built towers so that guards could look out for invaders from the north. Much of the Great Wall of China is still standing today. It is so long that, if you stretched it out across the United States, it would reach from Maine to Florida!

An Important Invention

Long ago, the Chinese came up with some important inventions. You can see a Chinese invention right in front of you. The Chinese invented paper! They made paper from the bark of mulberry trees, rags, and sometimes even old fishing nets. Chinese travelers showed people in other countries how to make paper. As the years went on, more and more people, in Asia and even in faraway Europe, learned how to make paper. Think about this: why was paper such an important invention?

This man is making paper the way the ancient Chinese did, one piece at a time. He lifts a screen out of water mixed with mashed vegetable fibers. The water drains out of the screen and then the fibers dry into a sheet of paper.

In the Language and Literature section of this book, you can read a folk tale from China called "The Magic Paintbrush." (See page 27.)

Smooth as Silk

Here is an old legend from China.

Once upon a time, an empress was having tea in her garden under the shade of some mulberry trees, when, *plunk!* something splashed into her teacup. She looked in and saw a small, white, fuzzy thing. It was a cocoon! It had fallen from the mulberry trees above, where little worms lived and ate the leaves.

Now, you might expect the empress to say "Yuck!" and throw out her tea, but she was a calm and curious person. She noticed something coming off the cocoon. When she looked closer, she saw it was a thread. When she touched the thread, it felt smooth and strong. And she thought, "If we had a lot of this thread, and if we could weave it, we could make a very special cloth."

Soon the empress and her servants were feeding all the worms in the mulberry trees and gathering many cocoons. And from the thread they wove a new kind of cloth. It was like no cloth that anyone had ever felt before—so smooth, soft, shiny, and cool. The empress, the emperor, and all the noble people began wearing clothes made of this

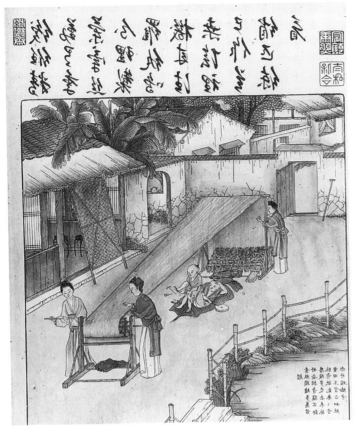

new cloth, called silk. Visitors from other countries saw these fine silk clothes and said, "We want silk, too."

That's the legend, and parts of it are really true. Silkworms do eat mulberry leaves. When the worms make their cocoons, they do produce a thread that can be made into silk cloth. And, many people did want silk from China.

The Chinese people made a lot of silk and traded it with people from other countries. Merchants from as far away as Europe and Arabia traveled to China to buy silk and then took it back home to sell.

This very old picture shows Chinese women weaving silk.

Silk feels so fine and smooth that even today, if things are going very well, people say that everything is "smooth as silk."

Chinese New Year

From as long ago as the time of Confucius up to the present day, the Chinese people have enjoyed celebrating the New Year Festival. On New Year's Day, Chinese families gather together—grandparents, parents, and children. They decorate their homes and shops with bright colors, especially red, and often wear red outfits, because in China red means good luck and happiness. The New Year Festival can go on for many days, with fireworks and parades in which people dress up in dragon costumes and dance in the streets.

The Chinese New Year does not happen on the first day of January, because the date of the Chinese New Year is based on a special calendar that follows the cycles of the moon. Usually, the Chinese New Year happens on a day somewhere between the middle of January and the middle of February.

In the Chinese lunar calendar ("lunar" means "of the moon"), each year is under the protection of one of twelve different animals. Find out what animal goes with the year you were born in— maybe a donkey, dragon, rabbit, tiger, or dog— by checking your library for books on the Chinese New Year, such as *Cat and Rat: The Legend of the Chinese Zodiac* by Ed Young (Henry Holt, 1995).

Dragon dancers whirl at a modern Chinese New Year Festival.

Let's Visit Japan

You've been learning about the long-ago times in India and China. Now, let's jump ahead in time and look at life as it is today in an important Asian country, Japan.

Japan is a country far to the east in Asia. Since the sun rises in the east, Japan has long been called "the land of the rising sun." A rising sun is pictured on the flag of Japan, which has a red circle on a white background.

Compared to China, Japan is a very small country. Japan is made up of many islands. The four main islands are really the tops of a great mountain range. There are many volcanoes in Japan, and there are many earthquakes.

In Japan you'll find one of the largest cities in the world, called Tokyo. Tokyo is a busy, crowded, modern city, with many banks, stores, restaurants, museums, colleges, and apartment buildings.

If you were to visit a Japanese family living in an apartment in Tokyo, the first thing you would do when you entered their home would be to take off your shoes. You would wear socks or special slippers, but you would *never* wear your outside shoes indoors!

If your Japanese friends invited you to stay for dinner, you might not sit in a chair but instead kneel on a cushion around a low table.

In the Language and Literature section of this book, you can read a folk tale from Japan, called "The Tongue-Cut Sparrow." (See page 42.)

Mount Fuji.

Here's a busy market on a crowded street in modern Tokyo.

To pick up your food, you would not use a fork—and no, you wouldn't use your fingers, but two slender pieces of wood about the size of pencils, called chopsticks.

In many ways, Japan is a very modern country. It has busy factories that make cars, televisions, radios, cameras, and other products that are bought by people around the world.

But there is more to Japan than a lot of modern business and industry. In Japan the people also care about their old ways and customs. For example, children in Japan learn a very old art form called *origami*. To do *origami*, you fold paper in special ways, without cutting or pasting it, to make lovely figures such as a bird or a swan.

On special holidays, many Japanese people—men and women, boys and girls—wear a *kimono*, a beautiful robe that is tied at the waist. In Japan, *Shogatsu*, New Year's Day, is a special holiday. The Japanese also celebrate two holidays that we don't have in America: one is called Girls' Day (in March), and the other is Boys' Day (in May). On these days the children dress in bright costumes, play games, and often receive presents.

These Japanese children are wearing traditional kimonos.

Ancient Greece

Birthplace of the Olympics and More

Have you ever watched the Olympics on television or been lucky enough to see the games live? If you have, then you know how exciting it is to see some of the best athletes from all around the world come together to compete in many sports, such as running and swimming in the Summer Olympics, or skiing and sledding in the Winter Olympics.

Do you know where the Olympics got started? In a land that is now the country called Greece. Did you know that the first Olympics were held in Greece more than 2,500 years ago?

The ancient Greeks loved athletics. Every four years, they would hold a week of games at a place called Olympia. The best athletes would gather to run, jump, wrestle, throw weapons, and race chariots and horses.

The Olympics of the ancient Greeks were in some ways different from our Olympics today. The ancient Greeks held contests in music and poetry, which are not part of our modern games. In ancient Greece, only men were allowed to compete, and they did not wear uniforms—in fact, they didn't wear anything! Today, the winners get medals, but in ancient Greece winners were crowned with a wreath made of wild olive leaves.

The ancient Greeks gave us the Olympics, but they also gave us much more. Ancient Greece is the birthplace of many of the ideas and beliefs that are still important to us today. Let's find out more about the civilization of the ancient Greeks.

A Civilization of City-States

In ancient Greece, did civilization begin by a big, flooding river? No! Greece is different. Greece has no flooding river like the Nile in Egypt. Greece is mostly a rocky, dry land, broken by many hills and mountains. The hills and mountains kept groups of people apart. Each

1988 Olympic medal-winner Jackie Joyner-Kersee sails through the air.

group didn't have much to do with its neighbors, because its neighbors were so far away. Some of these groups of people grew into large communities, which were called city-states. Look at the map on page 116 to find some of the most important city-states: Athens, Sparta, and Thebes.

These Olympic athletes were painted on a vase in ancient Greece.

The people in these separate city-states all spoke the Greek language. They told many of the same stories, and worshipped many of the same gods. (Like people in other ancient civilizations you've learned about, the Greeks believed in many gods, whom you can read about in this book, starting on page 56.) But the Greeks did not have a single ruler. In fact, the city-states often argued and sometimes fought against each other.

Most people in ancient Greece lived near the sea. Look at the map on page 116 and find the Mediterranean Sea and the Aegean [ih-JEE-un] Sea. Can you also find the island in the Mediterranean called Crete [rhymes with "street"]?

Athens: Birthplace of Democracy

Many things important to us today got their start in the ancient civilizations—things like agriculture (growing food crops), cities, and writing. From the ancient Greeks, we got many new ideas, including a very important idea from the city of Athens. Let's find out about this idea, called democracy.

For hundreds of years, the Athenians had tried different ways of governing their city. They argued a lot about the best way. Some Athenians got tired of being ruled by a small group of powerful and strict leaders. They spoke up and said, "Why should just a few people make laws for everyone else, especially when they make bad laws?"

Leaders who make bad laws and are cruel to the people are called "tyrants." Many

When you look at Greece on the map, you will see that it is a *peninsula*. A peninsula is a large piece of land that sticks out into the water and is almost surrounded by water. Look at a map of the United States and you will see that Florida is also a peninsula.

Ancient Greece and nearby regions.

Athenians got tired of being ruled by a few tyrants. "Let's get rid of the tyrants and rule ourselves!" they said. And that is what the Athenians did. They invented a new kind of government, in which the people chose their leaders. And if those leaders began to act like tyrants, then the people had the power to choose new leaders. This new kind of government, born in Athens and still with us today, is called "democracy." Democracy means "rule by the people" or "people power."

In Athens, democracy was not perfect. Not all the people had power. Not all the

There's a famous old story about a fierce monster that lived on the island of Crete. You can read the story of "Theseus and the Minotaur," as well as many other Greek myths, in the Language and Literature section of this book. (See pages 56–73.)

people were allowed to take part in the government. Only citizens were allowed to vote, and not every adult was a citizen. Women and slaves were not citizens, so they could not vote. It would take many more years for human beings to figure out that all people are created equal and should have equal rights, not just grown men who own a lot of property.

Still, even though democracy in Athens left out women and slaves, it was the beginning of an idea that is very important today in our own country—the idea that ordinary people can help make the laws and choose their own leaders. This idea of democracy made ancient Athens different from most other places on earth at that time, where the laws were made by a king, or a small group of warriors or priests. Where would you rather live? In a place where you helped make the laws and pick the leaders, or where you never had any say?

Rough, Tough Sparta

Not far from Athens there was another Greek city-state called Sparta. The Spartans were tough. They were great warriors. When Spartan boys were only seven years old, they were taken from their families and trained to be soldiers. Their heads were shaved and they were given only rough clothing, no shoes, and very little food to eat. They slept on hard beds with no covers. Why? To make them tough and ready for war.

Even the Spartan girls were trained to compete in sporting events. To the people of Athens, this was shocking. The Athenians believed that young girls should learn to take care of the home and children, and should grow up to be quiet and gentle. But not the Spartans. They wanted the girls to grow up to be strong and tough. Still, like the Athenians, the Spartans did not let women vote or take part in the government of the city-state.

Today, people use the word "Spartan" to describe something that is very plain and basic, with nothing fancy or frilly about it. To live a "Spartan" life means to live a life with very few comforts. For example, if you lived a Spartan life, you might get up very early, take only a cold shower, wear plain clothes, and never eat any sweet snacks.

The United States is a democracy. Today, the law in the United States says that if you are born in this country, then you are an American citizen. And as a citizen, as soon as you turn eighteen years old, you have the right to vote and help choose the people who will lead the country and make the laws.

The Persian Wars

While the city-states of ancient Greece, such as Athens and Sparta, were growing bigger and stronger, another civilization was growing to the east. These people were the Persians. The Persians had conquered the people in both Babylon and Egypt.

When a country conquers and takes charge of other lands, it makes those lands part of its "empire." About 2,500 years ago, the Persian empire was the mightiest in the world. The Persians ruled over most of the lands between the Indus River and the Mediterranean Sea. Wherever the Persians went, they spread their civilization. They gave the different peoples they conquered one government, one kind of money to use, and even a postal system.

As the Persians pushed farther west, their empire came closer and closer to Greece. The Persians came first to some Greek cities in the area called Ionia [eye-OH-nee-uh]. Look at the map on page 116 and you'll see that Ionia was not far to the east of Athens and Sparta. The Persian armies conquered Ionia. But then the Ionian people surprised the Persians: they didn't just act sad

This tablet shows Persian King Darius in his chariot hunting a lion. Do you see the cuneiform writing on the left?

and defeated. The Ionians wanted to be free, so they fought back. The Ionians asked Athens for help, and the Athenians sent ships and soldiers. The Persian king, named Darius [duh-RYE-us], was furious: "How dare these Greeks fight back?!" he thought. Darius gave orders for many soldiers and a large fleet of ships to prepare to attack the mainland of Greece.

And so the Greeks and Persians were at war. Darius believed that he would easily defeat the Greeks because, after all, the Greek city-states were always fighting each other. But, as you will see, Darius was wrong.

Battles That Live in Memory

Even though the Greeks and Persians fought more than two thousand years ago, people still remember and tell the stories of some famous battles.

Marathon

King Darius sent six hundred ships with thousands of soldiers to conquer Athens. The Athenians knew they needed help. So they turned to the city-state that had sometimes been their enemy, Sparta.

Back then, there were of course no telephones or any other way of quickly getting a message to someone far away. The fastest way to get a message to Sparta was to send a runner. The Athenians chose a runner named Pheidippides [fie-DIH-pih-deez]. For two days and nights, he ran, swam, climbed, and ran some more until he reached Sparta.

When Pheidippides asked the Spartans for help, they said, "We will send two thousand men to help you, but they cannot come until the next full moon, when they are finished with our religious festival." Pheidippides ran back to Athens with the news. The Athenians said, "We cannot wait. The Persians are close by. Get ready for battle."

Meanwhile, the Persian soldiers of King Darius had sailed their ships to a place called Marathon. From there they planned to march to the city of Athens. (Find Marathon and Athens on the map on page 116.) The Greek general knew that the Persians had many more soldiers, so he came up with a daring plan. At Marathon, he ordered the Greek soldiers to attack the Persians! The Greeks ran furiously right into the Persian lines. The Persians were surprised, and many of them ran back to their ships. By the end of the battle, many more Persians lay dead than Greeks.

The Greek general then turned to Pheidippides, who was already weary from the battle, and said, "Run to Athens with the news of our victory." For more than twenty miles, Pheidippides ran and ran, as fast as he could. He reached the city and managed to gasp out the good news—"We are victorious!"—then the poor man dropped dead.

Today, people still run in long-distance races called "marathons." A marathon is about twenty-six miles.

Thermopylae

"The Greeks have won for now," said King Darius, "but I promise, we will crush them all!"

Before he could keep his promise, however, Darius died. His son, named Xerxes [ZURK-seez], became king. "I will keep my father's promise," he said, and he prepared a great army. Hundreds of thousands of Persian soldiers attacked Greece from the north. They marched southward, toward Athens and Sparta. Could anything stop them?

The Persians came to a narrow strip of land between the mountains and the sea. At this place, called Thermopylae [ther-MOP-ih-lee], a group of about three hundred Spartan soldiers, with some other Greeks to help them, waited for the Persians. How could a handful of men hope to stand against so many thousands?

Bravely the Spartans faced their foes. To the Spartans, there was no such thing as fear. The Persians came forward, only to meet death at the points of the Spartan spears.

But there were so many more Persians than Spartans that, one by one, the Spartans

The battle of Thermopylae.

fell. At last their spears were broken. Yet still they stood side by side, fighting to the last. Some fought with swords, some with daggers, and some with only their fists. All day long they fought and held back the Persians. But when the sun went down, not one Spartan was left alive. Each and every one had died for his country.

Great Thinkers in Athens

After the Persian wars the people of Athens enjoyed some years of peace, and they worked hard to rebuild their city. During the leadership of a wise man named Pericles [PER-ih-cleez], they built a big new temple and dedicated it to Athena, the goddess they believed watched over their city. They built this temple out of marble and filled it with beautiful statues. It was called the Parthenon. (You can learn more about the Parthenon in the Visual Arts section of this book.)

Pericles examines plans for the building of the Parthenon.

The ancient Greeks wrote a lot about philosophy and history. They also wrote many poems and plays. The ancient Greeks used an alphabet which is still used in Greece today. Here are its first four letters.

A	B	Λ	Δ
alpha	beta	gamma	delta

The first two letters are called "alpha" and "beta." Do you see where our word "alphabet" comes from?

Many great thinkers lived in Athens. These thinkers were called philosophers, which means "lovers of wisdom." The philosophers asked big questions, such as, How should we live? What are our duties? What is the best form of government?

Let's meet three of the most important Greek philosophers: Socrates [SOCK-ruh-teez], Plato [PLAY-toe], and Aristotle [AIR-ih-stot'l].

Young men from all over Greece came to learn from Socrates. Socrates once said, "There is only one good, knowledge, and one evil, ignorance." He loved to ask questions. He made his students think by asking lots of questions and then questioning their answers! Some people felt that Socrates asked too many questions, and they got angry at him and threatened him. But Socrates did not stop asking questions. He wanted to know the truth.

Plato was a student of Socrates, and he wrote down much of what he learned from his wise teacher. Plato believed in the importance of education. Near Athens, he started a school called the Academy. Plato said, "The direction in which education starts a man will determine his future life."

Plato's best student was Aristotle. Aristotle was interested in everything around him. He loved to look closely at plants and animals, and to think about how things work. He thought a lot about people as well. He asked, what makes a person a good ruler? What are the best ways for people to live so that they get along with each other?

Alexander the Great

Aristotle had a student named Alexander. When he grew up, Alexander became so powerful and famous that he was called "Alexander the Great."

From the time that he was very young, Alexander's mother told him that he would do wonderful things. From his teacher, Aristotle, Alexander learned much about the world, about people, and about how a good king should rule. From others, Alexander learned how to fight well.

Alexander was the son of King Philip, the ruler of Macedonia [mass-ih-DOE-nee-uh] in the northern part of Greece (see the map on page 116). By the time Alexander was a young man, his father had already led his armies to the south and conquered many Greek city-states, including Athens.

There is a story that, one day, King Philip took the twelve-year-old Alexander to a sale of horses. One horse kept snorting and bucking furiously. "No one can ride so wild and savage a beast," the men said. King Philip ordered the servants to take the horse away, but Alexander spoke up. "Those men do not know how to treat him," he said.

"Perhaps you can do better?" said his father doubtfully.

"Yes," said Alexander confidently. He ran to the horse and quickly turned his head

toward the sun, because he had noticed that the horse was afraid of his
own shadow. He then spoke gently
to the horse and patted him with his
hand. When he had quieted him a
little, he quickly leaped on the
horse's back.

Everybody expected to see the
boy tossed to his death. But Alexander held on tight and let the horse
run as fast as he could. By and by,
the horse became tired, and Alexander rode him back to where his father was standing.

"My son," said King Philip,
"Macedonia is too small a place for
you. You must seek a larger kingdom
that will be worthy of you."

A few years later, after his father
died, that is just what Alexander
did. When he was only twenty-two
years old, Alexander set off on his
horse, which he named Bucephalus
[byoo-SEF-ah-lus], to conquer the
world.

Young Alexander tames the wild Bucephalus.

The Gordian Knot

Alexander was a strong, intelligent ruler, but he could also be hot-tempered and cruel.
Not long after he became king, the Greek city-state of Thebes decided that it no longer
wanted to be ruled by Alexander. The young king moved quickly to show his strength:
he burned the city to the ground and ordered that the citizens be sold as slaves.

Alexander and his army could not be stopped. With Greece under his control, he
marched eastward.

There is a famous legend about Alexander. The legend says that, hundreds of years
before Alexander, a king named Gordius made a knot with so many twists and turns
that nobody could untie it, a knot more tangled than the worst knot you've ever gotten
in your shoelaces. This famous knot, called "the Gordian knot," was tied in a rope on
an oxcart. People said that anyone who could undo the knot would have the world for
his kingdom.

When Alexander heard about the Gordian knot, he said, "Take me to it." The people took him to a little temple. There stood the oxcart, with the famous knot tied to it.

"Tell me again," said Alexander, "what you believe about this knot."

"It is said," the people replied, "that the man who can undo it shall have the world for his kingdom."

Alexander looked carefully at the knot. He could not find the ends of the rope—but what did that matter? He raised his sharp sword and, with one stroke, sliced through the knot. The rope fell to the ground, and the people cheered.

"The world is my kingdom," said Alexander.

What Lies Beyond?

Over the next few years, Alexander conquered a huge empire. He led his armies into Egypt. There, near the Nile River, he built a splendid new city which he named after himself, Alexandria. He then attacked the heart of the once mighty Persian empire, near the Tigris River. The people of Persia accepted Alexander as their king.

Alexander now ruled over most of the ancient world. (See the map below.) But that was not enough for Alexander. Always, as soon as he had conquered one land, he

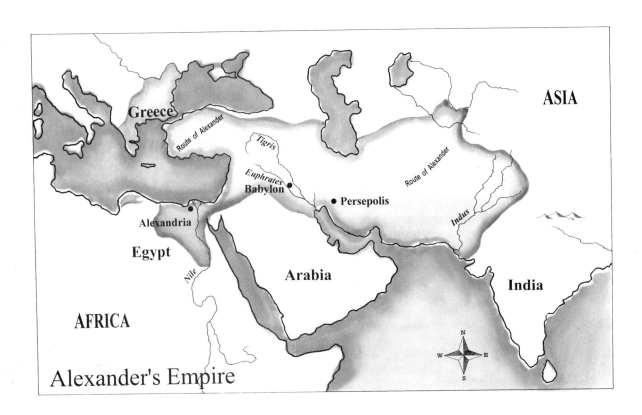

Alexander's Empire

would ask, "What lies beyond?" He pushed his army forward into battle after battle. But the soldiers were tired of fighting. They grumbled and argued and often drank too much wine. Finally, they refused to go any farther. Alexander was furious, but many of his men had been marching and fighting for eight years, and they had had enough. And so Alexander gave the order to return home.

We will never know whether Alexander would have been a good ruler of his empire, because he soon fell ill and died. He was only thirty-three years old.

In just ten years, Alexander had conquered the largest empire the world has ever known. But soon after his death, his empire fell apart. Other leaders got into fights about who should rule, and none of these leaders was as strong as Alexander. Still, even though his empire did not last, Alexander had a lasting effect on the world because everywhere he went, he spread Greek ideas and learning that are still important today.

Alexander speaks to his soldiers.

American History and Geography

A Quick Look Back

If you've read the first-grade book in this series, then put on your thinking cap, and let's see what you remember.

Let's take a quick look back to the times long, long, long ago, all the way back to pre-historic times. Way back then, wandering groups of people followed the animals they were hunting. The wandering hunters who lived on the continent of Asia followed the animals across what was, back then, a "land bridge." Where did this land bridge lead them? To another continent—our continent, North America.

Over many years, these people kept moving south. After a long time they settled down and started civilizations. Can you tell me something about some of the earliest Native American civilizations, like the Aztec, or the Maya, or the Inca?

Now, think about some of the first explorers who came from Europe to North and South America. (Find these continents on a world map or globe.) In 1492, who "sailed the ocean blue"?

A Pilgrim family aboard the *Mayflower*.

After Columbus, people from England crossed the Atlantic and settled in Virginia. In 1607 they arrived at a place they called Jamestown. They soon met the Powhatan Indians. Do you remember the brave young woman named Pocahontas?

More people came here from England. The Pilgrims and the Puritans settled in the Massachusetts Bay colony. Over the next hundred years, thirteen English colonies grew in America. Can you name some of these colonies? (If you don't remember their names, look ahead to the map on page 128.)

As the American colonies grew, they decided that they no longer wanted to be ruled by England and King George III. They wanted to be their own country and rule themselves. And so, one day in the year 1776, representatives of the thirteen colonies signed the Declaration of Independence, which said that from now on, we would be our own country. Now we celebrate that day as Independence Day, the birthday of our nation. Do you remember the exact date? (July 4, 1776.)

After we declared our independence from England, we had to fight for it. Many lives were lost in the American Revolution. But in the end a new country was born: the United States of America.

You've learned a lot about American history! Now it's time to find out more. We're going to begin by going back to the years just before George Washington became our first president. Let's start with what happened to our country just after the American Revolution.

Our Constitution

Democracy: A Big Challenge

You might think that after our country gained its freedom from England, everything was just fine. After all, we won the Revolutionary War. We were no longer ruled by a far-away king. We were no longer thirteen colonies of England. We were our own country. We could choose our own leaders. So, democracy was safe and sound in our new country, right?

Well, not quite. Democracy doesn't just happen. Do you remember what the word "democracy" means? It means "rule by the people." But the people don't always agree. Just think about your own family, or your classroom. Do you always agree?

Back in the 1780s, Americans did not always agree. They had fought hard to become the United States of America, but

Long before there was radio or television, the "town crier" in colonial times announced important news to keep the people informed.

they did not act very united. "United" means "joined together, working together." But each of the first thirteen states wanted to be in charge of itself. None of the new states wanted a strong central government telling them what to do. Each state wanted to

After the Revolutionary War, the thirteen colonies became the first thirteen states of the new United States of America. The dotted lines show the state boundaries as they exist today.

make its own laws and have its own rulers. Pennsylvanians wanted to make their own laws for Pennsylvania. But Virginians wanted to pass laws for Virginia. And Georgians would take care of themselves, too, thank you. And Rhode Island disagreed so much with its neighbors that once the little state almost got into a fight with Massachusetts and Connecticut!

So, the new states couldn't agree on much. They couldn't even agree to use the same kind of money.

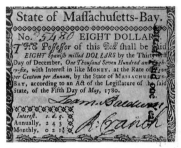

The states could not agree. They even issued different kinds of money.

With each state looking out for itself, how was the United States to be united? After all, sometimes the states would *have* to join together. What if England or another country attacked the United States? Then who would organize an American army? Who would pay the soldiers? Who would be in charge? Who would watch out for the *whole* country, not just each state on its own, but all together, *united*?

Many of the leaders knew they had to figure out some way for the states to work together. Fortunately, we had some very smart leaders. And one of the smartest was James Madison.

James Madison: Father of the Constitution

James was the oldest of the twelve children in the Madison family. His father called him Jemmy. He was often sick, but that didn't stop him from reading. On the big plantation in Virginia where they lived, his father had a room with eighty-five books, not children's books but big books about science and history. James started reading them when he was nine. By the time he was eleven, he had read every one!

So his father sent him to a school. There young Jemmy learned math and science. He learned to read

Leaders from the states met at the Constitutional Convention in 1787. Do you recognize the tall man standing on the platform at the right? (He would soon become our first president.)

in other languages, including French, Latin, and Greek. Later, James went to college in New Jersey. Most students took four years to finish their college studies, but James finished in only two.

All this reading and studying came in handy after the Revolutionary War. James Madison knew that if the United States was to be strong, the states had to learn to work together. But how? James started thinking—and, of course, he read some more. He asked his good friend, Thomas Jefferson, to send him books about history and government. Jefferson sent the books—hundreds of them! James Madison read them. He thought very hard. And he came up with a plan.

His plan was shared at a meeting in the city of Philadelphia. There, about fifty men from twelve of the thirteen states met in a building now called Independence Hall. (No one came from Rhode Island—they still disagreed with almost everyone else!) Along with James Madison, George Washington was at this meeting. So was Benjamin Franklin. Even though it was a terribly hot summer, they kept the windows closed, because they didn't want people outside to hear what they were arguing about.

And oh, how they argued! Although James Madison was usually a quiet person, even a little shy, he spoke up often at this meeting. Many men disagreed with him. But finally, after months of arguing in the hot, sticky building, the men accepted many of Madison's ideas.

They wrote down those ideas, and when they were finished, they had produced the Constitution of the United States. In the Constitution, they said how they wanted to set up the government of the new nation. They said:

The United States Constitution states the basic rules, the most important laws, of our country. Even today, the Constitution is the highest law in our land.

When the men in Philadelphia finished writing the Constitution, they sent copies to all the states. The American people read it. Many people liked it. Just as many people argued loudly against it. But after all the arguing was over, the representatives from each state voted to accept the Constitution. And because James Madison worked so hard to get the Constitution written, and because so many of his good ideas are in it, he is remembered as "the father of the Constitution."

James Madison.

Look closely at the picture of the Constitution below. Can you see what the biggest words are? They are the first three words:

We the People

Why are they so important? Because they say that we Americans ourselves chose this new kind of government. They say that the Constitution is not a law laid down by a mighty king. It's not what some all-powerful pharaoh or emperor says that everyone must do. Instead, the United States Constitution is the law of **We the People.**

The first page of our Constitution.

The War of 1812

Another War Already?

Not long after the Revolution, our young country faced another war. A war against whom? Oh no—not again—but yes, England!

It happened like this. In the year 1812, our president was "the father of the Constitution," James Madison. At this time, England and France were at war—again. (These two countries had a long habit of fighting each other.) But England and France are across the Atlantic Ocean in Europe. How did America get drawn into a faraway war?

It happened partly out on the rolling waves of the Atlantic Ocean. There, American ships were stopped by both French and British ships. ("British," you remember, is another way of saying "English.") You see, the British didn't want Americans selling supplies to the French, and the French didn't want Americans selling supplies to the British. So they *both* stopped American ships, and sometimes shot cannonballs at us, and sometimes even captured our ships and sailors.

In 1811, France let go all the American ships she had captured. But not England. The British navy kept on stopping American ships and sometimes "impressing" American sailors. That doesn't mean they did something to impress or amaze them! This kind of "impressment" means that the British captured some of our sailors and forced them to work for the British navy.

Many Americans were angry at England for impressing our sailors. They cried, "Let's fight the British!" But President Madison knew that the American navy was still young and not very strong, while the British had the most powerful navy in the world. So at first he did not want America to get into any fights with England.

But other people were saying, "We should fight England anyway, for another reason." These people, who were called the "War Hawks," had their eyes on the land to the north of the United States. They had their eyes on Canada.

Back then, Canada was still a British colony—just as the United States had been a British colony before we won our independence in the Revolutionary War. The War Hawks said, "Look, the English are busy fighting against France, so they won't be able to defend Canada. This is our big chance. Let's declare war on England. Then our American soldiers can march north and take over Canada. That will teach the British a lesson!"

Eventually President Madison came to agree with the War Hawks. With the battle cry of, "On to Canada!" the United States declared war on England. The War of 1812 had begun.

At first things did not go well for the Americans. The British surprised us. They sent many soldiers and fought hard to protect their northern territory. They beat back the American soldiers.

Even though the British were beating the Americans badly, the Americans did win some important battles at sea. That was a big surprise because the British had the most powerful navy in the world. But the Americans had some very good ships and commanders too. The ship called the *Constitution* won several naval battles. The sailors liked to say that British cannonballs bounced off of her sides as if she were made of iron. So they nicknamed her "Old Ironsides." *Old Ironsides* is docked in Boston harbor for tourists to see. She is the oldest warship afloat in any of the world's navies.

Old Ironsides is still sailing today!

Dolley Madison: A Brave Woman

Dolley Madison.

The Americans won some battles at sea, but things were not going well for the Americans elsewhere. British ships sailed into the Chesapeake Bay, bringing more soldiers. The soldiers were headed to our nation's capital, Washington, D.C.! What if they were to capture President Madison? What a disaster that would be!

Fortunately, James Madison was not in Washington at the time. But his wife, Dolley Madison, was there. From the president's house, she could hear gunfire as the British soldiers approached. The British had already burned the Capitol, the building where Congress met. Now they were heading toward the president's house.

Dolley Madison acted quickly. She ordered some men to remove a famous painting of George Washington and get it out of the city. She had many boxes of important papers loaded into a cart—including the Declaration of Independence and the Constitution! She even grabbed the silverware and two sets of beautiful red curtains. She tossed them all into a horse-drawn carriage. Then she disguised herself as a farmer's wife and drove quickly out of town.

Just in time! The British arrived soon after she left. They ate the dinner that Dolley had left on the table. Then they burned down the president's house, as well as many other buildings in Washington.

The British captured and burned Washington, D.C.

On the other side of the Potomac River, Dolley Madison met her husband. Because of her bravery and quick thinking, part of America's past had been saved.

The president's house was not repaired until 1818. Even then, the workmen could not re-move the burn marks the fire had made on the outside walls. So they covered the marks by painting the walls white. Pretty soon, people started calling the president's house by the name we still use today—the White House.

Dolley Madison saved this famous painting of George Washington before the British burned the president's house.

Oh, Say, Can You See . . .

For three days, fires blazed in Washington. Then the British troops sailed north to Baltimore. Baltimore was a very important city for the Americans, because many American ships sailed out of the Baltimore harbor. The British wanted to stop those ships. They wanted to smash Baltimore to the ground.

But this time it was the British who were surprised. The Americans were ready. As the British ships sailed into the Baltimore harbor, they approached Fort McHenry, which guarded the harbor. There they saw an American flag flying—and what a flag! It was huge! It measured forty-two feet by thirty feet.

The British ships were met by an American ship. But this ship did not come to fight. It came in peace. On it was an American lawyer named Francis Scott Key. He had been sent to ask the British to release an American doctor they were holding as a prisoner. The British released the doctor, but they would not allow the American ship to go back to Baltimore—at least not until after the battle.

Imagine that you're with Francis Scott Key on that ship. The battle begins. Cannons crash like thunder. Through the night the British ships keep bombing Fort

Francis Scott Key sees the American flag still waving over Fort McHenry.

McHenry. You wonder, what is happening to the Americans? Through the darkness, the smoke, and the noise, you can't tell. As the bombs keep bursting in the air, you fear the worst. Maybe Fort McHenry has fallen to the British.

Finally, the morning comes. By the dawn's early light, you look through the misty air. You strain your eyes to see Fort McHenry. What's that you see? Yes, our flag is still there! When you see that big American flag, with its broad stripes and bright stars still flying, you want to shout, "Hooray!" And you know that Baltimore is safe—the British have not won.

Francis Scott Key must have seen something like that. He wrote a poem about what he saw. People liked the poem and began to sing its words to a familiar tune. And in time that poem became the song that is our national anthem, "The Star-Spangled Banner." It has four parts; you may know the first part well:

> Oh, say, can you see by the dawn's early light,
> What so proudly we hailed at the twilight's last gleaming?
> Whose broad stripes and bright stars, through the perilous fight,
> O'er the ramparts we watched were so gallantly streaming?
> And the rockets' red glare, the bombs bursting in air,
> Gave proof through the night that our flag was still there.
> Oh, say, does that star-spangled banner yet wave
> O'er the land of the free and the home of the brave?

Our Changing Flag

The flag that Francis Scott Key saw waving over Fort McHenry was not exactly the same as our flag today. The flag he saw looks like the top flag here.

Since Key's time, our flag has changed many times. The bottom flag here looks like our flag today (though this picture doesn't show you the colors—red, white, and blue).

What are some of the differences between the flag that Key saw and our flag today? Compare the number of stripes on each flag. Our flag today has thirteen stripes. They stand for the thirteen original states of our country.

Count the number of stars on the older flag. Over the years, the American flag got more and more stars. Our flag today has fifty stars. Do you know what they stand for? (The fifty stars stand for the fifty states now in the United States of America.)

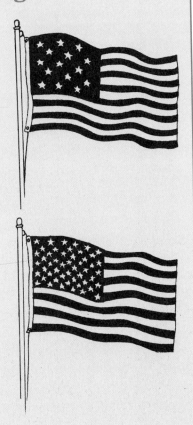

The Battle After the War

The War of 1812 dragged on. In fact, it was now late in 1814, and both sides were tired of fighting. In Europe, British and American leaders were talking and trying to find a way to end the war. They finally signed a peace treaty on December 24, 1814.

Now, if America were in a war today, and the war ended, you would know the news instantly. That's because we have satellites, radios, televisions, telephones, and other ways to get news around the world in the blink of an eye. But none of that was around in 1814. So the news of the peace treaty traveled slowly from Europe across the big Atlantic Ocean to America. And before the news arrived, American and British soldiers fought another big battle.

The Battle of New Orleans happened in early January of 1815, a couple of weeks after the peace treaty had been signed. General Andrew Jackson was in charge of the American troops. He and his men dug trenches around the city. They crouched down and waited.

The British marched straight toward General Jackson and his soldiers. And almost as fast as they marched, they were shot down. The battle was a big victory for the United States. It made Andrew Jackson a popular hero. He became so popular that, years later, he was elected our seventh president.

After the War of 1812 ended, England and the United States would never fight each other again. Today, the two countries are good friends.

The Battle of New Orleans. General Andrew Jackson is on horseback.

Westward Ho!

The Call of the West

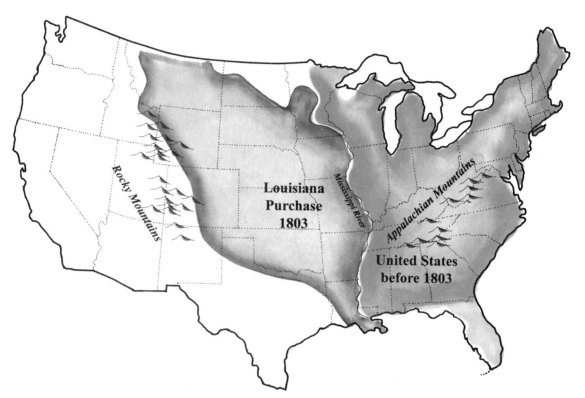

The United States at the time of the Louisiana Purchase.

Do you remember (from the first-grade book of this series) the Louisiana Purchase? It was a great bargain for the United States. France claimed a lot of land in North America but wanted to sell it. So President Thomas Jefferson bought it. And *zing*, just like that, the Louisiana Purchase doubled the size of our country!

Many Americans wanted to go to the new land. They wanted to farm the land and make new homes in the West. They had heard stories about how well the crops grew in the rich land between the Appalachian Mountains and the Mississippi River. (Can you find these on the map above?) Why, some people said that potatoes popped right out of the ground, and pumpkins grew to the size of mighty boulders! And some said there were so many animals to hunt you might trip over them when you walked!

But if you wanted to get to this land, there was something in your way—thick forests and a mountain range.

It was hard, slow going to cross the mountains on foot or in a horse-drawn wagon. If only there were some other way! Pretty soon, there was.

To get to the West, you had to cross the Appalachian Mountains.

Boats and Canals

Things changed when a man named Robert Fulton developed a new kind of boat, called the steamboat. Steamboats didn't need oars or sails. You just put wood or coal into a furnace that heated water, which made steam, which ran the engine, which made the boat go! Steamboats could take settlers up and down rivers and lakes faster than people had ever gone before.

But what if the rivers and lakes didn't go exactly where you wanted to go? Not even a steamboat can travel on land. For some of the settlers moving West, there was no way to go except by land. And this made their lives even harder. If they ran out of supplies like flour, or if

A steamboat chugs down a river.

they needed a new ax, it could take a month or more to get what they needed from the merchants back in the East.

Some people said, "It's so much faster and cheaper to move things in boats on the water. We've got lots of rivers and lakes—really big lakes, too, like the Great Lakes. If only we could join them together." But how?

Well, one man had an idea. The governor of New York, named DeWitt Clinton, wanted to build a canal—a big, man-made ditch. He wanted the canal to connect the Hudson River and Lake Erie. But such a canal would be over three hundred miles long! And it would have to be dug in hard, rocky ground, and through forests with snakes and wildcats.

Clinton got people to believe that his idea would work, and so they began digging the canal. Many of the workers were people who had recently come to America from Ireland. They were poor and hungry and willing to do the very hard and sometimes dangerous work.

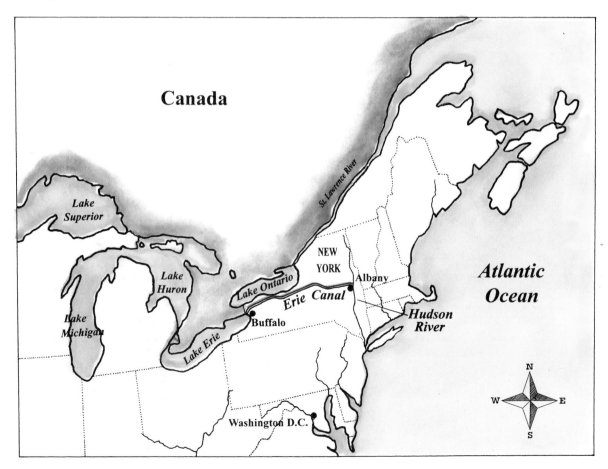

On this map, find the Hudson River, the Erie Canal, and the five Great Lakes.

Horses pull a packet boat along the Erie Canal.

At first people laughed at what they called "Clinton's Ditch." But in about seven years, nobody was laughing. The work was done. The Erie Canal was finished! Look at the map on page 142 to see how the canal connects the Hudson River and Lake Erie. The canal made traveling West a lot easier and cheaper. For many years people used the canal to move loads of cargo on big flat boats called barges. The barges were pulled by mules or horses walking along the banks of the canal. But people didn't use the canal as much when a new kind of transportation came along—the railroads.

The Erie Canal

Here's part of a well-known American folk song.

I've got a mule, her name is Sal,
Fifteen miles on the Erie Canal.
She's a good ol' worker and a good ol' pal,
Fifteen miles on the Erie Canal.

We've hauled some barges in our day,
Filled with lumber, coal, and hay,
And we know every inch of the way
From Albany to Buffalo.

Low bridge, everybody down!
Low bridge, for we're comin' to a town.
And you'll always know your neighbor,
You'll always know your pal,
If you've ever navigated on the Erie Canal.

The Iron Horse

It didn't take long for people to realize that if you could use a steam engine to power a boat, then maybe you could use it for other kinds of transportation, too. Soon, steam engines were pulling trains. These early, steam-powered railroads might seem slow to us today, but back then, people were frightened to be speeding along at twenty miles per hour!

The passengers on these early trains had other reasons to be frightened, too. The engines puffed out soot that could turn your nice white shirt a dirty gray. Even worse, the engines sometimes spit out sparks. One might land on you and set your coat on fire!

When people first heard a steam-powered train puffing and snorting along, they came up with a name for it. They called it an "iron horse." An American writer named Henry David Thoreau (thuh-ROW) was so excited to hear the railroad go past his house in the woods that he wrote, "I hear the iron horse make the hills echo with his snort like thunder, shaking the earth with his feet, and breathing fire and smoke from his nostrils."

Thousands and thousands of miles of railroad tracks soon crossed America. In 1869, Americans celebrated when work was finished on a track joining the eastern and western parts of this country. This track went almost all the way from the Atlantic to the

Workers lay track for the railroad.

Pacific oceans, across the whole continent. And so it was called the "Transcontinental Railroad" ("trans" means "across"). If you lived in the East and wanted to go West, all you had to do was buy a ticket, hop on board, and wave good-bye!

Many immigrants from China and Ireland helped build the Transcontinental Railroad. You can read about immigrants in America later in this book, beginning on page 164.

Wagons West

Boats, canals, and trains made it easier to head West. After the War of 1812, many thousands of Americans moved beyond the Appalachians. More and more people came from Europe, too. Some of these people had been poor and hungry in their old countries. In America, they hoped to find land to farm and the chance for a better life.

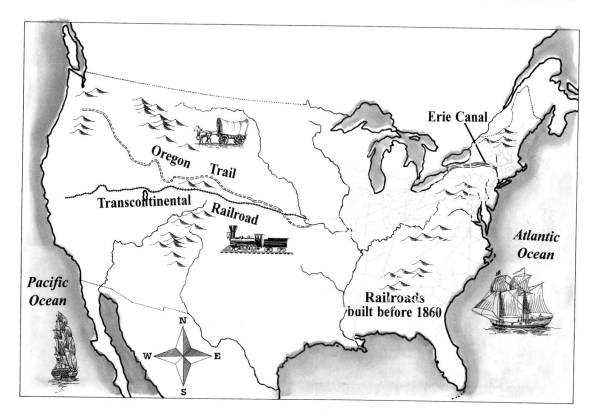

Some railroads and routes to the West.

Pioneers traveled in covered wagons.

The people who moved West, leaving behind their old lives and heading into an unknown future, were called pioneers. The pioneers prepared the way for the millions of people who would move West in later years.

Even before the railroads were built, many pioneers went West in a train—but not the "iron horse" kind of train. They went in a very different kind of train, called a wagon train. A wagon train was a group of covered wagons. The wagons had big wooden wheels, and were pulled by oxen, horses, or mules.

Why was it called a "covered wagon"? Because it was covered by a big canvas cloth stretched over wooden hoops. Inside a covered wagon a pioneer family would pack in as much as they could. Of course there were no supermarkets out West, so they had to take a lot of food, such as flour, potatoes, beans, and dried meat. They would also take a barrel of fresh water.

What else do you think the pioneers would need to take with them? Well, they needed clothes, of course, and needles and thread to sew new clothes or fix rips in the old clothes. And they needed blankets to keep them warm at night. And things to cook and eat with: pots and pans, metal plates, knives, forks, and spoons. And tools, like an ax to chop with, and a hammer and nails. And some soap to wash with, and some candles. And a rifle, so they could hunt for more food. And maybe, for the children, a favorite book or toy—but not more than one or two, because there just wasn't room enough in the covered wagon to hold more.

The family might also bring some animals like cows or sheep—but not *in* the wagon, of course! The animals were tied to ropes and walked behind the wagons.

A Family Goes West

Not every pioneer family traveled in a group with other families. Sometimes a family would load their covered wagon and head West on their own. Here is a part of story that tells about the journey of one family. The story is called *Going West*.

One day in early spring we packed everything we had into our wagon, tied our milk cow Sadie on behind, and set out to find a new home.

Going West.

There were five of us: Papa and Mama; me, Hannah, just turned seven; my little brother Jake; and Rebecca, a fat baby with yellow curls.

Mama cried. She was leaving her three sisters and all our furniture and the piano she loved to play. But Papa said we were going to a place where anything you planted would grow and a farm could stretch out as far as the eye could see.

We left behind the town we knew, the woods, the hills. We rode, bouncing and swaying in the creaking wagon, day after day.

At night Mama cooked over a campfire and we slept close together on the wagon floor, with stars winking through the opening in our canvas roof.

Here is what was in our wagon: blankets and pillows and quilts, Mama's favorite rocking chair, trunks full of clothes, barrels full of food, a cookstove, a box of tin dishes, all of Mama's cooking pots, all of Papa's tools, a Bible, a rifle, and a spinning wheel.

There was barely room for us.

Sometimes it rained. Our wagon got stuck in the mud and we all had to get out and push. Once it rained so hard that the wagon leaked. That night we slept in wet clothes in wet beds, without any supper. Rebecca cried, and Jake said he wanted to go home. Mama didn't say anything, but I think she felt the same.

We were all tired of the rocking wagon and the dust and the same sights day after day. Jake fell out and hurt his arm. Rebecca caught a cold. At night she coughed and coughed. Mama looked worried, but still we rode on.

Going West.

Going West.

A log cabin home.

We came to a river, all muddy and wide. "How will we get across?" I asked Papa.

"The horses will take us," he said.

First the water came up to the horses' knees. And then their chests.

Suddenly Papa shouted, "Hold on tight!"

The horses were swimming. Water was pouring into the wagon. Mama held me tight, until at last I felt the horses' feet touch bottom again.

We had crossed the river.

On the other side of the river the land was flat, with no trees. There was not a bush and not a stone; nothing but green, waving grass and blue sky and a constant, whispering wind. It seemed a lonely, empty place.

But Papa said, "This is the land we've been looking for."

As the sun was setting, we came upon a place where wildflowers bloomed in mounds of pink and lavender and blue, like soft pillows.

"Look," said Mama smiling.

And Papa said, "Here is where we will build our house."

The next day we began. Papa took the horses and rode away. When he came back, he brought logs from the creek. For many days he worked. Slowly, with Mama helping, he built walls, a roof, a door.

Finally he took Mama's rocking chair and set it next to our new fireplace. It was only one room, with dirt for a floor, but at last we slept in a house again.

Mama planted a garden. Jake carried water from the creek to do the washing. I minded the baby and swept the dirt floor and helped Mama hang checked curtains on the window.

"There," she said. "We are ready for visitors."

But no visitors came. We were alone on the vast prairie.

Papa rode away again, many miles to town. For three long days we watched and waited. And then Papa came back. He brought flour and bacon and six sheep that he traded for one of the horses and a surprise: real white sugar.

Mama baked a cake and it reminded me of home.

There's more to this story, and you can read it in *Going West* by Jean Van Leeuwen (Dial Books for Young Readers, 1992). You might also enjoy *Wagon Wheels* by Barbara Brenner (HarperCollins, 1978) and *Little House in the Big Woods* by Laura Ingalls Wilder (HarperCollins, 1932, 1971).

The Pony Express

Have you ever run a relay race? That's when you run part of the race, then you tag another runner, and he or she runs to tag the next runner, and so on.

If you imagine a relay race, then you'll understand how the Pony Express worked. The Pony Express was set up to get mail to the people who were settling out West, as far as California. It could take over a month to get a letter out there, and people got tired of waiting. So two businessmen decided to set up the Pony Express, a kind of relay race on horseback from Missouri to California.

Here's how it worked. A young rider would grab a mailbag then jump on a horse and ride for ten miles at top speed. Then he would jump on a fresh horse and keep going. He would change horses seven times, and then he would pass the mailbag to another rider, who would keep on riding on another seven horses for another seventy miles until he reached the next rider!

A Pony Express rider waves to workers putting up telegraph poles.

With the Pony Express, the mail got all the way to California in only ten days! But in just a couple of years, there was no need for the Pony Express. People could use a brand-new, electric way to send messages, the telegraph. With the telegraph, you could send a message in only seconds. That was a *lot* quicker than the Pony Express—but not as exciting!

Women's Work

Back in the pioneer days, many women worked hard, but they didn't leave their homes to go to work. Their work was at home, and they had their hands full.

Remember, this was before supermarkets, refrigerators, dishwashers, electric lights, and store-bought clothes. It was a big job to take care of a home and family, and the women did most of it. Women gardened and grew vegetables. They milked cows, collected eggs, and churned butter. They cooked the family meals and baked the family breads and pies. They canned fruits, made jelly, and preserved meats to last through the winter. They boiled lye to make soap and collected beeswax to make candles. They spun, knitted, and wove cloth, making blankets and much of the clothing for their families. Then, of course, the clothes got dirty and the women washed them too!

As if that weren't enough, pioneer women in America did one of the most important jobs done anywhere at any time—they raised the children. Their job was to teach their children how to be good people and how to be good helpers around the home and farm. Many mothers taught their children to read before they ever sent them off to school.

The Oregon Trail

Some pioneers wanted to go way far West, all the way to the Oregon Territory. To get there they followed a path called the Oregon Trail. The trail started in Missouri then stretched west. And what a stretch! The trail went on for about two thousand miles!(Look at the map on page 145.)

A journey on the Oregon Trail took a long time, usually about six months. It was a hard and dangerous trip. Pioneers who traveled the Oregon Trail usually started their journey in the spring. Often they would be soaked by bitter cold rains. Later they would have to make it through the hot, dry desert. After the desert, they came to the high, rough Rocky Mountains. It was very hard to get a covered wagon over the mountains. Sometimes a wagon would slip down a steep mountainside and a family would lose everything. Some pioneers got sick or starved and died on the way.

But many made it. With bravery, hard work, and a little luck, they pressed on till they came to the new land where they could start a new life.

Already There: The American Indians

But the lands out West were not new for everyone. For many American Indians, this land was their home.

Out West there were many different tribes. Each tribe had its own way of life. For example, in the dry and hot Southwest, the Pueblo Indians were mostly farmers, and they lived in houses they made of adobe, a mixture of clay, sand, and straw. Another tribe in the Southwest, the Apache, did not settle down and farm, but instead roamed the mountains and deserts and hunted for food.

Many American Indians lived in the big, grassy land between the Mississippi River and the Rocky Mountains, called the Great Plains. The Great Plains were home to tribes such as the Iowa, the Lakota (also called the Sioux), the Crow, the Blackfoot, and the Cheyenne.

For many of the Plains Indians, the big, shaggy animal called the buffalo was very important. Thousands and thousands of buffalo roamed across the Great Plains. The Indians hunted the buffalo for food. They used the buffalo's hide to make clothing. Some also used the hide to make a tent called a teepee.

For the American Indians living in the West, imagine what a shock it would be to

Some American Indian lands.

see black smoke pouring from a metal monster roaring right through the lands where you hunted. Imagine what a surprise it would be to see a wagon train rolling on to your land, bringing people who look and talk in such strange ways. Sometimes you might feel friendly toward these strangers. Maybe you would trade with them. They would give you a thick blanket or some metal fish hooks in exchange for some moccasins, the strong shoes you made out of buffalo hide.

But sometimes you would not feel friendly. More and more of the covered wagons keep coming. And sometimes they don't keep going. They stop. And the strange people begin cutting down trees and building odd box-shaped houses. And they start to hunt for the same animals that you have been hunting for many years.

These strangers come with very different ideas about the land. They say that they "claim" the land. Some say they have bought it, and so they own it. But you have lived on this land for years. You wonder, how can anybody *own* it? You do not see the land as something that any person can keep just for himself. You have always thought of the land, and the animals and the plants on it, as a gift that should be used carefully by all.

Railroads ran through American Indian lands.

One night, you hear the leaders of your tribe talking in serious voices around a campfire. One man sounds angry. He says that the strangers are bad. He says that they have driven away the animals you need, and that your people are going hungry. He says that you must fight the strangers and drive them away. You do not want this to happen, but something inside you knows that you cannot stop it. The fighting will come.

Many Plains Indians depended on the buffalo. They used the buffalo for food, shelter, clothing, and more. But as more settlers came West, they shot and killed many, many buffalo. They shot some for meat to feed the men working to build railroads. They shot others to sell the hides, which were worth a lot of money back in the East. They shot so many that soon the great herds of buffalo began to die out. There were once millions of buffalo, and then there were only hundreds. The buffalo almost became extinct. And that was a terrible threat to the Plains Indians, who needed the buffalo to live. No wonder they fought back.

Hunters killed the buffalo that the Plains Indians needed to live.

Forced from Their Lands

As the pioneers moved West, they often fought with the Indians. The pioneers thought of the land as their new home. They did not worry about taking away the land and homes of the Indians who already lived there.

In some ways, the pioneers were doing what the United States government had already been doing for years—pushing Native Americans off the lands where they lived, and forcing them to move far away.

One American leader who forced many Indians to move was President Andrew Jackson. He did not care about treating the Indians fairly. He just wanted them off the land that he wanted for the United States. Although many Americans did not agree with President Jackson, he went ahead with his plan to force thousands of Native Americans off their land. They had to move many hundreds of miles away to "Indian Territory," which was mostly dry, dusty land west of the Mississippi River. Later, as wagon trains brought more and more pioneers to this land, the American government forced the Indians to move onto smaller pieces of land, called reservations.

In the southeast part of our country, in what is now the state of Georgia, one tribe refused to go. The Cherokee people did not want to leave their good land and their homes. But the American government wanted their land because there was gold on it. So American soldiers were sent in. They used rifles to threaten the Cherokee people. The soldiers forced them to get onto railroad cars

Sequoyah's invention. A Cherokee named Sequoyah did an amazing thing. Many Native Americans did not use a written language, but Sequoyah worked for twelve years to make an alphabet for the Cherokee people. With the alphabet Sequoyah invented, many Cherokee people learned to read and write in their own language.

and steamboats, which took the people only part of the way to the Indian Territory. There were still hundreds of miles to go. The Cherokee people were forced to walk. Many got very sick. Many starved. Many did not make it. Thousands of Cherokee men, women, and children died along the way. The journey was so awful and so sad that it is now known as the "Trail of Tears."

Many Cherokee suffered or died on the Trail of Tears when they were forced to move from their homeland.

To learn more about the history of the Cherokee people and about how some live today, look for these books in your library: *The Cherokee* by Emilie Lepthien (Childrens Press, 1985); and *Cherokee Summer* by Diane Hoyt-Goldsmith (Holiday House, 1993).

At the Cherokee Nation library in Oklahoma, a ten-year-old girl uses a computer to study the Cherokee language.

The Civil War

Fighting Against Each Other

As you know, many years ago Americans fought the British in two wars—the Revolutionary War and the War of 1812. Now you're going to learn about another war—but this one was different. In this war, Americans fought against each other. It is called the Civil War, because a "civil war" is a war between two parts of a single country.

Our Civil War was a war between the North and the South of the United States. Why would Americans fight against each other? There were many reasons. One big reason was that people could not agree about slavery.

Slavery in America

Slavery started early in the United States. It started when we were still a group of colonies. Not long after the English first settled in Jamestown, ships brought the first Africans to America. Soon, more and more ships brought more and more people from

Africa. But these people did not come here because they wanted to. They were forced to come as slaves. Many had been kidnapped, taken against their will, from their homes in Africa. They were crammed into ships, and many of them died on the hard voyage across the Atlantic Ocean. Some were taken to Europe, others to North and South America.

The Africans who survived the terrible voyage were sold into slavery. Think about that—these were people, human beings, but they were *sold*, like furniture or cattle. They were mainly sold to farmers in the Southern states, like Virginia, North Carolina, South Carolina, and Georgia.

Slaves were packed tightly into ships and brought to America.

These Southern states had big farms, called plantations. On the plantations, the owners grew crops that they sold for money, such as tobacco and cotton. The farm owners wanted slaves to work on their farms. The owners were the masters, and they could do what they wanted with the slaves. Many masters forced the slaves to work hard from dawn to dark, with almost no rest. They gave the slaves very little to eat, and only worn-out clothes to wear. If a master did not like the way a slave was working, he could have the slave whipped.

Stop Slavery or Let It Spread?

Although there were many, many slaves in America, mostly in the South, not everyone agreed that slavery was right. In fact, many people were saying that slavery was

This very old photograph shows a slave family in South Carolina.

When Africans were forced to come to America as slaves, they combined their music with the music they heard in America. The songs they sang, called spirituals, often told of their hard lives and of their hopes for better times to come. Here are the words to a well-known spiritual.

Swing Low, Sweet Chariot

Swing low, sweet chariot,
Comin' for to carry me home,
Swing low, sweet chariot,
Comin' for to carry me home.

I looked over Jordan and what did I see
Comin' for to carry me home,
A band of angels comin' after me,
Comin' for to carry me home.

If you get there before I do,
Comin' for to carry me home,
Tell all my friends I'm comin' there too,
Comin' for to carry me home.

wrong and that it should be ended. They said that no one should be allowed to own people. They said the slaves should be given their freedom.

The people who wanted to end slavery lived mostly in the Northern states. But in the Southern states, where slaves worked on the big farms, most people wanted to keep slavery going. The Northerners and Southerners also disagreed about whether slavery should be allowed to spread. As more Americans moved out West, some wanted to take slaves to work for them. They said, "We own these slaves. They are our property. You can't stop us from taking what we own." But many Northerners said, "No! Slavery must not spread. People are not property."

Southerners did not want to change their way of life. They said, "The United States government cannot tell us what to do. We Southern states have the right to make our own decisions."

Another Kind of Railroad

While the North and South argued over slavery, some brave people worked to help slaves escape to freedom. One of the people who helped slaves escape had been a slave herself. Her name was Harriet Tubman.

When Harriet was a little girl, she had worked as a slave for a mistress who often beat her. Harriet wanted to run away. She dreamed of being free.

Harriet Tubman.

As she worked in the fields, Harriet heard other slaves whispering about a railroad. But it wasn't a real railroad. It was called the Underground Railroad, and it was a way for slaves to escape to freedom. It wasn't really underground, but it was called that because it was secret. It was a secret way to go North to freedom. Along the way many people, both white and black, took great risks by hiding and feeding slaves who had run away from their masters.

With help from people on the Underground Railroad, Harriet Tubman escaped to the North. There she was free. But she didn't just sit still and enjoy her freedom. She started to work for the Underground Railroad herself. She went back and helped her family escape. And she kept going back, over and over. It's hard to tell exactly how many people Harriet Tubman helped, but some say that she led three hundred slaves to freedom.

Follow the Drinking Gourd

Here is part of a song that some slaves sang about the Underground Railroad. The "drinking gourd" is another name for the stars known as the Big Dipper. To follow it was to go North to freedom.

When the sun comes back and the
    first quail calls,
Follow the drinking gourd.
For the old man is a-waiting for to
    carry you to freedom
If you follow the drinking gourd.

Follow the drinking gourd,
Follow the drinking gourd,
For the old man is a-waiting for to
    carry you to freedom
If you follow the drinking gourd.

The river ends between two hills,
Follow the drinking gourd.
There's another river on the other side,
Follow the drinking gourd.

Follow the drinking gourd,
Follow the drinking gourd,
For the old man is a-waiting for to carry you to freedom
If you follow the drinking gourd.

Yankees Against Rebels

Meanwhile, the Northern and Southern states kept arguing. The Southern states said that the United States government had no right to tell them what to do. Finally, the arguing turned to fighting.

In 1861, the Civil War started. It lasted until 1865. It was American against American, North against South. The Southerners called Northerners "Yankees." Northerners

A Northern "Yankee" soldier.

A Southern "Rebel" soldier.

called Southerners "Rebels" or "Rebs" for short.

General Robert E. Lee was in charge of the Southern army. General Ulysses S. Grant was in charge of the Northern army. They were very different men. General Lee was a quiet, tall, dignified gentleman. General Grant was scruffy-looking and, to tell the truth, he drank too much. But both men were brilliant military leaders.

Robert E. Lee.

Ulysses S. Grant.

Songs of the North and South

When Johnny Comes Marching Home

This is part of a popular marching song for the Northern army.

> When Johnny comes marching home again,
> Hurrah, hurrah!
> We'll give him a hearty welcome then,
> Hurrah, hurrah!
> The men will cheer and the boys will shout,
> The ladies they will all turn out,
> And we'll all feel gay when Johnny comes marching home.

Dixie

The most popular song in the South was actually written by a Northerner!

> I wish I was in the land of cotton,
> Old times there are not forgotten,
> Look away! Look away! Look away!
> Dixie Land.
>
> In Dixie Land where I was born in,
> Early on one frosty mornin',
> Look away! Look away! Look away!
> Dixie Land.
>
> Then I wish I was in Dixie,
> Hooray! Hooray!
> In Dixie Land, I'll take my stand,
> To live and die in Dixie,
> Away, away, away down south in Dixie.
> Away, away, away down south in Dixie!

Abraham Lincoln:
A Man for the Union

Just before the fighting started, the Southern states decided that they did not want to be part of the United States anymore. They said, "We will be in charge of ourselves," and they set up their own government and their own army.

But many people in the North did not think the Southern states should be allowed to leave the United States. There was one man who especially wanted the United States to stay together as a union—which means, to stay as one country, all united. This was President Abraham Lincoln.

If you say the Pledge of Allegiance at school in the morning, then you say the words, "one nation, indivisible." That's what President Lincoln wanted—a nation that could not be divided. He wanted to keep the country together.

President Lincoln said he would fight to save the Union. But he did not know how awful the fighting would be. Nobody knew. Many people thought the war would be over in a few months. But the Civil War turned out to be the largest and most deadly war Americans have ever fought—*ever!* Hundreds of thousands of men and boys died—many in battle, and many more from the diseases that spread in their dirty, crowded camps.

More Americans died in the Civil War than in any other war Americans have fought in.

When the Civil War started, a brave woman named Clara Barton gathered medicine and supplies and went to nurse the wounded soldiers. Clara's care meant a lot to the soldiers and she became known as the "Angel of the Battlefield."

Her work did not end when the war was over. After the war she formed an organization to look for missing soldiers and mark their graves. Then she began to think about people who needed help not just in wars but in disasters like floods, hurricanes, or droughts. She became the founder of the American Red Cross, which provided food, clothing, and medicine whenever disaster struck (and still does today).

Clara Barton, the "Angel of the Battlefield."

The Emancipation Proclamation

In the middle of the Civil War, President Lincoln wrote the Emancipation Proclamation. To "emancipate" means to set someone free. To "proclaim" is to announce something. In the Emancipation Proclamation, Lincoln announced that all slaves in the Southern states were now free. The Emancipation Proclamation did not end slavery overnight, but it was a big and important step toward ending slavery.

President Lincoln wanted this country to be one nation with liberty and justice for all. At Gettysburg, Pennsylvania, after a terrible battle in which many soldiers died, President Lincoln made a famous speech.

After the Emancipation Proclamation, many brave African American men joined the Northern army.

He said that the soldiers who died in battle died for a very important reason:

> . . . *that this nation, under God, shall have a new birth of freedom—and that government of the people, by the people, for the people, shall not perish from the earth.*

When the Civil War ended, the North won. Our country made it through the worst time in our history. The United States was united again.

A Nation of Immigrants

E Pluribus Unum

Let's talk about food for a minute. Do you like spaghetti or ravioli? Tacos or burritos? How about egg rolls or fried rice?

Many Americans love these foods. The funny thing is, all these foods came to America from other countries.

It's not just the food, it's also the people. People have come to America from all over the world.

The United States is a nation of *immigrants*. An immigrant is a person who leaves his or her home to settle in another land. People from countries all around the world have immigrated to America. They have chosen to come and settle here. They have come from Ireland, Italy, Poland, Cuba, Mexico, China, Vietnam, and many other countries. New immigrants are coming to America every day.

Do you know where your family originally came from? Were you born in America? How about your parents and grandparents?

American Indians had lived in this country a long time when people from Europe began to immigrate to North America. You've learned how the English settled at Jamestown in Virginia, and at Plymouth in Massachusetts. Pretty soon the English were joined by people from Holland and Scotland, who settled in New York and New Jersey. Germans began to settle in Pennsylvania. Immigrants from France made new homes in New York, New Hampshire, and Louisiana. People from Spain settled in Florida and Texas.

How could people from so many different countries settle here and live together peacefully? It wasn't always easy. People from different countries didn't always trust or like each other. But since the earliest days of this country, people knew that if America was going to succeed, all these different people must try to get along.

After the Revolutionary War, our country adopted a motto: "E Pluribus Unum." Look on the back of any coin, or on the back of a dollar bill and you will find the words "E Pluribus Unum." They are in an old language called Latin, and they mean, "One from many." That means Americans are determined to make one country out of people from many different countries—and we are still trying to do it today.

This is the back of a national symbol called the Great Seal of the United States. Do you see the motto, "E Pluribus Unum"?

Why Did Immigrants Come to America?

Would you be willing to move to a faraway country and never see your home or grandparents and aunts and uncles and cousins and friends again?

Why would people choose to immigrate? What made them want to leave their old countries and come to the United States? For many immigrants, it was a combination of bad times at home and the hope for something better in America.

Do you remember why the Pilgrims and the Puritans came to America? They wanted religious freedom. In England they were not allowed to worship in the way they believed was right. So they looked for a place where they could practice their religion and live as they wanted to. They left their homes in England and made the hard trip across the Atlantic Ocean to America.

Many immigrants have continued to come to America looking for religious freedom. Quakers, Catholics, and Jews left their home countries and came to America because they wanted to be free to follow their own beliefs.

Some immigrants have come to America to get away from awful things happening in their old countries. Once in Ireland a deadly disease almost wiped out one of the most important crops, potatoes. Without potatoes, many poor families in Ireland went hungry. There was so little to eat that thousands of people were starving. Some of these Irish people decided that things were so bad they had to leave their country. And so they came to America. People came from other countries, too, such as Sweden and Germany and China, for the same reason—the land where they lived just wasn't producing enough food. They came to America with dreams of starting a farm, growing food, and never being hungry again.

A Land of Opportunity?

Most immigrants were sad to leave their old homes but hopeful about life in this New World. They thought America would be a land of opportunity, a place where they and their families would have a new chance for a better life. Their hopes gave them the courage they needed to make the hard trip to America.

Many immigrants came to America on crowded ships. For most of the passage across the ocean they were cramped in the big, dark bottom of the ship, called the "steerage." There were no separate rooms. Everybody was jammed together. There were no sinks or bathtubs. The air smelled awful. If you had hard crackers and dried cheese to eat, you were lucky. Some passengers got sick, and in the crowded space of the steerage, their diseases spread quickly. Weaker immigrants often died of disease before they ever saw America.

Immigrants were jammed together on this ship bound for America.

When they finally came near land, the tired immigrants rushed on deck to see their new country. After 1886, immigrants who arrived in New York Harbor were greeted by a special sight: the Statue of Liberty raised her torch in welcome.

But some immigrants did not feel very welcome. For example, many who arrived in New York had to stop at a big building on Ellis Island. They had to wait in long lines and go through medical examinations and answer a lot of questions. If they were sick or didn't have the proper papers, they might not be allowed to enter the country.

When they were allowed to enter, their lives were still hard. Many came to America

In New York Harbor, the Statue of Liberty welcomes newcomers to America. "Lady Liberty" was a gift from France to the United States. The statue is so large that it had to be delivered in parts to the United States.

hoping to buy a little land and start a farm, but most were so poor that they had to stop and look for work in the cities where they arrived—cities like New York, Philadelphia, Boston, and San Francisco.

Immigrants often took the low-paying jobs no one else wanted. They sold newspapers or washed clothes. They did the backbreaking work of building the canals and railroads. Many Irish immigrants worked to build the Erie Canal. Many Chinese immigrants helped build the Transcontinental Railroad. In hot factories, women and even children worked at spinning cloth or sewing clothes.

Immigrants were often treated badly. Americans who had been in the country for many years did not like the different languages, religions, or customs of the new immigrants. These Americans forgot that there was a time when their ancestors had been immigrants, too.

Even though many immigrants were not welcomed, they worked hard and made a better life for themselves in America. Some saved enough money to buy a little land to farm, or to open their own business in the cities. They built homes. They educated their children, and they watched their sons and daughters become suc-

To make ends meet, the children in this immigrant family had to work very hard.

cessful people. They became the country's teachers, professors, writers, businessmen, nurses, and doctors. They became our newest and proudest citizens.

Becoming a Citizen

What does it mean to be a "citizen" of a country? It means you are a legal member of a country. As a citizen of the United States, you have certain rights and responsibilities. For example, all adult American citizens have the right to vote in elections, and the right to be elected to a position in the government (if enough people vote for you!). All citizens have the responsibility to obey the laws and pay taxes.

How do you get to be an American citizen? If you are born in the United States, you are automatically a citizen of this country. But you don't have to be born here to be a citizen. Immigrants can become United States citizens, too, if they want to. First they have to live in the United States for at least five years. During that time, they have to obey the law. Then they take a test on American history and government. The test asks questions like, What is the basic law of our country called? Who was president during the Civil War? (You know the answers, right?)

After passing the test, you make a pledge to be loyal to the United States—and then, you are a new citizen.

These new citizens are promising to be loyal to the United States.

Civil Rights:
Liberty and Justice for All

All Men Are Created Equal

You know these words from the Declaration of Independence: *"We hold these truths to be self-evident, that all men are created equal."*

Does that mean that all people are alike? No, as you can easily see. Instead, it means that people are born with equal rights. It means that everyone should have a fair chance. It means you should have the same freedom as everyone else to do things like get an education, get the best job you can, and vote for the leaders you want, or even try to become a leader.

That's what it means, but that's not always the way it has worked out. The Africans who were brought here and forced to work as slaves were not given equal rights and opportunities. The American Indians who were forced to leave their homelands were not given a fair chance.

Our country was very young when Thomas Jefferson wrote those words, "All men are created equal." Now, more than two hundred years later, we are still working to make this country a place where everyone has a fair chance. In our history, many brave people have worked hard to help bring equal rights to all Americans. Let's learn about some of these people who have worked for our civil rights.

Susan B. Anthony and Votes for Women

Let's look at those important words one more time: "All men are created equal." Wait a minute. Does that mean only "all *men* are created equal," not women and girls? No, not really. When the Declaration of Independence was written, people sometimes used the word "man" to mean all people, all of humanity. Do you see the word "man" in humanity?

But for a long time in this country, women did *not* have the same rights as men. For a long time women were kept out of many jobs. They were not even allowed to vote.

That wasn't fair, and Susan B. Anthony knew it. For many years after the Civil War, she made

Susan B. Anthony.

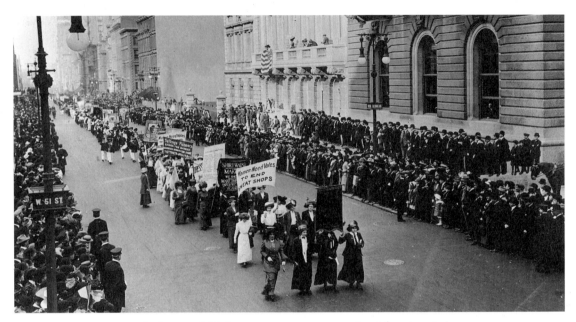

In New York City in 1912, many women marched for the right to vote.

speeches and she published a magazine in which she said that women should have equal rights, including the right to vote. She asked: Why should only men have the right to choose our leaders? Why should women be left out?

In the year 1872, Americans were voting for a new president. Well, American *men* were voting. Women still weren't allowed to vote. But that didn't stop Susan B. Anthony. Bright and early, at seven o'clock in the morning, she walked to the polls (the voting place) and she cast her vote for president. Then she was arrested. A judge said she had to pay a fine of one hundred dollars! She refused to pay the fine because she did not believe she had done anything wrong. She thought she wasn't wrong for voting. Instead, the country was wrong for not allowing women to vote.

Susan B. Anthony kept working for women's rights till the end of her life. Fourteen years after she died, her hard work paid off. In 1920, all American women gained the right to vote.

Eleanor Roosevelt

In the United States, the wife of the president is known as the First Lady. One of the most famous First Ladies ever was Eleanor Roosevelt, the wife of President Franklin Roosevelt (you can see his face on a dime). She was full of energy. She once wrote a book called *It's Up to the Women*. In it she said that women must actively work to make the nation better. She followed her own advice. She tried to help wherever she could.

When Franklin Roosevelt was first elected president in 1932, this country was going through a very hard time known as the Great Depression. Many people had lost their jobs and were poor and hungry. President Roosevelt started government programs to give people jobs. Eleanor Roosevelt did not stay cooped up in the White House. She volunteered to work in the soup kitchens that served meals to hungry people. She visited factories and coal mines, and she talked with the workers to see what the government could do to help them.

Eleanor Roosevelt spoke out for equal rights for all Americans. In many speeches, she said that everyone in America should be given a fair chance, and she meant everyone—women, black people, American Indians, poor people, *everyone*. She said, "We are all brothers, regardless of race, creed, or color."

Eleanor Roosevelt addresses Americans by radio.

Equality Regardless of Color

You know that after the Civil War slavery was ended in the United States. But that didn't suddenly make life easy for African Americans. They still faced many struggles. Many people did not want to give equal rights to African Americans and other people with dark skin. But there were many other people who were determined to get equal rights for all people, regardless of color.

Mary McLeod Bethune

Mary McLeod Bethune wanted to be sure that African Americans got their chance through a good education. In 1904 she opened a small school for black girls in Daytona, Florida. She didn't have much money. The students used boxes for desks. And there were only five students at first.

But in the next few years, her school grew and grew. In time it became Bethune-Cookman College. Mary McLeod Bethune served as president of the college. Later, President Franklin Roosevelt asked Mary McLeod Bethune to work for him, and when she said yes, she became the first African American woman to be in charge of a government office.

Mary McLeod Bethune.

Jackie Robinson.

Near the end of her life, Mary McLeod Bethune wrote down what she wanted to leave behind after she was gone. In strong capital letters, she wrote, "I leave you LOVE; I leave you HOPE; I leave you a THIRST FOR EDUCATION."

Jackie Robinson

In college, Jackie Robinson was a good student. And he was an amazing athlete. He won awards in four different sports, including baseball. You would think that the major league baseball teams would all be crying, "Play for us, Jackie." "No, play for us!"

But that didn't happen. Back then—and this was only about fifty years ago—blacks weren't allowed to play in the major leagues. There was a separate league for black baseball players.

Think about it. There were dozens and dozens of great baseball players, but they couldn't play in the major leagues, simply because they were black. That would be like saying to Michael Jordan, "You can't play in the NBA because you're black." Good grief!

But then Jackie Robinson joined the Brooklyn Dodgers. He was the first black player on a major league team. And he was terrific! He could hit, run, steal bases, and play second base like nobody else.

At first he had to put up with more than most people could stand. People spit on him and called him terrible names. Pitchers would throw balls and try to hit him.

But Jackie Robinson stayed tough. He played his best, and people respected him. By the end of his first year in the major leagues, he was named the Rookie of the Year. And two years later he was named the league's Most Valuable Player.

Jackie Robinson opened the way for many great African American athletes who have come after him.

Rosa Parks

Even after Jackie Robinson joined the major leagues, many African Americans were kept out of many things. Especially in the southern states, black people were kept separate and apart from white people. In restaurants, black people were told to sit in a separate section, or often they weren't allowed in at all. Black children went to separate schools from white children. There were even separate drinking fountains for white people and black people.

This separating of people just because of their skin color is called "segregation." Segregation is wrong. It's just about as far from the idea that "all men are created equal" as you can get.

Rosa Parks.

In 1955, even the buses in southern states were segregated. If you were white, you could sit in the front. If you were black, you had to sit in the back, or give up your seat to a white person if there were no empty seats left.

One day in 1955, a black woman named Rosa Parks got on a bus in Montgomery, Alabama. She had worked hard all day and she was tired. She sat down in a seat at the back of the bus. But later the bus got crowded and all the seats in the white section were filled. Well, the next time the bus stopped, a white man got on, and the bus driver told Rosa Parks to get up and give her seat to the white man.

Rosa Parks did not give up her seat. She was not going to move, even if the law said she should move. It was a bad, stupid law. Still, it was a law. And so she was arrested.

When people heard that Rosa Parks had been arrested, they got very angry. African Americans in the city of Montgomery decided that they would stop riding the buses. They would walk or share rides in cars. But they would not pay the bus company to ride as long as the company practiced segregation.

For a whole year, African Americans refused to ride the buses in Montgomery. This became known as the Montgomery Bus Boycott. (To "boycott" is to refuse to buy or use something.)

A little more than a year after Rosa Parks was arrested, the highest court in our land, the Supreme Court, said that she was right and Alabama law was wrong. Her determination helped to end a bad law.

Martin Luther King, Jr.

In the Montgomery Bus Boycott, African Americans had a strong leader. He was a young minister named Martin Luther King, Jr.

Dr. King went on to lead people in other cities, too. He brought many people together, black and white, to show that segregation was wrong. He said that wherever white and black people were separated by the law, it was wrong. In schools, hospitals, restaurants, or hotels, it was wrong to keep people apart just because of the color of their skin.

Dr. King would go on to fight for civil rights as long as he lived. But he believed in fighting peacefully. He wanted to change the bad laws, but he did not believe in using violence to change them. He told people not to use their fists, or throw rocks, or shoot guns. Instead, they should join together and march peacefully. Or they could go to a restaurant for white people only and ask to be served. If the restaurant refused to serve them because they were black, they should just sit patiently.

But that wasn't always easy. Even when people marched peacefully or sat in restaurants, they were often shouted at, hit, and sometimes thrown into jail. Once someone threw a bomb into Dr. King's home. He was arrested and thrown into jail many times. But this didn't stop Dr. King. He kept right on peacefully fighting for what he knew was right.

Many Americans shared Dr. King's dream of equal rights for all people. But not everyone agreed with him. Some people even hated him, because these people did not want blacks to have equal rights. And in the spring of 1968, one of these people shot and killed Martin Luther King, Jr.

Dr. King moved our country closer to its dream of equality. To honor him and his work, the United States government has made the third Monday in January a holiday in memory of Martin Luther King, Jr.

Martin Luther King, Jr.

Cesar Chavez

Once when he was a teenager, Cesar Chavez was arrested for refusing to leave a section of a movie theater reserved for white people only. Cesar Chavez wasn't black. He was Mexican American.

For many years, in the Southwest part of this country and in California, Mexican Americans were treated as black people were in the South. They had to go to separate schools and were kept out of restaurants and hotels.

Many Mexican American people worked as migrant workers. They moved around from farm to farm, hoping to find work picking fruits and vegetables. It was very hard work. They didn't get paid much. At night they were often crowded into dirty shacks to sleep.

Cesar Chavez came from a family of migrant workers. As a boy, before he left the eighth grade, he had gone to thirty-eight different schools. When he grew up, he decided to try to make life better for migrant workers. He brought the workers together to ask for what they deserved, like more pay and a clean place to eat and sleep.

Cesar Chavez.

Like Martin Luther King, Jr., Cesar Chavez wanted to fight peacefully for equal rights. He told people not to use violence.

Have you ever walked a mile? Imagine what Cesar Chavez felt when he and many workers made a march of *three hundred miles* across California. He wanted to draw attention to the suffering of the farm workers. He wanted more Americans to understand that the workers deserved a better life. On the news on television, people across the country saw Cesar Chavez and the workers marching. And in the years ahead, the workers got better pay and better living conditions, thanks largely to the dedication of Cesar Chavez.

GEOGRAPHY OF THE AMERICAS

The United States Today

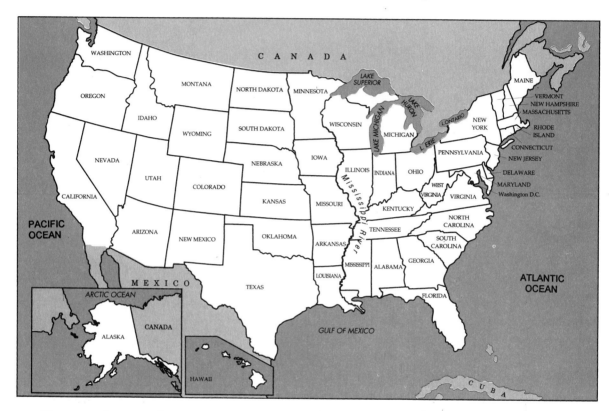

Here are five quick review questions. Ready? What continent is the United States on? What country is our neighbor to the north? What country is our neighbor to the south? What ocean is to the east of the United States? What ocean is to the west of the United States?

(The answers, in order, are: North America, Canada, Mexico, Atlantic, Pacific.)

Take a look at the map on this page, which shows you the United States as it is today. Can you find the state where you live?

Do you know how many states are in the United States today? There are fifty states (and that's why our country's flag has fifty stars on it).

On the map you can see that forty-eight of the states are "contiguous," which means "touching." But two states do not touch any others. One of these states is Alaska, way up north. The other is Hawaii, a group of islands in the Pacific Ocean. There are little pictures of Alaska and Hawaii on the map, but to see where they really are, you need to find them on a globe.

On the map, find the big Mississippi River. Now find the five big lakes in the north called the Great Lakes. (To help remember their names, think of the word "HOMES," which is made up of the first letter of each lake: Huron, Ontario, Michigan, Erie, Superior.) Now look south and find the warm body of water called the Gulf of Mexico. Which states touch the Gulf of Mexico?

There are some islands that are part of the United States, but they are not states. These islands are called "territories" of the United States. For example, the little island of Guam in the Pacific Ocean is a U.S. territory.

Central America and the Caribbean

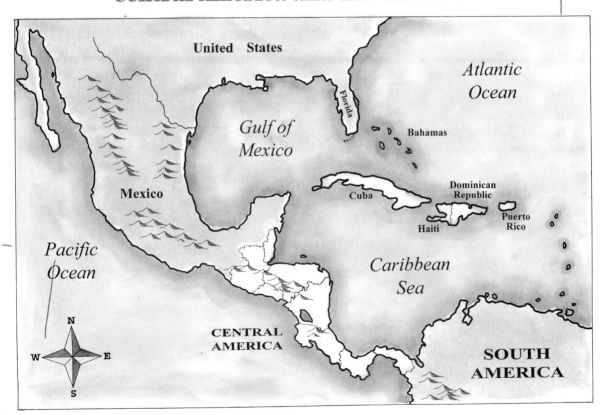

On a globe or a map of the world find the continents of North America and South America. Put your finger on Mexico, then move it down to the narrow land just before South America. On a map, it looks almost like a tail hanging off the end of a kite.

We call this narrow region Central America. Look at the map above. Central America is not a continent. In fact, it is part of North America. Central America is the name people use for the seven countries that are in the center, between the two big continents of North America and South America. (In first grade, you learned about the ancient Maya who lived in Central America.)

What body of water is to the west of Central America? Yes, it's the Pacific Ocean. To the east you'll find the warm, crystal-blue waters of the Caribbean Sea [pronounced CARE-uh-BEE-un or kuh-RIB-ee-un]. In the Caribbean there is a large group of islands called the West Indies. (Do you remember why Christopher Columbus called these islands the "Indies"?) On the map, find these big islands in the West Indies: Cuba, Puerto Rico [PWHERE-toe REE-koh], and the island with the countries of Haiti [HAY-tee] and the Dominican Republic.

Central America and the West Indies are near the equator, so what does that make you think the climate is like there? It's often very warm, except in the high lands of the mountains, where it stays pretty cool. The climate is good for growing crops like coffee, bananas, and sugarcane. But many hurricanes also hit this region.

South America

Look at South America on the map. The continent looks like a triangle. Its shape reminds some people of an ice cream cone. Two favorite flavors of ice cream come from crops grown in South America: chocolate from cocoa beans, and vanilla from vanilla beans!

South America

Most people in South America today speak Spanish. That's because long ago Spanish explorers and soldiers conquered the Native Americans living in South America. Do you remember learning in first grade about the Inca people, and how they were defeated by the Spanish conqueror named Pizarro?

The Incas built their civilization high in the Andes Mountains. Find the Andes Mountains on the map. They run along the Pacific coast of South America. Starting in the south, the Andes run through the long narrow country called Chile. They go on through the countries of Bolivia, Peru, Ecuador, and Colombia, and a little bit into Venezuela. (Find all these countries on the map.) The Andes are the longest mountain chain in the world. They go on for more than five thousand miles!

On the map find the second-largest country in South America, called Argentina. Part of this country is a big desert. But part of Argentina is a great grassy area called the *pampas*. On the pampas, farmers grow crops like wheat and cotton, and they also raise many sheep and cattle.

The largest country in South America is Brazil. Brazil was never conquered by Spain, but it was conquered by another European country, Portugal. That's why most people in Brazil today speak the Portuguese language.

Find Brazil on the map

The country called Bolivia is named after a great leader named Simón Bolívar. He helped the people of five South American countries win their independence from Spain. Bolívar is known as "The Liberator" (to "liberate" means to set free).

This spider monkey lives in the rainforest.

and run your finger along the line that shows the world's second longest river, the Amazon. (Do you remember the longest? It's the Nile, in Africa.) The line on the map may look short, but the Amazon is almost four thousand miles long!

The Amazon River flows through the biggest rain forest in the world. In the warm, steamy rain forest, you'll find more different kinds of plants, animals, and insects than you could count, even if you had years to do it.

The rainforest is filled with many different plants and trees.

III.

Visual Arts

INTRODUCTION

A book alone cannot adequately convey the experience of music or the impact of visual art. While this book *can* hope to provide some basic knowledge about art, nothing can replace visiting museums, attending performances, listening to recordings, and encouraging children to sing, dance, paint, sculpt, and playact for themselves.

For the second grader, art should mostly take the form of *doing*: drawing, painting, cutting and pasting, working with clay and other materials. In this section, we suggest many activities your child can do, sometimes with your help. You can also find good art activities in some of the books recommended below.

By reading this section aloud with your child, you can also help him or her learn some of the ways that we talk about art, and introduce some wonderful works of art. In this way, your child will come to understand that, while art is *doing*, it is also *seeing and thinking*. By looking closely at art, and talking about it, your child will begin to develop a love of art and a habit of enjoying it in thoughtful, active ways.

But let us repeat: beyond looking at art and talking about it, do try to provide your child with materials and opportunities to be a practicing artist!

Suggested Resources

Art Activity Books

Mudworks: Creative Clay, Dough, and Modeling Experiences and *Scribble Cookies and Other Independent Creative Art Experiences for Children* by MaryAnn F. Krohl (Bright Ring Publishing, 1985 and 1989)

Kids Create: Art and Craft Experiences for 3- to 9-Year-Olds by Laurie Carlson (Williamson Publishing, 1990)

Books That Reprint Artworks for Children

The *Come Look with Me* series by Gladys Blizzard (Lickle Publishing); titles include *Come Look with Me: Enjoying Art with Children* (1990); *Come Look with Me: Animals in Art* (1992); *Come Look with Me: World of Play* (1993); *Come Look with Me: Exploring Landscape Art with Children* (1992)

Books about Artists

The *Getting to Know the World's Greatest Artists* series by Mike Venezia (Childrens Press); titles include *Paul Klee; Henri Matisse; Picasso; Van Gogh;* and many more.

For more good resources, see *Books to Build On: A Grade-by-Grade Resource Guide for Parents and Teachers* edited by John Holdren and E. D. Hirsch, Jr. (Dell, 1996).

Taking a Line for a Walk

An artist named Paul Klee [pronounced "clay"] once said drawing is taking a line for a walk.

When you draw a picture, notice the different lines you use. Let's say you want to draw a tree. You might start with the trunk by drawing two straight lines. Lines that go up and down are called *vertical* lines. If you want to draw the ground under the tree, you might draw a line across the bottom of the page. Lines that run from side to side are called *horizontal* lines. And you might want to draw a ladder leaning up against the tree. Lines that lean are called *diagonal* lines.

Think of where you might see these different kinds of lines. You see vertical lines in

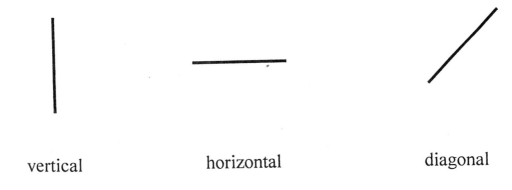

vertical   horizontal   diagonal

tree trunks, telephone poles, fence posts, and skyscrapers. You see horizontal lines in a mattress or the edge of a table, or on the horizon. You see diagonal lines in slides, hills, and ramps.

You probably know the names for other kinds of lines, too.

zigzag   curved   spiral   wavy

Lines can be thick or thin. In the picture above, which lines are thick? Which ones are thin?

Activity: Get a piece of paper and a pencil. Turn the paper so the long edge is at the top. Then fold it in half to make a dividing line down the middle. On the left side draw your favorite animal using only straight lines. They can be horizontal, vertical or diagonal, but all the lines have to be straight. On the other side of the paper, try drawing the same animal in the same pose using only curved or wavy or zigzag lines. Now do the same thing, but this time draw a house or building instead.

Mother and Child.

The arrangement of the figures suggests a
line. What kind of line is it?

Let's look at a beautiful painting called *Mother and Child* by the Spanish artist Pablo Picasso. Take your finger and follow the lines in the picture. Do you find more straight or more curved lines? The many curving lines add to the gentle feel of this picture.

Sometimes an artist can suggest a line rather than actually paint one. In *Mother and Child* the tilt of the mother's head suggests a line. Look at the tilt of the mother's head. If you could draw a line to follow the tilt of her head, would the line be horizontal or diagonal?

Now look at the child's body. The same diagonal line extends from the mother's head along the child's body. Picasso united mother and child with a single suggested line to show how close they feel to each other. What else in the painting shows how close they feel?

Lines and Movement

Have you ever been swimming at the beach and been knocked down by a big wave? Well, be glad it wasn't as big as the wave in this picture by the Japanese artist Hokusai [HOE-coo-sye]. (You can read about Japan in the World History section of this book.)

This painting is called *The Great Wave at Kanagawa Nami-Ura.* Imagine this picture is part of a movie. What will happen next? What is the great wave about to crash on? Can you spot the men huddled together in wooden fishing boats? Hokusai has drawn the great wave as if it were alive, with curling fingers reaching out to grab the boats.

Do you see the many curving lines in the picture? Put your finger on the top of the water on the right side of the picture. Now move your finger to the left, following the curving line up and under the big wave. Do you see how the line pushes up and around, almost as if it wants to keep on until it makes a big circle? Now put your finger on the top of the water on the left side of the page and follow the curve along the top of the great wave. This line seems to want to keep going, too. What kind of shape would it make?

The Great Wave at Kanagawa Nami-Ura.

Looking at Sculptures

You can walk around a sculpture or statue. It's not flat like a picture. Things like chairs and tables—things that aren't flat—are said to have mass. Your body has mass. So does a sculpture. Sculptures can be made of stone, wood, or metal. Let's look at a stone sculpture from ancient Greece called the *Discus Thrower*. (In the World History section of this book, you can read about how the Olympic Games started in ancient Greece.)

This statue shows a man who is trying to throw a discus farther than anyone else. A discus looks like a big Frisbee made out of metal. Find the discus in this picture.

Although the *Discus Thrower* is a sculpture, not a drawing, it still has lines. Let's see how.

Activity: Put a piece of tracing paper over this picture of the *Discus Thrower*. Draw a straight line from the hand holding the discus to his chin. Draw another straight line from his chin to his hip. Now draw a straight line from his hip to his knee. Finally, draw a straight line from his knee to the heel that sticks up in the air. Now lift the tracing paper and see what you have drawn. A zigzag line! Even though this statue does not move, the zigzag line helps show energy or action. Throwing a discus takes a lot of energy. A discus may look like a Frisbee, but it's much heavier. Hold a big book in one hand. Now try to stand like the *Discus Thrower*. Bend your knees, move your arms to one side of your body, and look over your shoulder. Can you feel that your body would have to work hard to throw a discus?

The Discus Thrower.

Now let's look at a sculpture often called *Flying Horse*. It was found in a tomb in China and is about two thousand years old. (You can read about ancient China in the World History section of this book.) Even though the sculpture is made of a heavy metal called bronze, it seems light. Why? Look at the legs. See how thin they are? How many legs are in the air? All the weight of the horse is perfectly balanced on one hoof. This makes the sculpture seem as if it's floating or even flying!

Flying Horse.

What do you think the man is doing in this sculpture by the French artist Auguste Rodin (row-DAN)? See how he rests his chin on his fist. Have you ever sat this way? The sculpture is called *The Thinker*. Rodin modeled this sculpture in clay first and then had it cast in bronze. Several copies have been made of it, some small and others twice as big as a real man! Look at how Rodin posed the figure. Try to sit this way with your right elbow resting on your left knee. Is this a comfortable pose? No, you have to strain your muscles to hold this position. The strained pose, the powerful muscles, and stern expression all show that thinking can be hard work!

The Thinker.

Looking at Landscapes

If you've read the first-grade book in this series, then you learned about two kinds of painting: portraits and still lifes. Now let's learn about another special kind of painting called a landscape. The most important thing in a landscape is the scenery, which includes the land, the trees, and the sky. A painter can put people in a landscape, but they are not the main focus of the painting. When you look at a landscape painting, try to notice the weather, season, location, and time of day.

This painting by the American artist Thomas Cole has a very long name, but it's usually called *The Oxbow*. An oxbow is a U-shaped collar placed around the neck of an ox so that it can be hitched to a plow. Can you find something U-shaped in this scene? (Do you see the bend in the Connecticut River?)

You could almost divide this painting in two parts. One part shows the landscape close-up. The other shows the landscape far away. Look at the left side of the painting, which shows the close-up part of the landscape. What is the weather like here? Do you see the broken tree trunk? What do you think might have happened to this tree?

Now look at the faraway landscape on the right side of the painting. What is the weather like? This painting shows two very different views of nature. On the left, close to us, nature is dark and wild. But on the right, nature looks bright and peaceful. Now that

The Oxbow.

you've looked carefully at the weather in this painting, its real name won't surprise you: it's called *View of Mount Holyoke, Northampton, Massachusetts, After a Thunderstorm*.

Did you notice a person in this painting? The picture in this book is *much* smaller than the real painting so it may be hard to find him. Look near the bottom, a little to the right of the center. Who is it? An artist—why, it must be Thomas Cole painting a landscape! But in this painting, it's easy to tell that the landscape is more important than the person.

Now let's look at a landscape by the Spanish artist called El Greco. This picture, *View of Toledo*, shows us the city of Toledo in Spain where the artist lived four hundred years ago. Can you point out a river, a bridge, and many buildings? What is the weather like? What time of day do you think the artist is showing? It might be daytime with the sky darkened by a thunderstorm. Or maybe it's nighttime with moonlight breaking through storm clouds. Either way, the sky casts a spooky light over the whole scene. What kind of mood or feeling do you have when you see this painting? Is it the kind of picture you would want to use on a poster saying, "For your next vacation, visit Toledo"?

View of Toledo.

Landscapes don't have to be of real places. They can also be of places you imagine. The French artist Henri Rousseau [on-REE roo-SO] never visited a tropical jungle, but he did many paintings like this one, called *Virgin Forest*. Rousseau

Virgin Forest.

learned about jungle plants and animals like monkeys and lions from encyclopedias, science books, and visits to the zoo, but he did not try to copy them in a lifelike way. Look at the plants here. Rousseau painted many plants and made them very big. Does this landscape look like a place you would want to visit? Before you answer, did you notice the man wrestling with a jaguar? Rousseau's colorful, dreamlike jungle is beautiful, but it is also dangerous.

Look at the painting called *The Starry Night* by the Dutch artist Vincent van Gogh [van GO*]. What do you notice first in the painting? What do you see in the bottom half of the painting? What do you see in the top half? Van Gogh's sky is full of circles.

The Starry Night.

Use your finger to follow some of the curving lines that Van Gogh painted in the sky. The sky seems to be moving and swirling around, while the town below is calm and still. Van Gogh applied the paint in bold, thick strokes. Even though this is just a picture of the painting, you can almost feel its rough texture.

Activity: Make a landscape of your own. First you need to decide whether it will be a real landscape or an imaginary one. Then decide what you will use: you could use watercolors, tempera paint, colored pencils, or markers. Think about the mood or feeling you want your picture to have. Think about the weather, the time of day, and the light. Will it be dark and stormy and spooky? Or bright and sunny and peaceful? Or something else? Will you put any people or animals in your landscape?

* You may also hear his name pronounced van-KHOKH, especially outside the United States.

Animals Real and Imagined

Let's look at some different pictures of animals. Some artists want us to know exactly what an animal looks like. They are careful to include every detail and to get the colors exactly the way they are in nature. The German artist Albrecht Dürer [DUR-er], who lived about five hundred years ago, painted the picture called *Young Hare*. Doesn't it look real? It seems as though the bunny might wiggle its nose and hop away at any moment. Can you see how Dürer used separate, short brush strokes and touches of white to imitate the fluffy texture of the hare's fur?

The nineteenth-century American artist John James Audubon [AH-da-BAHN] also wanted to make very lifelike pictures of animals, especially birds. He traveled throughout North America from Florida to Canada studying and sketching birds. He became famous when his illustrations were published in a book called *Birds of America*. Look at Audubon's picture of passenger pigeons. The one on the lower branch is a male and the other one is a female. Do they look alike? How do their colors differ?

Dürer and Audubon wanted their pictures of animals to look like real animals. But other artists try to show us animals in a new or unusual way.

Look at the painting on the next page by Paul Klee [clay] called *Cat and Bird*. Klee had many cats, including a pet tomcat named Fritzi, who inspired this painting. But does this painting show what Fritzi really looked like? No! Klee painted only the head, and he made it huge, with eyes that

(Top) *Young Hare.* (Right) *Passenger Pigeon.*

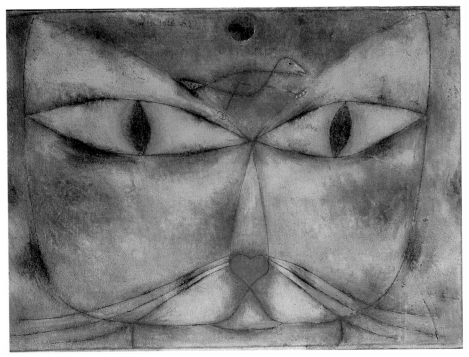

Cat and Bird.

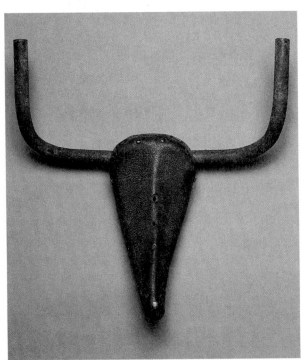

are much bigger than life, and an unusual shade of green. Klee did not try to show the cat's soft fur, the way that Dürer painted the fur of the young hare. Instead Klee used only simple lines and shapes. Look for these shapes in the painting: an oval, diamond, triangle, and circle. And look at the shape Klee used for the tip of the cat's nose—a heart! Why do you think he might have put a heart in this painting? Also, you probably noticed what Klee painted on the cat's forehead—a bird! Why do you think he did that? What do cats like to do to birds?

Now let's look at a sculpture by Pablo Picasso. What do you think it's a sculpture of? Do you see an animal? If you don't, look again and think about the title of the sculpture, *Bull's Head*. What two things did Picasso put together to create the image of a bull's head? A bicycle seat and handlebars! By using his imagination, Picasso turned everyday objects into a piece of art that makes us see the lines and shapes of a bull's head in a new and interesting way.

You can see the bull's head in Picasso's sculpture, but you might have a little trouble at first seeing the animal in this picture. It's by the French artist, Henri Matisse [on-REE ma-TEECE]. Can you guess what it is?

Activity: Find a photograph of an animal you would like to draw. Look at it closely. Now decide if you would like to make a realistic, lifelike drawing of the animal, or just sketch its main lines and shapes, and maybe add some unusual touches, the way Klee drew his cat. If you want to color your picture, then, like Audubon, you can use realistic colors, or like Klee you can use unusual colors, and perhaps add something that your animal is thinking about.

Matisse called this picture *The Snail.* It is made from cut-out pieces of colored paper stuck on a white background. At first it might look like a bunch of colored shapes. But how has Matisse arranged the shapes? With your finger, make a counterclockwise circle around the green shape in the center. Continue moving your finger so that it goes to the black shape. From the black shape take your finger along the outside edges of the other shapes that curve around the central green shape. Do you see how your finger moved in a spiral path? So, Matisse has arranged the shapes to suggest a spiral. His picture doesn't show you what a snail looks like in real life—instead, it shows how much the shape of a snail is made up of a spiral line.

The Snail.

Activity: It's fun to use your imagination to see the basic lines and shapes in animals. You can make your own animal cut-out, like Matisse. Start by tearing or cutting out various shapes from pieces of colored construction paper. Experiment with placing them in a variety of positions on a white piece of paper. If you want, arrange them in a way that reminds you of some animal's basic shape—for example, the big oval of an elephant's body. When you have made a picture you like, paste the pieces onto the paper. What title will you give your picture?

Abstract Art

We call art like Dürer's *Young Hare* or Audubon's bird pictures *realistic* art, because it looks very real and lifelike. There's a different name for art like Picasso's *Bull's Head* or Matisse's *The Snail*. We call such art *abstract* art. Abstract art doesn't look exactly like the real thing, but it may remind you of things you've seen. Or it may make you see something in a new way, not by showing you every little detail but instead drawing your attention to the basic lines and shapes.

I and the Village.

Have you ever had a dream full of crazy things happening? Some people think the next painting looks like something from a dream. Look at this abstract painting by the Russian painter Marc Chagall [sha-GALL].

What do you see? You can recognize some of the things in this painting, such as a woman milking a cow, or a man and a woman walking near a group of buildings. But how are the things in this painting arranged? Some of them are upside down and some are much bigger than others. Some, like the woman milking the cow, are in very strange places. And what about the colors? What colors seem unusual to you?

Chagall called his painting *I and the Village*. He painted it just after he left the small village in Russia where he grew up and moved far away to Paris, France. Do you think he missed home?

Activity: **Make a Dreamscape** Now it's your turn to make an abstract picture that shows things in a dreamlike way. What will your picture be about? It can be a place you like a lot, like the beach, or it can be a time of year, like autumn when the leaves fall. Think of all the things you want to include in your picture. Make some much bigger and others much smaller than they really are. What colors do you want to use? How do you want to arrange things on the page?

Sculpture can be abstract, too. Look at this sculpture by Constantin Brancusi [bran-KOO-zee], an artist from Romania. What does it look like to you? The title, *Bird in Space,* may help you see what the artist was thinking. Brancusi did many sculptures of birds. The first ones he did still looked somewhat like birds. But this one doesn't look much like a bird at all.

Or does it? Have you ever watched a bird fly? Think about a bird flying, then look at this sculpture again. Brancusi made a tall, thin, pointed, gently curving shape that seems to soar. Its shiny metal surface reflects the light and seems almost weightless. So, while this sculpture does not show you the image of a bird with a beak and feathers, it shows you something about a bird in flight. It gives the feeling of rising into the air in one quick *swoosh!*

Bird in Space.

Architecture: The Art of Designing Buildings

Architecture is the art of designing and planning buildings. A person who designs buildings is called an architect.

Here is a photograph of a very famous building in Greece called the Parthenon [PAR-thuh-non]. More than two thousand years ago, the ancient Greeks built the Parthenon as a temple to honor the goddess Athena. (You can read about the ancient Greeks in the World History section of this book.)

You can see that the Parthenon

The Parthenon as it is today.

has been worn down through the years. But here is a picture that shows a model of what the Parthenon looked like when it was first built. Now, think about the kinds of lines you've learned about. Do you see how the roof and the steps of the Parthenon make long horizontal lines? But even more, you probably notice all the up-and-down vertical lines made by the many columns. The columns hold up the roof. They also point upward to the sky. Why does that seem right for a temple?

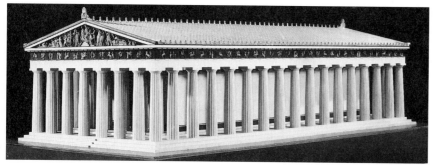

A model of the Parthenon.

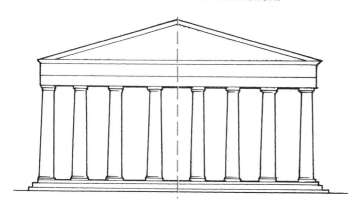

The front of the Parthenon, with a line of symmetry.

Now look at this drawing of the front of the Parthenon. We've put a vertical dotted line right down the middle to help you see something about the way this building is designed. First, count the number of columns on the left side of the dotted line. Now count the number of columns on the right side of the dotted line. Did you get four columns on each side?

When something is the same on both sides of an imaginary line running down the middle, we say it is *symmetric* [sih-MET-rik]. We call the imaginary line running down the middle a line of symmetry [SIM-ih-tree]. The Parthenon is a symmetric building. (You can read more about symmetry in the Mathematics section of this book on page 287.)

A valentine heart is a symmetric figure. So is Picasso's sculpture of a bull's head. Where else can you see symmetry—not just in art or buildings, but in nature, too? Look in a mirror at your body. You are symmetric! Can you think of something else that's symmetric?

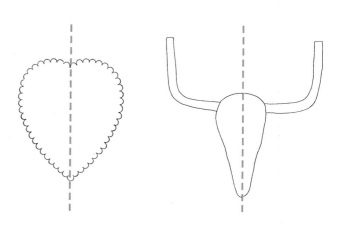

The ancient Greeks designed beautiful buildings, and many architects learned from them in later years. For example, in America today you can find many buildings with columns. Are there any buildings with columns where you live?

Thomas Jefferson designed columns at his home, Monticello.

A Building of Curves

The Great Stupa.

In the World History section of this book, you can read about how Buddhism began in India. This building is a temple for Buddha. It is called the Great Stupa, and it is in Sanchi, India.

Think of what you know about different kinds of lines. Now, look again at the Parthenon (on page 198), then look at the picture of the Great Stupa. What big differences do you see? The Parthenon is mostly straight lines—many vertical, some horizontal, some diagonal. But the Great Stupa has many curved lines. If you walked around it, you would walk in a circle. A line running from one side of the Stupa across the top to the other side would be curved. In fact, it would be half a circle.

You know what a sphere is, right? A sphere has the same shape as a ball. The Great Stupa is half a sphere. In architecture, this shape is called a dome. The outside of a dome may remind you of the shape of hills. People in India say that when you walk around the Great Stupa, you are walking the Path of Life around the World Mountain.

A Beautiful Castle

You've looked at one building with straight lines and one with curved lines. Now let's look at Himeji [hih-MAY-gee] Castle in Japan. (You can read about Japan in the World History section of this book.) The castle is made of wood covered with white plaster, and was built over four hundred years ago during a time when the Japanese were often at war. What do you think the castle's barred windows and gates were for?

There's something unusual about the design of Himeji Castle. Look at the way each story is smaller than the one below it. The overall shape of this building is like a triangle with its top cut off. This shape and the curving roofs make the castle seem to point upward. Himeji Castle is also called "White Heron Castle" because it reminded people of a favorite bird, the white heron in flight.

Himeji Castle (White Heron Castle).

A Modern Museum

Have you ever been to a museum? They're wonderful places to visit. In many museums, you'll find beautiful works of art. When Frank Lloyd Wright, an American architect, was asked to design a new museum, he decided to make the building itself a work of art!

The Guggenheim Museum is in New York City. What is unusual about it? Its shape! The outside looks like a teacup made of four circular disks. If you go inside, you're in for another surprise. A ramp spirals up to the top, leaving a tall opening in the center. To see the paintings on display, you walk along the ramp. It's like walking inside a big sculpture. Every step you take gives you a different view of the museum's inside, too.

The Guggenheim Museum.

Inside the Guggenheim Museum.

IV.

Music

INTRODUCTION

A book alone cannot adequately convey the experience of music or the impact of visual art. While this book *can* hope to provide some basic knowledge about art, nothing can replace visiting museums, attending performances, listening to recordings, and encouraging children to sing, dance, paint, sculpt, and playact for themselves.

When it comes to music, one of the best activities, and one of the easiest, is singing with your child. We suggest some familiar children's favorites in this section. The more you sing with your child, the more you'll enjoy music together.

We also encourage you to listen to recordings with your child and attend musical performances to help build his or her love of different kinds of music. In the first-grade book in this series, we introduced jazz, classical music, and opera, as well as different kinds of dance. In this book we build on that earlier knowledge by introducing patriotic music and folk music, and by extending the discussion of classical music to include more composers. We also build on the first-grade introduction to melody, harmony, and rhythm by exploring a few of the basics about how music is written down.

While some families will choose to provide lessons that will lift children to a level of musical competence beyond what we describe in the following pages, it is important for everyone to enjoy music. We hope this book will help increase that enjoyment.

In the following section we suggest a number of recordings. For more good resources, see *Books to Build On: A Grade-by-Grade Resource Guide for Parents and Teachers* edited by John Holdren and E. D. Hirsch, Jr. (Dell, 1996).

Many Kinds of Music

People around the world love to sing and play music. Here in the United States, where we have many different kinds of people, we have many different kinds of music. If you turn on a radio, you might hear rock-and-roll, jazz, classical, soul, country, or salsa.

Let's find out more now about three kinds of music: patriotic music, folk music, and classical music. Whenever you can, sing the songs that we give the words for, and try to listen to recordings of all these kinds of music.

Patriotic Music

It's a tradition to sing our national anthem before the ball game begins.

Have you ever been to a baseball game or a football game where, just before the game begins, everyone stands and sings "The Star-Spangled Banner"? That's our national anthem—which means, our country's official song.

Songs and music that honor our country are called *patriotic* music. Just about every country has its own patriotic music. Patriotic music makes people feel proud of their country. Besides "The Star-Spangled Banner," do you know any other patriotic songs about America?

In first grade, did you sing "America the Beautiful"? It begins with, "O beautiful for spacious skies . . ."

Here are the words to part of a favorite patriotic song called "This Land Is Your Land," written by Woody Guthrie. What do the words say about our country?

As I was walking that ribbon of highway
I saw above me that endless skyway.
I saw below me that golden valley
This land was made for you and me.

This land is your land, this land is my land,
From California to the New York island.
From the redwood forest to the Gulf Stream waters,
This land was made for you and me.

Woody Guthrie.

Folk Music

Do you know the song called "I've Been Working on the Railroad"? Here are the words. Let's sing it.

I've been working on the railroad,
All the live long day.
I've been working on the railroad,
Just to pass the time away.
Can't you hear the whistle blowin'?
Rise up so early in the morn',
Can't you hear the captain shoutin',
"Dinah, blow your horn!"

Dinah, won't you blow?
Dinah, won't you blow?
Dinah, won't you blow your horn?
Dinah, won't you blow?
Dinah, won't you blow?
Dinah, won't you blow your horn?

Who wrote "I've Been Working on the Railroad"? No one knows. It's a song that has been passed down from parents to children for many years. We call this kind of song a *folk song*. Another word for "folk" is "people." Folk songs have been sung and enjoyed by people for so long that, most of the time, we don't know who made them up. Many of the melodies of our favorite American folk songs were brought to this country by immigrants from other countries. (You can read about immigrants in the American History section of this book, beginning on page 164.)

Wherever you go in a country, people often know the same folk songs. In America, folks who have never lived near a railroad can sing "I've Been Working on the Railroad."

Just about every country has its own folk music. In France, people enjoy singing a folk song about "Frère Jacques" (Brother John). You probably know the English words for this song: "Are you sleeping, Brother John?"

Mozart (born in Austria, 1756).

Classical Music

Do you know who **Wolfgang Amadeus Mozart** [MOTES-art] is? Perhaps you've heard some of his music (and read about him in the first-grade book in this series). He was one of the greatest composers of all time. He began composing music when he was only five years old!

We call the kind of music Mozart wrote *classical music*. Some classical music is played by a large group, called an orchestra. An orchestra is made up of many musicians who play many different instruments—violins, clarinets, trumpets, drums, and a lot more. Do you remember what the person who leads the orchestra is called? (The conductor.) A long piece of mu-

An orchestra.

sic played by an orchestra is called a symphony. Although Mozart did not live to be very old, he wrote forty-one symphonies!

Meet Some Great Composers

You've met Mozart, and I hope you've heard some of his music. Now let's meet some other great composers of classical music. Try to hear their music, too.

When he was a boy growing up in Italy, **Antonio Vivaldi** [vih-VAHL-dee] learned to play the violin from his father. When Vivaldi grew up, he became a priest. He was nicknamed the Red Priest, because of his curly red hair, and because he sometimes wore a bright red robe. He worked at an orphanage for girls. He taught the girls to play the violin. Many people came to the concerts given by the orchestra of orphan girls, and everyone said they played beautifully.

Vivaldi (born in Italy, 1678).

Vivaldi composed hundreds of pieces of music. One of his most famous works is called *The Four Seasons*. For each season, Vivaldi wrote a concerto [con-CHAIR-toe]. A concerto is played by an orchestra, and usually one instrument or a group of instruments gets to show off a bit. When one instrument gets the most attention, the person who plays this instrument is called the soloist. In Vivaldi's *Four Seasons*, the soloist plays a violin, and he or she gets to make sounds that make you think of birds singing in the spring or lightning flashing in a summer storm.

Johann Sebastian Bach [BAHKH] came from a family filled with music. When Bach grew up, he became a great organist. He composed *tons* of music,

Bach (born in Germany, 1685).

Beethoven (born in Germany, 1770).

including organ music, concertos, and a lot of choral music for the church. Bach had many children—twenty in all! Four of them grew up to be composers.

Ludwig van Beethoven [BAY-toe-vun] did not have a happy childhood. When the boy was four years old, his father started to give him piano lessons. He made the boy practice for hours, sometimes late into the night. If young Ludwig made a mistake, his father would shout or hit the boy's knuckles.

You might think that Beethoven would grow up hating music. But music was his whole life. He became famous as the greatest pianist in Europe, and as a great composer.

Beethoven wrote nine symphonies. Try to listen to his Sixth Symphony. It's also known as the "Pastoral" Symphony, because the music is full of peaceful feelings about Beethoven's love of nature and the countryside. But Beethoven was not a peaceful man. He was often moody and he had a fiery temper. By the time he wrote his great Ninth Symphony, a very sad thing had happened. Beethoven had become deaf. He could not hear the orchestra play his wonderful music.

Composers and Their Music

• The *Classical Kids* series (produced by Susan Hammond) offers a fun way to get to know some composers and their music. Titles (on cassette tapes or compact discs) include *Mr. Bach Comes to Call, Beethoven Lives Upstairs, Mozart's Magic Fantasy,* and *Vivaldi's Ring of Mystery.* Each title weaves the composer's music into a lively story.

• The *Greatest Hits* series (Sony Classics) and the *Best of . . .* series (Naxos) offer budget-priced compact discs with favorite works by Vivaldi, Bach, Beethoven, and more.

• The classic Walt Disney animated movie *Fantasia,* available on video, features works by Bach and Beethoven, as well as other favorites.

Families of Instruments: A Closer Look

If you've read the first-grade book in this series, then you may remember that an orchestra is made up of different families of instruments. Can you name an instrument in the *brass* family? How about an instrument in the *wind* family? In the *percussion* family? In the *string* family?

Let's take a closer look now at the string family and the percussion family.

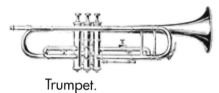

Trumpet.

Clarinet.

The String Family

This man is playing a banjo.

You may know two stringed instruments: the guitar and the banjo. You play them by using the fingers of one hand to press on the strings that run up the long neck of the instrument, while you use your other hand to strum or pick the strings.

The guitar and banjo are popular stringed instruments, especially for folk music, but you won't find them in an orchestra. The main stringed instruments in an orchestra are the violin, viola, cello, and double bass. The violin is the smallest: the others look like bigger and bigger violins.

Violin and bow.

Each of these instruments has four strings. You can pluck the strings to make a sound, but most of the time you play them by sliding a bow back and forth over the strings. When you play the violin or viola, the instrument rests between your shoulder and chin. But the cello is much bigger: you sit on a chair and hold the instrument between your legs. To play the big double bass, you either have to stand beside it or sit on a tall stool.

Of these four stringed instruments, the violin makes the highest sounds. The viola makes slightly lower sounds. The cello's sounds are even lower, while the double bass plays the lowest pitches of all the stringed instruments.

The French composer Camille Saint-Saëns [san-sahn] wrote a work for orchestra called *The Carnival of the Animals*, in which he used the sounds of different instruments to make us think of different animals. He used a cello to make us think of a lovely swan floating gracefully on the water. And what stringed instrument do you think he used to make us think of big, heavy elephants? The double bass!

The boy on the left is playing a cello. The teacher and the other boy are playing violins.

The Percussion Family

The instruments in the string family look like each other, but the instruments in the percussion family are as different as can be. The percussion family includes tiny clicking castanets, a triangle that goes *ding-a-ling-a-ling*, and a big bass drum that goes *boom-boom-boom*.

Castanets.   Triangle.

Why are all these instruments in the same family? What do they have in common?

Bass drum.

They are all percussion instruments because you *hit* them. You play most percussion instruments by hitting them with your hand or with a stick. You shake some percussion instruments, like the maracas.

Maracas.

Some percussion instruments can add excitement to music. When the French composer Georges Bizet [bee-ZAY] wrote the overture to his opera *Carmen*, he used cymbals to give a big, bright splash of sound.

Smaller percussion instruments can add a kind of decoration to music. For example, when you shake sleigh bells, or hit a wooden block, you can make sounds that are just right for Christmas music, since they make you think of a horse pulling a sled down a snowy path.

The main job of percussion instruments is to beat out the rhythm. In a marching band, the big bass drum helps keep a steady beat.

Some percussion instruments can also play melodies. You can play songs on the xylophone or marimba, which have keys that you strike with mallets.

Carlos Chavez, a Mexican composer, wrote some music just for percussion instruments. His *Toccata for Percussion* is exciting to hear. (A recording is available on a compact disc on the Dorian label.)

These big drums are called timpani. Sometimes they're called "kettle drums" because they look like big, tubby kettles.

Keyboard Instruments

Is there a piano at your school? On a piano you can play many different kinds of music: classical, jazz, rock, as well as melodies to go along with songs you might sing at home or school.

A piano has eighty-eight keys. When you push the keys, it causes little wooden hammers covered with hard felt to strike the strings inside the piano, and that's what makes the sound. On the piano, you can push one key with a single finger, or you can play many notes at the same time.

A piano is a *keyboard instrument*. Another keyboard instrument is the organ. Some organs have

Grand piano.

two, three, or even four keyboards. That keeps the organist's hands very busy! But that's not all: really big organs have many pedals that the organist plays with his or her feet. In some churches or auditoriums, you might see a big organ called a pipe organ. When you press a key, it allows air to be sent through a pipe.

A big pipe organ.

Mr. Bach at the Keyboard

A lot of wonderful music for the organ was composed by Johann Sebastian Bach, who was himself a great organist. Did Bach also play the piano? No—but that's because the piano had not been invented in Bach's time (about three hundred years ago). Bach played other keyboard instruments that were the ancestors of the piano, such as the harpsichord. The harpsichord looks like a piano, but it makes a more plucky, jangly sound.

Harpsichord.

When Johann Sebastian Bach was only ten years old, both his parents died, so he went to live with his older brother, Johann Christoph. The whole Bach family was very musical: Johann Christoph was the church organist in the town where he lived. He gave his younger brother music lessons, but he was a very hard, strict teacher. He would not let his brother study a very valuable book of organ music that he kept locked in a bookcase. But Johann Sebastian wanted so much to learn and play the music in that book! So, at night, while his brother was asleep, Johann Sebastian would creep downstairs in the dim moonlight, squeeze his hand between the bars of the bookcase door, take out the valuable book, and then copy the music, note by note! He did this every night until he had copied the whole book. But then his stern brother found the copies, and he took them away as a punishment.

But do you know what? Even without the copies, young Johann Sebastian could play much of the music, because it was in his head! The music in that book was now in his memory!

There is so much wonderful music written for the piano or organ that it's hard to say where to begin! But for starters, try listening to these:

"Minuet in G major" from J. S. Bach's *Anna Magdalena Notebook*
Rondo "Alla turca" from *Piano Sonata No. 11*, K. 331 by Mozart
"Für Elise" by Beethoven
"Spring Song" from *Songs Without Words* by Felix Mendelssohn
"Toccata and Fugue in D minor" (for organ) by J. S. Bach

Writing Music Down

You've read about some famous composers, such as Bach and Mozart. Now, imagine that *you* are a composer. You have written a song. How can you get other people to play it as you want it to sound? Well, you could play the song for them and they could follow along. But what about people far away, who can't be right there with you to hear your song? If you want them to play the song just right, then you have to write it down.

When composers write down music, they use special marks and follow rules that they all agree on. Music that is written down is like directions that tell you what to do. Here is how part of a song you probably know looks when it's written down.

Twin-kle, twin-kle,   lit-tle star, how I won-der what you are.

Sing aloud the first words: "Twinkle, twinkle, little star." Now, sing it again, but clap along with the strong sounds, like this:

Twin	kle	twin	kle	lit	tle	star
clap		clap		clap		clap

When you clap at the strong sounds, you get the *beat*.

Now sing the words again, but this time clap on each sound, like this:

Twin	kle	twin	kle	lit	tle	star
clap	clap	clap	clap	clap	clap	clap

When you clap on each sound, you get the *rhythm*.

Now hum the tune, but don't say the words, like this:

him   hum   him   hum   him   hum   himmm

When you hum the sounds, you get the *melody*.

When you sing the song, then you get it all: the beat, the rhythm, the melody, and the words, all at once.

Follow the Notes

When composers write music down, they use special marks called *notes*. Here are some musical notes:

whole   half   quarter
note   note   note

The notes tell us the rhythm. They tell us how the music moves. That's because each note has a different length. Another way of saying that is, each note stands for a sound that lasts for a different amount of time. On the whole note, you count to four. On the half note, you count to two. The quarter note gets one count. (You might also hear people say that a whole note gets four beats, a half note gets two beats, and a quarter note gets one beat.)

Try this: find a clock with a second hand, the kind that goes "tick-tick-tick" loud enough for you to hear. Now, say "ahh" for four ticks. You've just made a sound that lasts as long as a whole note. (Really, in different songs, notes can last for different times, but we can use the seconds of a clock as an example of how long notes can last.) If a whole note lasts for four ticks of the clock, then how long would a half note last? Say "ahh" for two ticks—that's how long a half note lasts. Now, say "ah" four times, in time with the ticking of the clock like this: "ah—ah—ah—ah." You've just made the sound of four quarter notes.

A half note lasts twice as long as a quarter note. It takes two half notes to make up a whole note. How many quarter notes do you think it takes to make up a whole note? (Four.)

Look again at this music from "Twinkle, Twinkle Little Star." Can you put your finger on the quarter notes? On the half notes?

Twin-kle, twin-kle,   lit-tle star, how I won-der what you are.

Pitch: High and Low

Let's think of some high sounds and low sounds. What are some high sounds? How about a bird chirping, or the brakes on a car squeaking? Can you think of some low sounds? How about thunder rumbling, or a big dog growling?

When we talk about how high or low a sound is, we are talking about *pitch*. Pitch is how high or low the sounds are.

When you sing a song, your voice goes higher and lower. Listen to yourself as you sing just the first two words of "Twinkle, Twinkle Little Star." Do you hear how your voice goes higher on the second "twinkle"?

When composers write music, they tell us how high or low the notes should be by placing the notes in different positions on a *staff*. A staff looks like a wide ladder:

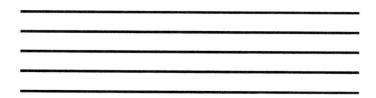

When you follow the notes as they go up and down on the staff, you get the melody. When you put notes near the top of a staff, they are high notes. The notes near the bottom of the staff are lower notes.

Often at the beginning of a staff you will see a special mark called a treble clef. When a staff has a treble clef at the beginning of it, then the lines and spaces of the staff have special names. These names tell musicians how high or low the notes are. The names for the pitches are taken from the alphabet. The music alphabet is **A B C D E F G.** Can you say the music alphabet forward and backward?

We use the music alphabet to name the lines and spaces of the staff. Count how many lines are in the staff. Now count the number of spaces between the lines. Did you count five lines and four spaces? Here are their names:

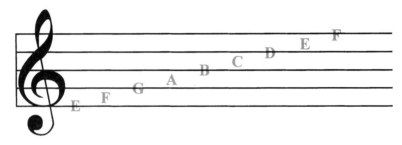

Do you see how the music alphabet is repeated? Look at the bottom line of the staff, which is an E. You go up to F, then G. What comes next? Not H. Instead, you start over again with A.

Sometimes a composer wants silence as part of the music. Then he or she writes a mark called a *rest.* A whole rest lasts as long as a whole note. It says to the musician, "Stay quiet for four counts." A half rest lasts as long as a half note. A quarter rest lasts as long as a quarter note.

| whole note | whole rest | half note | half rest | quarter note | quarter rest |

A Musical Scale

You've seen that musical notes have letter names: A B C D E F G. When you sing or play these notes in a row, one after the other, you are singing or playing a musical *scale*.

On a piano or electric keyboard, you can play a scale called the C major scale. It begins and ends with C, but the first C is a lower pitch than the last one. Begin with a white key just below two black keys, and play only the white keys. (Later books in this series will tell you what the black keys do.)

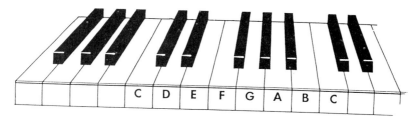

You can use letters to name the notes of the C major scale, or you can use some special sounds. Here are the sounds that go with each letter:

```
                                                      do
                                            ti         C
                                 la          B
                        sol       A
              fa         G
         mi    F
   re     E
do    D
 C
```

Here are the words to a song you can sing to help you learn the special names of the notes.

Do-Re-Mi

Doe—a deer, a female deer,
Ray—a drop of golden sun,
Me—a name I call myself,
Far—a long, long way to run,
Sew—a needle pulling thread,
La—a note to follow sew,
Tea—a drink with jam and bread,
That will bring us back to doe!
Do-re-mi-fa-sol-la-ti-do!

Some Songs for Second Grade

PARENTS: *Here we present the words to some favorite children's songs. You can find the music to these and other favorite songs in songbooks like* Gonna Sing My Head Off! American Folk Songs for Children *by Kathleen Krull (Knopf, 1992) and* American Folk Songs for Children *by Ruth Crawford Seeger (Doubleday, 1980). You might also want to play tapes or compact discs for your child to sing along with, such as:*

- A Child's Celebration of Folk Music, *available on tape or compact disc from Music for Little People (800-727-2233)*
- Wee Sing America *and other recordings in the* Wee Sing *series by Pam Beall and Susan Nipp (Price Stern Sloan)*

You can find more songs for second graders
elsewhere in this book, including:

Clementine

In a cavern, in a canyon,
Excavating for a mine,
Dwelt a miner, forty-niner,
And his daughter, Clementine.

(chorus)
Oh my darling, oh my darling,
Oh my darling, Clementine,
You are lost and gone forever,
Dreadful sorry, Clementine.

Light she was and like a fairy,
And her shoes were number nine,
Herring boxes without topses,
Sandals were for Clementine.
　(repeat chorus)

Drove she ducklings to the water,
Every morning just at nine,
Hit her foot against a splinter,
Fell into the foaming brine.
　(repeat chorus)

Ruby lips above the water,
Blowing bubbles soft and fine,
But, alas, I was no swimmer,
So I lost my Clementine.
　(repeat chorus)

Old Dan Tucker

I came to town the other night
To hear the noise and see the fight.
The watchman was a-runnin' round,
Cryin', "Old Dan Tucker's come to town."

(*chorus*)
So get out the way, Old Dan Tucker,
You're too late to get your supper.
Supper's over, breakfast cookin',
Old Dan Tucker standin' there a-lookin'.

Now Old Dan Tucker was a mighty man,
He washed his face in a frying pan,
Combed his hair with a wagon wheel,
And he died with a toothache in his heel.
(*repeat chorus*)

Home on the Range

Oh, give me a home where the buffalo roam,
Where the deer and the antelope play,
Where seldom is heard a discouraging word,
And the skies are not cloudy all day.

Home, home on the range,
Where the deer and the antelope play,
Where seldom is heard a discouraging word,
And the skies are not cloudy all day.

Goodbye, Old Paint

Goodbye, Old Paint, I'm leaving Cheyenne.
Goodbye, Old Paint, I'm leaving Cheyenne.
I'm leaving Cheyenne, I'm off for Montana,
Goodbye, Old Paint, I'm leaving Cheyenne,
Goodbye, Old Paint, I'm leaving Cheyenne.

Buffalo Gals

This American song from the 1840s is not about buffalo but about the women of Buffalo, New York—or of any other town where the boys like to dance with the girls.

As I was walking down the street,
Down the street, down the street,
A pretty gal I chanced to meet
Under the silvery moon.

Buffalo gals, won't you come out
   tonight,
Come out tonight, come out tonight,
Buffalo gals won't you come out
   tonight,
And dance by the light of the moon.

Casey Jones

Maybe you know the story of the railroad engineer Casey Jones (if you don't, you can find it in What Your Kindergartner Needs to Know). Casey Jones was famous for always getting his train in on time. But one day, as his train was speeding along the tracks, there was a stalled train on the tracks just ahead—and that's how Casey met his end. Casey Jones has become a tall-tale legend in America, and his story lives on in song. There are many versions of the song about him; here are some verses you can sing. (You can read about some other tall-tale heroes in the Language and Literature section of this book.)

Come all you rounders if you want to hear
The story of a brave engineer.
Casey Jones was the rounder's name;
On a big eight-wheeler, boys, he won his fame.

Early one mornin' about half past four
He kissed his wife at the station door,
He mounted to the cabin with his orders in his hand
And he took his farewell trip to that Promised Land.

(*chorus*)
Casey Jones mounted to the cabin,
Casey Jones, with his orders in his hand,
Casey Jones mounted to the cabin,
And he took his farewell trip to that Promised Land.

V.

Mathematics

INTRODUCTION

In school, any successful program for teaching math to young children follows these three cardinal rules: 1) practice, 2) practice, and 3) practice. Not mindless repetition, of course, but thoughtful and varied practice, in which children are given opportunities to approach problems from a variety of angles, and in which, as they proceed to learn new facts and operations, they consistently review and reinforce their earlier learning. Psychologists who specialize in the subject explain that the gaining of ability through practice is *not* opposed to mathematical understanding, but in fact is the prerequisite to thoughtful problem solving. Those who take extreme positions that polarize practice and problem solving are greatly oversimplifying the issues.

Some well-meaning people fear that practice in mathematics—for example, memorizing the addition and subtraction facts up to 18, or doing timed multiplication worksheets—leads to joyless, soul-killing drudgery. Nothing could be further from the truth. The destroyer of joy in learning mathematics is not practice but anxiety—the anxiety that comes from feeling that one is mathematically stupid or lacks any "special talent" for math.

The most effective school math programs that we know of incorporate the principle of incremental review. By incremental review psychologists mean that, once a concept or skill is introduced, it is consciously and regularly presented in later exercises, gradually increasing in depth and difficulty. This feature in mathematics materials helps to cultivate a child's automatic understanding of what is to be done. When children reach the point that they automatically know the basic facts—when, for example, they can instantly tell you what $9 + 8$ equals—then and only then are their minds left free to tackle more challenging problems that ask them to apply or extend the skills and concepts they have learned. School math programs that offer both incremental review and varied opportunities for problem solving tend to get the best results.

In the pages that follow we present a brief explanatory outline of math skills and concepts that should form part of a good second-grade education. But we must emphasize that this outline is *not meant to constitute a complete math program.* These pages can provide a useful supplement for checkup and review at home, but in school children need more extensive and regular opportunities for practice and review than these pages can offer.

Suggested Resources

Family Math by Jean Kerr Stenmark, Virginia Thompson, and Ruth Cossey (University of California, Berkeley, 1986); to order call 510- 642-1910.
Software: *Math Blaster* (Davidson); *Math Workshop* (Broderbund)

Working with Numbers to 100

Skip-Counting

Mario: Can you count to a hundred really fast?

Dana: Sure. One, two, skip a few, a hundred!

Dana's way is tricky, but you know better ways to count to a hundred, like counting by fives or by tens. Try it now. Count out loud by fives to a hundred. Then count out loud by tens to a hundred.

When you count by fives and tens, you are "skip-counting," because you skip over some numbers. You should also learn to skip-count by twos and by threes. Practice now by reading only the numbers in color in the lines below. Keep practicing until you can do it without looking at the numbers.

1, 2, 3, 4, 5, 6, 7, 8, 9, 10, 11, 12, 13, 14, 15, 16, 17, 18, 19, 20

1, 2, 3, 4, 5, 6, 7, 8, 9, 10, 11, 12, 13, 14, 15, 16, 17, 18, 19, 20

Some Special Math Words

When you add numbers together, the numbers you add are called the *addends*. The answer you get is called the *sum*.

$$\left.\begin{array}{r} 5 \\ +3 \end{array}\right\} \text{addends}$$
$$\overline{8}\ \text{sum}$$

You can have more than two addends. What are the addends here?

$$2 + 3 + 5 = 10$$

When you subtract, the number left over is called the *difference*. In $9 - 7 = 2$, the difference is 2. What is the difference here?

$$\begin{array}{r} 7 \\ -4 \\ \hline 3 \end{array}$$

Even and Odd Numbers

Try this. Gather a small pile of crayons. Count how many you have. Then arrange them in pairs. After you arrange them in pairs, are there any left over? If there are none left over, then you picked up an *even* number of crayons. If there is one left over, then you picked up an *odd* number of crayons.

There are 11 crayons here. 11 is an odd number.

When you start at 0 and count by twos, you are naming the even numbers. The even numbers up to 30 are:

0, 2, 4, 6, 8, 10, 12, 14, 16, 18, 20, 22, 24, 26, 28, 30

When you start at 1 and count by twos, you are naming the odd numbers. The odd numbers up to 30 are:

1, 3, 5, 7, 9, 11, 13, 15, 17, 19, 21, 23, 25, 27, 29

Can you name the next even number after 30? Can you name the next odd number after 29?

Between, One More, and One Less

When a number comes in the middle of two other numbers, we say it is *between* them. For example, 7 is between 6 and 8. What number is between 11 and 13? (12) What numbers are between 5 and 9? (6, 7, and 8)

You know that 9 comes just before 10. Another way of saying that is, 9 is one less than 10. You can say that 11 comes just after 10, or that 11 is one more than 10. If I give you a number, can you tell me what is one less and one more than the number? Let's try it. The number is 7. What is one less than 7? What is one more than 7? Practice telling what is one less and one more than any number up to 100. Try these:

5   19   30   43

Counting with a Tally

Imagine you're at a basketball game. You want to keep track of how many points your favorite player scores, so you use a *tally*. You mark down a small straight line for each point he scores. After his first basket, which is worth two points, you make two lines, like this:

| |

After his next basket, you mark down two more points, for a total of four, like this:

| | | |

Then he makes a free throw, which is worth only one point. How many points does that make in all? Five, so far. When you get to five in a tally, you make a line through the first four lines, like this:

卌

Later, when the game is over, you can quickly skip count by fives to see how many points your favorite player scored. Can you tell from this tally how many points he scored?

卌 卌 卌 卌 卌 ||

Wow, 27 points—that's a good game!

Using Graphs

The children in Mrs. Chen's class chose their favorite kind of fruit. They put their choices on a graph, like this:

Our Favorite Fruits							
bananas							
peaches							
apples							
grapes							

0 1 2 3 4 5 6 7

We call this kind of graph a "bar graph," because it shows information in the form of bars. A bar graph can also look like this:

This graph shows favorite pets of the children in Mr. Levy's class. Just by looking quickly at the graph, without reading any numbers, can you tell what pet is the favorite of most children? Now, read the graph and tell how many children liked dogs best, how many liked cats best, how many liked birds best, and how many liked fish best.

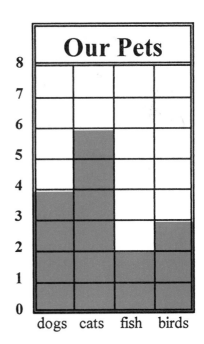

Writing Numbers as Words

Can you write the words for the numbers from 1 to 10? You should also learn to write the words for the numbers from eleven to twenty.

11	eleven	16	sixteen
12	twelve	17	seventeen
13	thirteen	18	eighteen
14	fourteen	19	nineteen
15	fifteen	20	twenty

Practice writing those words until you can do it easily. Also, practice writing the words for the tens up to a hundred:

10	ten	60	sixty
20	twenty	70	seventy
30	thirty	80	eighty
40	forty	90	ninety
50	fifty	100	one hundred

Be careful with "forty." It doesn't have a "u" in it, as "four" and "fourteen" do.

Once you know these words, you can write the words for any number up to 100. Here are some examples:

21 twenty-one   45 forty-five   83 eighty-three

Can you write the words for these numbers?

14   33   42   59   76

Reading a Number Line

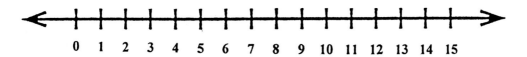

This is a number line. It shows the numbers in order. A number line has arrows because the numbers keep on going forever. All the numbers you've learned, and a whole lot more, can be shown on a number line.

You can use a number line to practice addition and subtraction. For example, to find the sum of 7 + 4 on a number line, first go forward to 7. Then go forward four more numbers. Where do you end? On 11. So, 7 + 4 = 11.

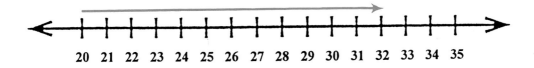

You can also use a number line to practice subtraction. For example, to find the difference of 32 − 7, first go forward on the number line to 32.

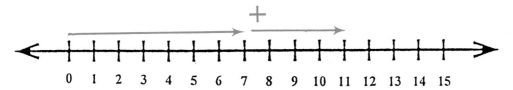

Then go backward 7 numbers.

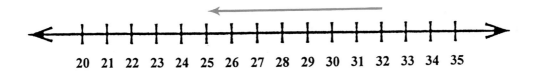

Where do you end up? At 25. So, with the help of a number line, you can figure out that 32 − 7 = 25.

Review: Addition Facts to 12

Review these addition facts with sums up to 12. Practice until you know the sums without having to stop to count.

Sum of 0	Sum of 1	Sum of 2	Sum of 3	Sum of 4
$0 + 0 = 0$	$1 + 0 = 1$	$2 + 0 = 2$	$3 + 0 = 3$	$4 + 0 = 4$
	$0 + 1 = 1$	$1 + 1 = 2$	$2 + 1 = 3$	$3 + 1 = 4$
		$0 + 2 = 2$	$1 + 2 = 3$	$2 + 2 = 4$
			$0 + 3 = 3$	$1 + 3 = 4$
				$0 + 4 = 4$

Sum of 5	Sum of 6	Sum of 7	Sum of 8
$5 + 0 = 5$	$6 + 0 = 6$	$7 + 0 = 7$	$8 + 0 = 8$
$4 + 1 = 5$	$5 + 1 = 6$	$6 + 1 = 7$	$7 + 1 = 8$
$3 + 2 = 5$	$4 + 2 = 6$	$5 + 2 = 7$	$6 + 2 = 8$
$2 + 3 = 5$	$3 + 3 = 6$	$4 + 3 = 7$	$5 + 3 = 8$
$1 + 4 = 5$	$2 + 4 = 6$	$3 + 4 = 7$	$4 + 4 = 8$
$0 + 5 = 5$	$1 + 5 = 6$	$2 + 5 = 7$	$3 + 5 = 8$
	$0 + 6 = 6$	$1 + 6 = 7$	$2 + 6 = 8$
		$0 + 7 = 7$	$1 + 7 = 8$
			$0 + 8 = 8$

Sum of 9	Sum of 10	Sum of 11	Sum of 12
$9 + 0 = 9$	$9 + 1 = 10$	$10 + 1 = 11$	$11 + 1 = 12$
$8 + 1 = 9$	$8 + 2 = 10$	$9 + 2 = 11$	$10 + 2 = 12$
$7 + 2 = 9$	$7 + 3 = 10$	$8 + 3 = 11$	$9 + 3 = 12$
$6 + 3 = 9$	$6 + 4 = 10$	$7 + 4 = 11$	$8 + 4 = 12$
$5 + 4 = 9$	$5 + 5 = 10$	$6 + 5 = 11$	$7 + 5 = 12$
$4 + 5 = 9$	$4 + 6 = 10$	$5 + 6 = 11$	$6 + 6 = 12$
$3 + 6 = 9$	$3 + 7 = 10$	$4 + 7 = 11$	$5 + 7 = 12$
$2 + 7 = 9$	$2 + 8 = 10$	$3 + 8 = 11$	$4 + 8 = 12$
$1 + 8 = 9$	$1 + 9 = 10$	$2 + 9 = 11$	$3 + 9 = 12$
$0 + 9 = 9$		$1 + 10 = 11$	$2 + 10 = 12$
			$1 + 11 = 12$

Review: Subtraction Facts from Numbers to 12

Review these subtraction facts from numbers up to 12. Practice until you know them by heart.

From 0	From 1	From 2	From 3	From 4
$0 - 0 = 0$	$1 - 0 = 1$	$2 - 0 = 2$	$3 - 0 = 3$	$4 - 0 = 4$
	$1 - 1 = 0$	$2 - 1 = 1$	$3 - 1 = 2$	$4 - 1 = 3$
		$2 - 2 = 0$	$3 - 2 = 1$	$4 - 2 = 2$
			$3 - 3 = 0$	$4 - 3 = 1$
				$4 - 4 = 0$

From 5	From 6	From 7	From 8
$5 - 0 = 5$	$6 - 0 = 6$	$7 - 0 = 7$	$8 - 0 = 8$
$5 - 1 = 4$	$6 - 1 = 5$	$7 - 1 = 6$	$8 - 1 = 7$
$5 - 2 = 3$	$6 - 2 = 4$	$7 - 2 = 5$	$8 - 2 = 6$
$5 - 3 = 2$	$6 - 3 = 3$	$7 - 3 = 4$	$8 - 3 = 5$
$5 - 4 = 1$	$6 - 4 = 2$	$7 - 4 = 3$	$8 - 4 = 4$
$5 - 5 = 0$	$6 - 5 = 1$	$7 - 5 = 2$	$8 - 5 = 3$
	$6 - 6 = 0$	$7 - 6 = 1$	$8 - 6 = 2$
		$7 - 7 = 0$	$8 - 7 = 1$
			$8 - 8 = 0$

From 9	From 10	From 11	From 12
$9 - 0 = 9$	$10 - 1 = 9$	$11 - 1 = 10$	$12 - 1 = 11$
$9 - 1 = 8$	$10 - 2 = 8$	$11 - 2 = 9$	$12 - 2 = 10$
$9 - 2 = 7$	$10 - 3 = 7$	$11 - 3 = 8$	$12 - 3 = 9$
$9 - 3 = 6$	$10 - 4 = 6$	$11 - 4 = 7$	$12 - 4 = 8$
$9 - 4 = 5$	$10 - 5 = 5$	$11 - 5 = 6$	$12 - 5 = 7$
$9 - 5 = 4$	$10 - 6 = 4$	$11 - 6 = 5$	$12 - 6 = 6$
$9 - 6 = 3$	$10 - 7 = 3$	$11 - 7 = 4$	$12 - 7 = 5$
$9 - 7 = 2$	$10 - 8 = 2$	$11 - 8 = 3$	$12 - 8 = 4$
$9 - 8 = 1$	$10 - 9 = 1$	$11 - 9 = 2$	$12 - 9 = 3$
$9 - 9 = 0$		$11 - 10 = 1$	$12 - 10 = 2$
			$12 - 11 = 1$

Addition Facts with Sums of 13, 14, 15, 16, 17, and 18

You know your addition facts with sums up to 12 very well, right? (See page 234 if you want to review or practice.) Now here are more addition facts with sums up to 18. Learn these by heart, so that you can give the sums quickly without having to stop to count.

Sum of 13	Sum of 14	Sum of 15	Sum of 16	Sum of 17	Sum of 18
$9 + 4 = 13$	$9 + 5 = 14$	$9 + 6 = 15$	$9 + 7 = 16$	$9 + 8 = 17$	$9 + 9 = 18$
$8 + 5 = 13$	$8 + 6 = 14$	$8 + 7 = 15$	$8 + 8 = 16$	$8 + 9 = 17$	
$7 + 6 = 13$	$7 + 7 = 14$	$7 + 8 = 15$	$7 + 9 = 16$		
$6 + 7 = 13$	$6 + 8 = 14$	$6 + 9 = 15$			
$5 + 8 = 13$	$5 + 9 = 14$				
$4 + 9 = 13$					

Subtraction Facts from 13, 14, 15, 16, 17, and 18

In first grade you learned the subtraction facts from numbers up to 12. (See page 235 if you want to review or practice.) Here are more subtraction facts with numbers up to 18. Learn these facts and you will be able to solve subtraction problems quickly and easily.

From 13	From 14	From 15	From 16	From 17	From 18
$13 - 4 = 9$	$14 - 5 = 9$	$15 - 6 = 9$	$16 - 7 = 9$	$17 - 8 = 9$	$18 - 9 = 9$
$13 - 5 = 8$	$14 - 6 = 8$	$15 - 7 = 8$	$16 - 8 = 8$	$17 - 9 = 8$	
$13 - 6 = 7$	$14 - 7 = 7$	$15 - 8 = 7$	$16 - 9 = 7$		
$13 - 7 = 6$	$14 - 8 = 6$	$15 - 9 = 6$			
$13 - 8 = 5$	$14 - 9 = 5$				
$13 - 9 = 4$					

Adding in Any Order, and Adding Three Numbers

It does not matter what order you add numbers in, the sum is still the same.

$$9 + 4 = 13 \text{ and } 4 + 9 = 13 \qquad 7 + 12 = 19 \text{ and } 12 + 7 = 19$$

That's why you can check your work by adding the numbers in a different order. For example, when you are adding three numbers, first add down, like this:

$$\begin{array}{r} 4 \\ 3 \\ +5 \\ \hline 12 \end{array} \Big\} \qquad \begin{array}{r} 7 \\ +5 \\ \hline 12 \end{array}$$

Then check by adding up, like this:

$$\begin{array}{r} 4 \\ 3 \\ +5 \\ \hline 12 \end{array} \Big\} \qquad \begin{array}{r} 4 \\ +8 \\ \hline 12 \end{array}$$

Either way, no matter what order you add in, you get the same sum.

Doubles and Halves

When you add a number to itself, you are doubling the number. When you add 3 and 3, you double 3. 3 + 3 = 6, so double 3 is 6. Another way to say that is "twice 3 is 6." Practice doubling the numbers from 1 to 9 until you know them by heart.

$$
\begin{array}{ccccccccc}
1 & 2 & 3 & 4 & 5 & 6 & 7 & 8 & 9 \\
+1 & +2 & +3 & +4 & +5 & +6 & +7 & +8 & +9 \\
\hline
2 & 4 & 6 & 8 & 10 & 12 & 14 & 16 & 18
\end{array}
$$

Look at the sums of the doubles. Do you see a pattern? Do you see how the sums go up by twos? Did you also notice that when you double any number, the result is an even number? Even if you double an odd number, the double turns out even. Try it: double 3, and you get 6. Double 5 and you get 10. So, all even numbers are a number doubled. What number is doubled to get 2? What number is doubled to get 6?

Doubles can help you when you're adding. If you know that 7 + 7 = 14, then you can quickly figure what 8 + 7 is. You know that 8 is one more than 7. So, 8 + 7 must be one more than 7 + 7.

7 + 8 is the same as 7 + 7 + 1

7 + 8 = 14 + 1

7 + 8 = 15

Try to work out some more of these "doubles-plus-one" problems. What is 6 + 7?

6 + 7 is the same as 6 + 6 + 1

6 + 7 = 12 + 1

6 + 7 = 13

Now try these doubles-plus-one problems on your own:

$$5 + 6 = 11 \qquad 9 + 8 = 17 \qquad 8 + 7 = 15$$

If you learn your doubles up to 20, then you'll also know how to divide numbers in half. If you cut a piece of bread in two equal parts, then each part is a half. When a number is divided in two equal parts, each part is a half.

What is half of 8? You know the answer if you know what number you double to make 8. You double 4 to make 8. So, 4 is half of 8.

What number do you double to get 4? To get 4, you double 2. So, half of 4 is 2. What number do you double to make 12? To get 12, you double 6. So, half of 12 is 6. Can you tell me what half of 6 is?

What is half of 6?

How many things make up a dozen? There are 12 in a dozen. So, if I ask you to buy half a dozen eggs, how many should you buy?

Sum of 10

All of the problems below have a sum of 10. See if you can give the missing number in each problem.

$$
\begin{array}{ccccccccc}
5 & 6 & 1 & 3 & 2 & 7 & 4 & 8 & 9 \\
+5 & +4 & +9 & +7 & +8 & +3 & +6 & +2 & +1 \\
\hline
10 & 10 & 10 & 10 & 10 & 10 & 10 & 10 & 10
\end{array}
$$

Practice your sums of 10, because you will be able to do lots of math problems more easily if you know by heart the numbers that add up to 10.

Checking Addition and Subtraction

Addition is the opposite of subtraction. So, you can always check a subtraction problem by doing addition, like this:

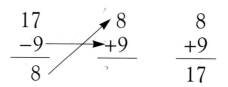

$$
\begin{array}{r} 17 \\ -9 \\ \hline 8 \end{array} \qquad
\begin{array}{r} 8 \\ +9 \\ \hline \end{array} \qquad
\begin{array}{r} 8 \\ +9 \\ \hline 17 \end{array}
$$

When you check, you should end up with the same number you began with. You began by subtracting from 17. When you check, you add 8 and 9 and you get 17, so you know you got the right answer.

You can also check addition by doing subtraction, like this:

$$
\begin{array}{r} 8 \\ +5 \\ \hline 13 \end{array} \qquad
\begin{array}{r} 13 \\ -5 \\ \hline \end{array} \qquad
\begin{array}{r} 13 \\ -5 \\ \hline 8 \end{array}
$$

Fact Families

A fact family brings together addition facts with their opposite subtraction facts. Here is a fact family you may know:

$$
5 + 2 = 7 \qquad 7 - 2 = 5
$$
$$
2 + 5 = 7 \qquad 7 - 5 = 2
$$

Practice forming fact families with the new addition and subtraction facts you've learned, using numbers up to 18. For example:

$$
9 + 4 = 13 \qquad 13 - 4 = 9
$$
$$
4 + 9 = 13 \qquad 13 - 9 = 4
$$

Do you see how making fact families is just like checking addition by subtraction and checking subtraction by addition?

Here are two more addition facts. Can you give the rest of the facts in each fact family?

$9 + 7 = 16$ _____ $8 + 5 = 13$ _____

_____ _____   _____ _____

Find the Missing Number

Practice finding the answers to problems with a missing number, like this:

$7 + \underline{} = 12$ (The missing number is 5.)

$\underline{} - 6 = 7$ (The missing number is 13.)

When you know your addition and subtraction facts by heart, then you can quickly solve a problem with a missing number. Just by looking at this problem, can you tell me the missing number?

$3 + \underline{2} = 5$

Sometimes you might need to figure out the missing number. You can do that by thinking about what you've learned from fact families, and from checking addition with subtraction, as well as checking subtraction with addition. You know that addition and subtraction are opposites. So, look at this problem:

$9 + \underline{} = 17$

If you don't know the missing number instantly, you can figure it out by turning the addition problem into a subtraction problem.

$17 - 9 = 8$

So, the missing number is 8.

$9 + 8 = 17.$

To figure out the missing number in a subtraction problem, you can turn it into an addition problem. For example:

$\underline{} - 8 = 5$

You can find the missing number by adding 5 and 8.

$$5 + 8 = 13$$

So, the missing number is 13.

$$13 - 8 = 5$$

Practice doing problems with missing numbers. Here are some to get you started.

$$8 + \underline{\ \ } = 14 \qquad 3 + \underline{\ \ } = 15 \qquad 9 + \underline{\ \ } = 18 \qquad 8 + \underline{\ \ } = 17$$

$$\underline{\ \ } - 6 = 6 \qquad \underline{\ \ } - 7 = 8 \qquad \underline{\ \ } - 6 = 9 \qquad \underline{\ \ } - 7 = 9$$

Missing Number Problems with Greater Than and Less Than

Do you remember the signs for greater than and less than? The sign > means "greater than." The sign < means "less than." When you see 10 > 8, you read that as "10 is greater than 8." Try reading the following out loud:

$$9 > 7 \qquad 7 + 6 > 5 + 6 \qquad 23 < 72 \qquad 15 - 8 < 11$$

You can do missing number problems with the greater than and less than signs. With these problems, there may be more than one right answer, like this:

$$15 - \underline{\ \ } > 11$$

You could fill in that blank with 0, 1, 2, or 3. They're all correct.
Try these problems:

$$7 + \underline{5} < 12 \qquad\qquad 13 - \underline{\ \ } > 8$$

Working with Equations

When you write $7 - 4 = 3$, or $5 + 3 = 8$, you are writing an *equation*. An equation compares numbers using an equals sign: =. As you know, the equals sign means "is the same as." All of these are equations:

$$7 + 7 = 14 \qquad 36 = 36 \qquad 4 + 1 = 9 - 4$$

Whenever you change one side of an equation, you have to make the same change to the other side so the two sides stay equal. For example, let's say that we're adding triangles. Look at the groups of triangles in this picture:

We can use an equation with numbers to stand for our groups of triangles:

$$3 + 5 = 8$$

Now, if I add 2 triangles to the side with 3 and 5 triangles, then what do I have to do to the side with 8 triangles, if I want the two sides to stay equal? I have to add 2 triangles to the 8 triangles as well.

In an equation when we add 2 to one side, we have to add 2 to the other side as well:

$$2 + 3 + 5 = 2 + 8$$

Tens and Ones

You know that 1 ten is the same as 10 ones.

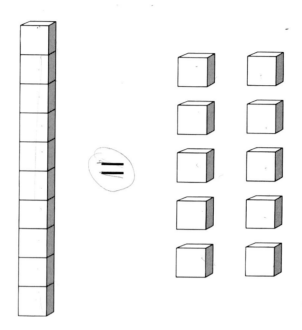

When you have 27 of something, you have 2 tens and 7 ones. You can write 27 as a sum of tens and ones:

$$27 = 20 + 7$$

How many tens are in 34? How many ones? So, you can write 34 as a sum of tens and ones:

34 is the same as 30 + 4

Practice writing some numbers as a sum of tens and ones. For example, you can write 46 as 40 + 6. Following that pattern, how would you write 77? How about 32, 56, and 98?

Adding Numbers with Two Digits

Another word for any of the numbers from 0 to 9 is a "digit." The number 43 has two digits, a 4 and a 3. As you know, 43 is 4 tens and 3 ones. When we look at the digits in the number 43, we say that the 4 is in the tens place and the 3 is in the ones place.

When you add two-digit numbers, first you add the ones, then you add the tens. When we write an addition problem with two-digit numbers, we say that the numbers in the ones place are in the ones column, and the numbers in the tens place are in the tens column. Let's figure out this sum:

$$\begin{array}{r} \text{tens ones} \\ 23 \\ +35 \\ \hline \end{array}$$

First we add the numbers in the ones column. Add 3 and 5, and you get 8. Then add the numbers in the tens column. Add 2 and 3 and you get 5. But you're really adding 2 tens and 3 tens, which makes 5 tens, or 50. So the sum is 5 tens plus 8 ones, or 50 + 8, which equals 58.

$$\begin{array}{r} \text{tens ones} \\ 23 \\ +35 \\ \hline 58 \end{array}$$

Sometimes when you add two-digit numbers, you have to "regroup." For example, look at this problem.

$$\begin{array}{r} 48 \\ +26 \\ \hline \end{array}$$

You begin by adding the numbers in the ones column. When you add 8 + 6, you get 14 ones. You know that 14 is the same as 10 + 4. So, you need to "regroup" 14 into 1 ten and 4 ones. You write the 4, which means 4 ones, at the bottom of the ones column. Then you write the 1, which means 1 ten, at the top of the tens column, and add it to the other tens.

Add the ones and regroup.

$$
\begin{array}{r}
1 \\
48 \\
+26 \\
\hline
4
\end{array}
$$

Now add the tens.

$$
\begin{array}{r}
1 \\
48 \\
+26 \\
\hline
74
\end{array}
$$

Altogether you have 7 tens and 4 ones, which makes a sum of 74.

Writing a new ten at the top of the tens column is also called "carrying." In the problem above, when you added the numbers in the ones column, you got 14. You wrote the 4 at the bottom of the ones column. Then you wrote a 1 (for 1 ten) at the top of the tens column, which is the same as saying that you "carried the 1" (for 1 ten) to the tens column.

Checking Addition by Changing the Order of Addends

It does not matter what order you add numbers in, the sum is still the same: $7 + 3 = 10$ and $3 + 7 = 10$. So, you can check your answer to an addition problem by writing the addends in a different order and then adding again. You should get the same sum both times. For example:

Change the order of the addends.

$$
\begin{array}{r} 37 \\ +55 \\ \hline 92 \end{array}
\qquad
\begin{array}{r} 55 \\ +37 \\ \hline 92 \end{array}
$$

Adding Three Numbers

Let's try adding three numbers. First you add the numbers in the ones column. If they add up to more than 10, you need to regroup and carry.

$$
\begin{array}{r}
\text{tens ones} \\
43 \\
28 \\
+14 \\
\hline
\end{array}
$$

When you add $3 + 8 + 4$, you get 15. So, you need to regroup. Write the 5 at the bottom of the ones column, then carry the 1 (for 1 ten) to the top of the tens column. Add the numbers in the tens column (don't forget to add the 1 you carried), and you'll get the sum.

$$
\begin{array}{r}
1 \\
43 \\
28 \\
+14 \\
\hline
85
\end{array}
$$

Subtracting Numbers with Two Digits

When you subtract from a two-digit number, first you subtract the numbers in the ones column. Here's an example:

$$97 - 55$$

You start by subtracting the ones: $7 - 5$ leaves 2. You write 2 at the bottom of the ones column. Then you subtract the tens. When you take 5 tens away from 9 tens, the difference is 4 tens. So you write 4 at the bottom of the tens column.

Subtract the ones.   *Subtract the tens.*

tens ones   tens ones

$$\begin{array}{r} 97 \\ -55 \\ \hline 2 \end{array} \qquad \begin{array}{r} 97 \\ -55 \\ \hline 42 \end{array}$$

Sometimes when you subtract you will need to regroup. But instead of changing 10 ones to 1 ten, you will regroup 1 ten into 10 ones. Let's see how it works.

Pretend you have 27 pencils. You want to take away 9 pencils. How many will you have left? Let's write that as a subtraction problem.

$$27 - 9$$

Look at the numbers in the ones column. You want to take away 9. But you only have 7 ones. Remember, however, that 27 is the same as 2 tens and 7 ones.

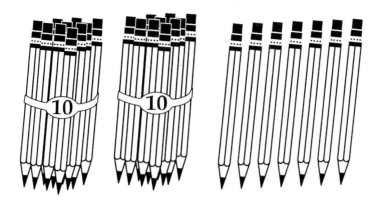

Take 1 of those tens and regroup it with the ones. That will leave you with 1 ten and 17 ones.

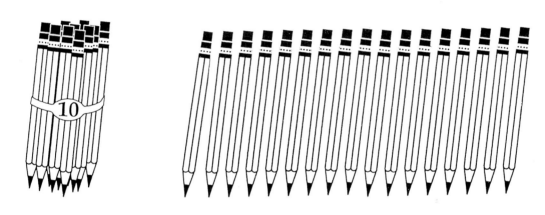

You have regrouped 2 tens and 7 ones into 1 ten and 17 ones. Some people say that you have "borrowed" 1 ten from the tens column and put it in the ones column. Now, you know how to take away 9 from 17. That leaves you with 8 ones. But don't forget you still have 1 ten left. So, $27 - 9 = 18$.

Let's do some more subtraction problems with regrouping, and learn a way to write the problems to keep each step clear as you go along. Look at the ones column in this problem:

$$\begin{array}{r} 65 \\ -48 \\ \hline \end{array}$$

8 is greater than 5, so you can't take away 8 from 5. You need to regroup. You know that 65 is the same as $60 + 5$, or 6 tens and 5 ones. Take 1 ten and add it to the 5 ones.

What does that leave you with? 5 tens and 15 ones. Cross out the 6 in the tens place and write 5 above it. Cross out the 5 in the ones place and write 15 above it. Now you can subtract easily. Remember, start with the ones first.

Subtract the ones.   *Now subtract the tens.*

$$
\begin{array}{r}
\overset{\text{tens}\ \text{ones}}{5\ \ 15} \\
\cancel{6}\ \ \cancel{5} \\
-4\ \ \ 8 \\
\hline
7
\end{array}
\qquad
\begin{array}{r}
\overset{\text{tens}\ \text{ones}}{5\ \ 15} \\
\cancel{6}\ \ \cancel{5} \\
-4\ \ \ 8 \\
\hline
1\ \ 7
\end{array}
$$

Checking Two-Digit Subtraction

Remember that addition is the opposite of subtraction, so you can check subtraction by addition. Here's a subtraction problem.

$$
\begin{array}{r}
62 \\
-35 \\
\hline
27
\end{array}
$$

You can check this by going from bottom to top and turning it into an addition problem. The sum should be the same as the number you first subtracted from, which is 62. Try it. Does it check?

$$
\begin{array}{r}
27 \\
+35 \\
\hline
\end{array}
$$

Adding and Subtracting Horizontally, Vertically, and in Your Head

You know that addition and subtraction problems can be written in two ways: across or up and down. We also say that a problem written across is written *horizontally*. A problem written up and down is written *vertically*. Either way, the answer comes out the same.

Horizontal

$11 + 17 = 28$ *is the same as*

Vertical

$$\begin{array}{r} 11 \\ +17 \\ \hline 28 \end{array}$$

$23 - 12 = 11$ *is the same as*

$$\begin{array}{r} 23 \\ -12 \\ \hline 11 \end{array}$$

When you see a two-digit addition problem written horizontally, it is sometimes easier to solve it by writing it over vertically. For example, what is the sum of $12 + 39$? Rewrite the problem vertically, and make sure you keep all the ones in the ones column and the tens in the tens column.

Rewrite the problem vertically.

tens ones

$$\begin{array}{r} 1\ 2 \\ +3\ 9 \\ \hline \end{array}$$

Add the ones and regroup.

tens ones

$$\begin{array}{r} 1\ \ \\ 1\ 2 \\ +3\ 9 \\ \hline 1 \end{array}$$

Add the tens.

tens ones

$$\begin{array}{r} 1\ \ \\ 1\ 2 \\ +3\ 9 \\ \hline 5\ 1 \end{array}$$

Here is a way to solve a horizontal two-digit addition problem in your head. Try this problem: find the sum of 57 + 32. First, you break the numbers into tens and ones: 57 is the same as 50 + 7. 32 is the same as 30 + 2. In your head, add the tens: 50 + 30 is 80. Now add the ones: 7 + 2 is 9. So the sum is 80 + 9, or 89.

If you need to solve a subtraction problem written horizontally, you can rewrite it vertically.

$$65 - 43 = \underline{} \qquad \textit{rewrite vertically as} \qquad \begin{array}{r} 65 \\ -\ 43 \\ \hline \end{array}$$

You can also look at the problem as it's written horizontally and try to solve it in your head. Try to find the difference of 65 − 43. Break the numbers into tens and ones: 65 is the same as 60 + 5, and 43 is the same as 40 + 3. 60 − 40 = 20, and 5 − 3 = 2. So the difference is 22.

It's not as easy to add and subtract in your head when you have to regroup. When you have to regroup, you will probably want to rewrite the problem vertically.

But, even when you need to regroup, you can learn to add and subtract in your head if you think of a math fact you already know. For example, to solve

$$28 + 6 = \underline{}$$

think first of what you know.

You know that $8 + 6 = 14$.
So in your head regroup 28 as $20 + 8$, like this: $\quad 20 + 8 + 6 = \underline{}$
Now add $8 + 6$, which you know is 14: $\quad 20 + 14 = \underline{}$
Now you can figure out the sum in your head: $\quad 20 + 14 = 34$

Let's try a subtraction problem in our heads.

$$35 - 8 = \underline{}$$

You know that $15 - 8 = 7$.
So in your head regroup 30 as $20 + 15$, like this: $\quad 20 + (15 - 8) = \underline{}$
Now subtract 8 from 15, which you know is 7. $\quad 20 + 7 = \underline{}$
Now you can figure out the answer in your head. $\quad 20 + 7 = 27$
So, $35 - 8 = 27$.

It may be tough at first to do problems like these in your head, but keep trying. With practice, it will get easier, and then you'll be ready to tackle even harder and more interesting math problems. When you're ready for a challenge, try doing these problems in your head:

$$38 + 7 = \underline{\quad} \qquad 43 - 8 = \underline{\quad} \qquad 25 + 8 = \underline{\quad} \qquad 65 - 6 = \underline{\quad}$$

Adding and Subtracting 9 in Your Head

You can use a little trick to solve problems that ask you to add or subtract 9. For example: $25 + 9 = \underline{\quad}$. Change the 9 to 10, and in your head you can quickly figure out that $25 + 10 = 35$. Now, just subtract 1 from 35 (because 10 is 1 more than 9) and you get the answer, 34. So, to add 9 in your head, a short cut is to add 10 then take away 1.

Now let's try subtracting 9. Here's the problem: $53 - 9 = \underline{\quad}$. Change the 9 to 10, and in your head you can quickly figure out that $53 - 10 = 43$. Now, because you're subtracting, and you've taken away 1 more than 9, you need to add that 1 back. Add 1 to 43 and you get the answer, 44. So, to subtract 9 in your head, a short cut is to subtract 10 then add 1.

Try doing these in your head:

$$37 + 9 = \underline{\quad} \qquad 76 - 9 = \underline{\quad} \qquad 45 + 9 = \underline{\quad} \qquad 58 - 9 = \underline{\quad}$$

Estimating and Rounding
to the Nearest Ten

Donny likes to collect baseball cards. When you visit him, he opens a box and pours out a pile of cards. "Wow! How many cards do you have?" you ask. "About 300," says Donny.

Sometimes it's easier to say *about* how many you have instead of exactly how many. When you say *about* how many, you are *estimating*.

Sometimes when you are adding and subtracting, you only need to know *about* what the answer is. When you don't need to know the exact answer, then you can estimate the answer—you can figure out *about* what it is. For example, how would you estimate the sum of $23 + 45$? To begin, you turn the numbers into numbers that are easier to work with in your head. It's easier to work with numbers like 10, 20, 30, 40, 50, and so on. So, you need to "round" the numbers to the nearest ten.

Let's see what it means to round 23 to the nearest ten. Look at this number line.

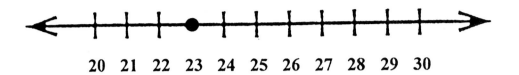

20 21 22 23 24 25 26 27 28 29 30

You can see that 23 is between 20 and 30. But it's closer to 20. So, 23 rounded to the nearest 10 is 20.

What is 45 rounded to the nearest ten? To answer that, you need to know a special rule: *When a number is exactly between two numbers, you round up to the greater number.*

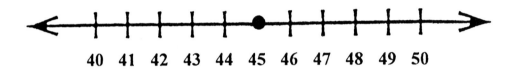

40 41 42 43 44 45 46 47 48 49 50

You can see on the number line that 45 is exactly between 40 and 50. So you round it up to 50.

Let's go back to our addition problem: how would you estimate the sum of 23 + 45?

$$23 \text{ rounds to } 20$$
$$+45 \text{ rounds to } +50$$
$$70$$

So, 23 + 45 is *about* 70.

You can also use estimation when you subtract two-digit numbers and only need to know *about* what the difference is. For example:

$$87 \text{ rounds to } 90$$
$$-41 \text{ rounds to } -40$$
$$50$$

So, 87 − 41 is *about* 50.

Fractions

A fraction is a part of something. In first grade you learned these fractions:

$^1/_2$

one half

$^1/_3$

one third

$^1/_4$

one fourth
(*also called one quarter*)

If something is divided into five equal parts, each part is one fifth, which in numbers is written as $^1/_5$. Here is a pizza divided into five equal slices. Each slice is $^1/_5$.

A fraction has a top number and a bottom number. The bottom number tells how many equal parts there are. The top number tells how many equal parts you are talking about. For example, look again at the pizza divided into five equal slices. If you ate two slices, what fraction of the whole pizza did you eat? You ate $^2/_5$ (two fifths).

Each slice is $^1/_5$ (one fifth).

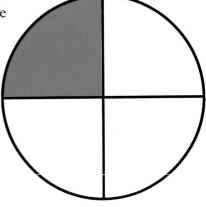

Look at this circle. It is divided into four equal parts. One part is blue. What fraction of the circle is blue?

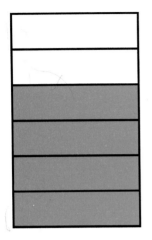

Here is a rectangle divided into six equal parts. Each part is $\frac{1}{6}$ (one sixth). Four parts of the rectangle are blue. What fraction is blue? $\frac{4}{6}$ (four sixths) of the rectangle is blue.

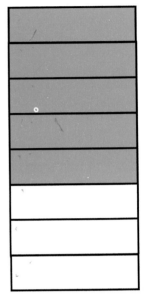

Here is another rectangle divided into eight equal parts. Each part is $\frac{1}{8}$ (one eighth). Five of the parts are blue. What fraction is blue? $\frac{5}{8}$ (five eighths) of the rectangle is blue.

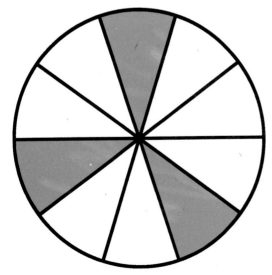

This circle has ten equal parts. What do you think each equal part is called? Each part is $\frac{1}{10}$ (one tenth). Count how many parts are blue. What fraction of the circle is blue?

You can also use fractions to talk about parts of a group. For example, there are eight girls in the class. Three of them are on the soccer team. What fraction of the girls are on the soccer team? $\frac{3}{8}$ (three eighths) of the girls are on the soccer team.

Working with Numbers to 1,000

The Hundreds

Count out loud by tens from 10 to 100. How many tens are in one hundred?

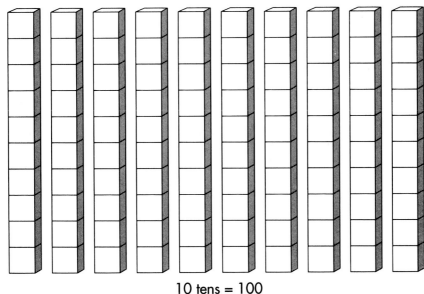

10 tens = 100

100 is the same as 10 tens. 100 is written in words as one hundred.

Here are the numbers and words for the hundreds. Learn to write the numbers and words, and practice counting the hundreds out loud.

100	one hundred
200	two hundred
300	three hundred
400	four hundred
500	five hundred
600	six hundred
700	seven hundred
800	eight hundred
900	nine hundred

Counting Between Hundreds

Let's count out loud by ones, starting with 100. After 100 comes

101, 102, 103, 104, 105, 106, 107, 108, 109, 110, 111, 112 . . .

Okay, you can stop for now. When you read those numbers, you say one hundred one, one hundred two, one hundred three, one hundred four, one hundred five, and so on. (Notice that you don't say "one hundred *and* one" or "one hundred *and* twelve"— there's no "and" in these numbers.)

Now, let's start at 189 and keep on counting.

189, 190, 191, 192, 193, 194, 195, 196, 197, 198, 199 . . .

What comes after 199? A new hundred, which is 200. After 200, you can keep counting in the same way:

200, 201, 202, 203, 204, 205, 206, 207, 208, 209, 210, 211, 212 . . .

What comes after 299? 300. You can keep counting till you get to 999 (nine hundred ninety-nine). What's the number after that? It's ten hundreds, but we use a new name for it:

1,000 one thousand

Count On!

Practice counting by hundreds from 100 to 1,000, like this:

100, 200, 300, 400, 500, 600, 700, 800, 900, 1,000

Now try counting by fifties to 1,000. We'll get you started, and you finish:

50, 100, 150, 200, 250, 300, 350 . . .

Practice counting by tens and by fives from any hundred to the next hundred. For example:

by tens (from 400): 400, 410, 420, 430, 440, 450, 460, 470, 480, 490, 500
by fives (from 525): 525, 530, 535, 540, 545, 550, 555, 560… *(on to 600)*

Now try this: count by tens from any old number. For example, start with 37. We'll get you started, then you go on a bit longer:

37, 47, 57, 67, 77, 87, 97, 107, 117, 127… *(go on to 227)*

Count by tens from 176. Again, we'll get you started.

176, 186, 196, 206, 216, 226… *(go on to 326)*

Practice until you can count easily by tens from any number. Also, practice counting *backward* by ten from any number. For example:

235, 225, 215, 205, 195, 185, 175… *(Can you keep going backward by tens to 25?)*

Practice writing the words for three-digit numbers. For example:

843   eight hundred forty-three
607   six hundred seven

You try writing the words for 156, 403, and 987.

Place Value

Remember that we call numbers like 21 and 73 "two-digit" numbers. Notice that 100 has one more digit. It is a three-digit number. We say that the first digit is the hundreds place. You know where the next digits are—in the tens place and the ones place.

100

Let's look at the number 245 (two hundred forty-five). The 2 in the hundreds place means there are 2 hundreds. The 4 in the tens place means there are 4 tens. And what does the 5 in the ones place mean?

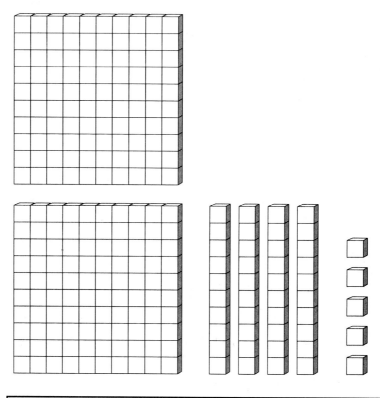

hundreds	tens	ones
2	4	5

You can use place-value blocks to help you understand what each digit in a three-digit number means, like this:

259

hundreds	tens	ones
2	5	9

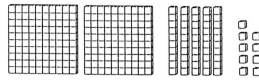

504

hundreds	tens	ones
5	0	4

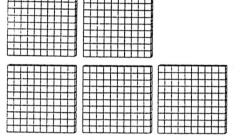

Only one of the following numbers has 8 tens and 4 hundreds. Can you tell which one? (You might find it helpful to write the numbers in a place-value block.)

418   884   814   148   481   448

Expanded Form

You know that 73 is 7 tens and 3 ones. You know that another way to write 73 is 70 + 3. When you write 73 as 70 + 3, you are writing the number in "expanded form." ("Expanded" means "stretched out.")

You can also write three-digit numbers in expanded form. For example, in expanded form, 273 is 200 + 70 + 3. Here are other examples:

$$359 = 300 + 50 + 9$$
$$603 = 600 + 3 \text{ (There are no tens in this number.)}$$
$$740 = 700 + 40 \text{ (There are no ones in this number.)}$$

Try writing these numbers in expanded form:

394   571   805   630   912

Comparing Three-Digit Numbers

Which number is greater: 689 or 869? When you compare a three-digit number, look at the hundreds place first. If you look at the hundreds place in 689 and 869, you'll see that 8 is greater than 6. So you can quickly say that 869 > 689.

If the number in the hundreds place is the same, then you need to look at the tens place. For example, 371 > 359.

If the numbers in both the hundreds place and the tens place are the same, then look at the ones place. For example, 863 < 867.

Put the correct sign between the following pairs of numbers.

$$> \qquad < \qquad =$$

greater than   less than   equal to

876___599   348___384   765___769   252___225

Adding Three-Digit Numbers

To find the sum of three-digit numbers, first add the ones. Then add the tens. And then add the hundreds.

Find the sum.   *Add the ones.*   *Add the tens.*   *Add the hundreds.*
          Regroup if necessary.

$$
\begin{array}{r}
253 \\
+338 \\
\hline
\end{array}
\qquad
\begin{array}{r}
1 \\
253 \\
+338 \\
\hline
1
\end{array}
\qquad
\begin{array}{r}
1 \\
253 \\
+338 \\
\hline
91
\end{array}
\qquad
\begin{array}{r}
1 \\
253 \\
+338 \\
\hline
591
\end{array}
$$

Regrouping Tens as Hundreds

In the addition example above, you needed to regroup ones as tens. Sometimes when you add you need to regroup tens as hundreds. It's not much different from regrouping ones as tens. Let's see by finding the sum of 80 + 40. How many tens are in 80? Yes, 8. And 40 is 4 tens.

$$8 \text{ tens} + 4 \text{ tens} = 12 \text{ tens}$$

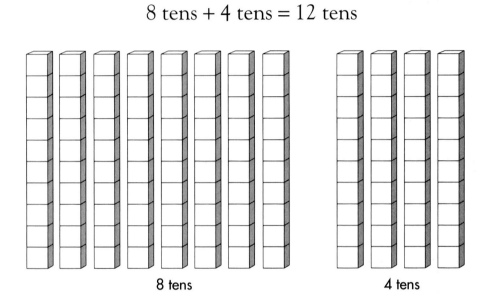

8 tens   4 tens

So, now you have 12 tens. You can take 10 of the tens and group them together to make 1 hundred, with 2 tens left over. So, 12 tens is the same as 1 hundred and 2 tens.

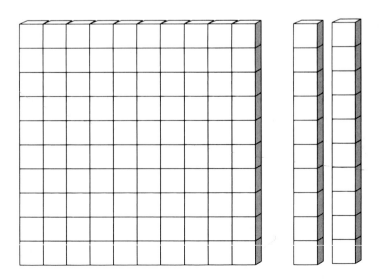

In an addition problem, when you have 10 or more tens, you need to regroup them as hundreds. Here is an example:

Find the sum.	*Add the ones.*	*Add the tens.* *Regroup if necessary.*	*Add the hundreds.*
		1	1
276 +663	276 +663 9	276 +663 39	276 +663 939

When you add the tens in this problem, you add 7 tens plus 6 tens. That makes 13 tens. 13 tens is the same as 1 hundred and 3 tens. So you write 3 at the bottom of the tens column, then you "carry the 1" (which stands for 1 hundred) to the top of the hundreds column.

Now let's do a problem in which you have to regroup both tens and ones.

Find the sum.	*Add the ones* *Regroup.*	*Add the tens.* *Regroup.*	*Add the hundreds.*
	1	11	11
638 +265	638 +265 3	638 +265 03	638 +265 903

Practice doing many three-digit addition problems until you can do them easily. Check your addition. Remember, you can check yourself by changing the order of the addends then adding again to see if you get the same answer.

Subtracting from a Three-Digit Number

To subtract from a three-digit number, first subtract the ones. Then subtract the tens. Then subtract the hundreds.

Find the difference.	*Subtract the ones. Regroup if necessary.*	*Subtract the tens.*	*Subtract the hundreds.*
	7 12	7 12	7 12
582	58̷2̷	58̷2̷	58̷2̷
− 269	− 26 9	− 26 9	− 26 9
	3	13	313

Remember, you can check subtraction by adding, like this:

$$
\begin{array}{cccc}
 & & & 1 \\
582 & & 313 & 313 \\
-269 & \longrightarrow & +269 & +269 \\
\hline
313 & & & 582 \\
\end{array}
$$

Subtraction and Regrouping Hundreds

As you know, sometimes when you subtract you need to regroup 1 ten as 10 ones. For example, you would need to regroup a ten as 10 ones in this problem:

$$
\begin{array}{r}
82 \\
- 57 \\
\hline
\end{array}
$$

In some problems, you may also need to regroup 1 hundred as 10 tens. Say that you have 230 pencils. They are bundled together in 2 hundreds and 3 tens.

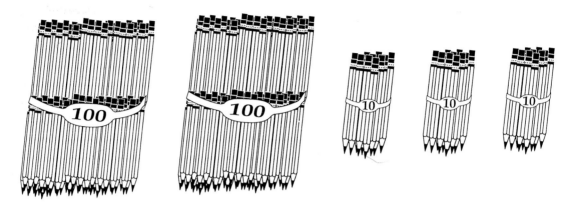

You want to give away 60 pencils. How can you do this? You only have 3 tens, but 60 is 6 tens. So, you need to regroup one of the hundreds into tens.

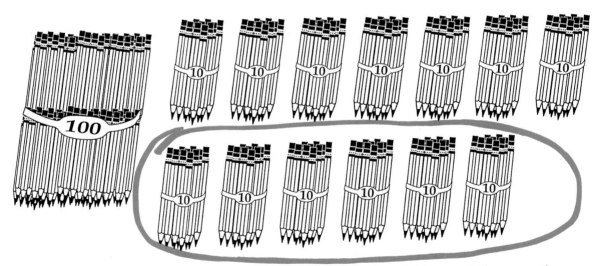

You can regroup 2 hundreds and 3 tens as 1 hundred and 13 tens. Take away 6 tens (the pencils circled in the picture), and that leaves you with 1 hundred and 7 tens, or 170 pencils. So, 230 − 60 = 170.

Now let's try another subtraction problem in which you need to regroup 1 hundred as 10 tens.

Find the difference. *Subtract the ones.* *Subtract the tens.* *Subtract the hundreds.*

556
−372
―――

55 6
−37 2
―――
    4

4 15
5̶5̶6
−3 72
―――
  84

4 15
5̶5̶6
−3 72
―――
1 84

> Practice doing many three-digit subtraction problems until you can do them easily.
> Remember, you can check your subtraction by adding.

Money

Coins and Dollar Bills

Can you name these coins, and tell how many cents each is worth?

Here's another coin that you may see sometimes, called a half dollar. It is worth 50 cents.

A half dollar.

Here is a picture of a one dollar bill.

Here is the way you write one dollar, using numbers and the dollar sign:

$$\$1.00$$

$1.00 is worth the same as 100 pennies.

$$\$1.00 = 100¢$$

You can write amounts of money using the cents sign or the dollar sign.

cents ¢   dollars $

When you write an amount of money with a dollar sign, the numbers to the right of the little dot (called a "decimal point") are cents. For example, $1.50 is 1 dollar and 50 cents. $2.98 is 2 dollars and 98 cents.

You can write amounts less than a dollar with a dollar sign or a cents sign.

$$\$0.89 = 89¢$$

You read $0.89 and 89¢ in the same way—89 cents.

How much does this toy car cost?

How would you write 79¢ using a dollar sign instead?

How Many Make Up a Dollar?

Let's learn how many coins of different types it takes to make up a dollar. At the same time, let's see what fraction of a dollar each coin is.

 =

Two half dollars equal one dollar. A half dollar is ½ of a dollar.

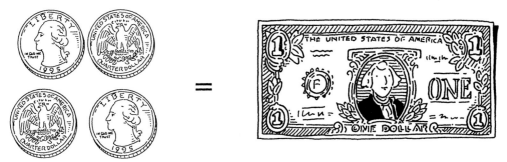

Four quarters equal one dollar. A quarter is ¼ of a dollar.

Ten dimes equal 1 dollar. A dime is ⅟10 of a dollar.

Quarters and Counting by 25

Henry wants to buy a popsicle at the school cafeteria. It costs 50¢. His mother gives him quarters to pay for the ice cream. How many quarters does she give him?

Mr. Jones buys a newspaper. It costs 25¢. He gives the man a dollar bill. The man gives him quarters for change. How many quarters does he give Mr. Jones?

Remember: 2 quarters make 50¢, and 3 quarters make 75¢, and 4 quarters make $1.00. When you count quarters, you count by 25s. Practice counting by 25s to 200:

25, 50, 75, 100, 125, 150, 175, 200

Counting Money

When you count coins, start with the coins that are worth most. For example, how much is this?

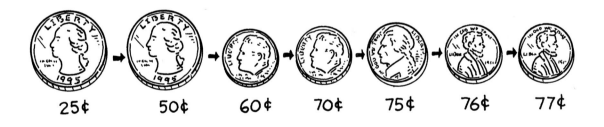

| 25¢ | 50¢ | 60¢ | 70¢ | 75¢ | 76¢ | 77¢ |

Those coins add up to 77¢. What is another way of writing 77¢, using the dollar sign?

Now let's count this money. Count the dollars before you count the coins.

Starting with the dollar bills, you have $2.00. Three quarters make 75¢ more, or $2.75 in all so far. Two dimes make $2.85, $2.95. Now for the three nickels. The first nickel makes $3.00 even. Then you get $3.05, $3.10. At last, the pennies. You count $3.11, $3.12, $3.13, $3.14. Altogether you have $3.14.

Practice counting money until you can do it quickly without making mistakes.

Adding and Subtracting Money

When you write down amounts of money, you add and subtract the amounts in the same way you add and subtract other numbers. For example:

$$
\begin{array}{ccc}
1 & 1 & 6\ 12 \\
67\text{¢} & \$1.85 & \$6.\cancel{7}\cancel{2} \\
+18\text{¢} & +3.64 & -4.2\ 6 \\
\hline
85\text{¢} & \$5.49 & \$2.46
\end{array}
$$

Notice that when you need to regroup in a money problem, you do the same as you would in a regular addition or subtraction problem. In a money problem, don't forget to write the $ or ¢ sign in your answer, and remember to bring down the decimal point, too.

Word Problems

As you practice math, you will do many word problems. The trick is figuring out what the word problem is asking you to do. Is it asking you to add? Or maybe to subtract?

What is this word problem asking you to do?

> *The second-grade classes at Brownsville Elementary collected cans for recycling. Ms. Johnson's class collected 345 cans. Mr. Franklin's class collected 275 cans. How many cans did they collect in all?*

This is an addition problem. To solve it:

You write:	You add:	You check:
	11	11
345	345	275
+275	+275	+345
	620	620

The second-grade classes collected 620 cans in all. Now, try another word problem:

> *Margaret brings $3.65 to a movie. The movie ticket costs $2.75. After she buys her ticket, how much money does she have left?*

This is a subtraction problem. To solve it:

You write:	You subtract:	You check:
	2 16	1
$3.65	$3.65	$0.90
− 2.75	− 2.75	+2.75
	$0.90	$3.65

How would you solve this problem?

At the museum gift shop, Tricia bought a poster for $6.47. Her friend, Joanie, bought a necklace for $4.29. How much more did Tricia spend than Joanie?

When a word problem asks you "how much more," you need to subtract, like this:

You write:	*You subtract:*	*You check:*
	317	1
$ 6.47	$6.4̶7̶	$2.18
− 4.29	− 4.29	+4.29
	$2.18	$6.47

So, Tricia spent $2.18 more than Joanie.

Measurement

Measuring Length

When you measure how long something is, you measure its length. Length can be measured in different units, such as inches and feet.

This paper clip is 1 inch long. The leaf is 3 inches long.

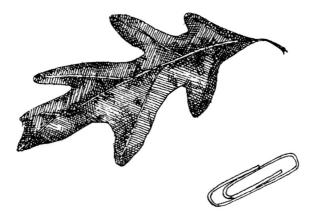

Practice measuring different objects in inches, using tools like a ruler or a tape measure.

Most things are not exactly a certain number of inches long. Sometimes you just need to estimate how long something is. For example, rounding to the nearest inch, this pencil is about 5 inches long.

At home or school, you may have a ruler that is 12 inches long. 12 inches is also called a foot.

12 inches = 1 foot

Practice measuring in feet and inches. You might start by measuring how tall you or your friends are.

In the United States, we use inches and feet to measure length, but in many other countries, such as Japan, France, and Germany, they use a unit called centimeters. This toy car is 5 centimeters long.

A centimeter is shorter than an inch; it's not quite half an inch. If you have a foot ruler at home or school, check to see if it also has centimeters on one edge, then practice measuring some objects in centimeters.

When we write measurements, we often use abbreviations, like this:

inches = in.   feet = ft.   centimeters = cm

Measuring Weight

When you measure how heavy something is, you are measuring weight. We often measure weight in pounds. The abbreviation for pounds is a little strange, but you can remember it: **lb.** The book in this picture weighs one pound.

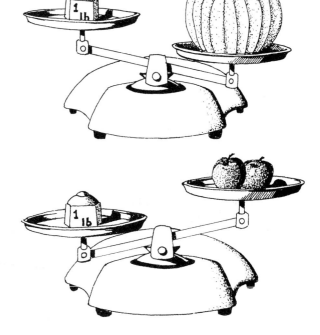

One tool for weighing is called a balance. When the balance is level, both sides weigh the same.

When one side of the balance is lower than the other, the lower side weighs more. Look at the balances in the pictures here. Does the pumpkin weigh more or less than one pound? Do the apples weigh more or less than one pound?

Look again at the pictures of the balances with the book, pumpkin, and apples. Then list the objects in order from the lightest to the heaviest. (From lightest to heaviest, they are the apples, the book, the pumpkin.)

Measuring Time: The Calendar

We measure time in many units, including years, months, and days. You probably know what year it is now, and what month, too: can you tell me? Sometimes you need to check a calendar to tell what day of the month it is. Practice reading a calendar to identify what day it is, as well as what day of the week it is.

On this calendar, the day marked in color is October fifteenth. What day of the week is it? You know it's a Tuesday, because the number is in the column under Tuesday. One day on this calendar is circled. Can you say the date that's circled, and what day of the week it is? (The circled day is October twenty-fifth, and it's a Friday.)

OCTOBER

SUNDAY	MONDAY	TUESDAY	WEDNESDAY	THURSDAY	FRIDAY	SATURDAY
		1	2	3	4	5
6	7	8	9	10	11	12
13	14	15	16	17	18	19
20	21	22	23	24	25	26
27	28	29	30	31		

You may have noticed that to say what day of the month it is, we use the ordinal numbers, which are numbers that tell what number something is in an order. Instead of saying, "Today is October five," we usually say, "Today is October fifth" or "Today is the fifth of October."

The months of the year have anywhere from 28 to 31 days. Practice saying and writing the ordinal numbers up to thirty-first. Here they are, written as numbers and words.

1st	first	17th	seventeenth
2nd	second	18th	eighteenth
3rd	third	19th	nineteenth
4th	fourth	20th	twentieth
5th	fifth	21st	twenty-first
6th	sixth	22nd	twenty-second
7th	seventh	23rd	twenty-third
8th	eighth	24th	twenty-fourth
9th	ninth	25th	twenty-fifth
10th	tenth	26th	twenty-sixth
11th	eleventh	27th	twenty-seventh
12th	twelfth	28th	twenty-eighth
13th	thirteenth	29th	twenty-ninth
14th	fourteenth	30th	thirtieth
15th	fifteenth	31st	thirty-first
16th	sixteenth		

Can you say and write the names of the twelve months of the year in order, starting with January? Do you know how many days are in each month? (Do you remember the poem that begins, "Thirty days hath September"?) Can you write the names of the days of the week?

Measuring Time: Clock Time to 5 Minutes

How many minutes does it take for the minute hand to go once all the way around the clock? Another way of asking that question is, How many minutes are in an hour?

There are 60 minutes in 1 hour. One hour (or 60 minutes) is how long it takes for the hour hand on a clock to move from one number to the next number. (The hour hand is the short hand.)

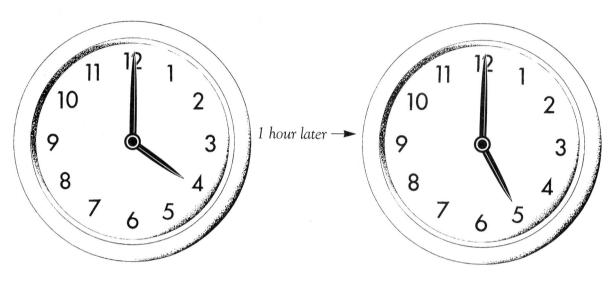

1 hour later →

On a clock, when the minute hand (the long hand) moves from one number to the next, 5 minutes have passed. For example, the time on this clock is 5 minutes after 4.

When the minute hand moves from the 1 to the 2, that means 5 more minutes have gone by. What time will it be then? It will be 10 minutes after 4.

You can count by fives for each new number on a clock face to find out how many minutes have passed since the hour. For example, look at this clock. The minute hand is on the 7. How many minutes have passed since the hour? Count by fives, starting with the 1 on the clock (touch each number on the clock face as you count aloud): 5, 10, 15, 20, 25, 30, 35.

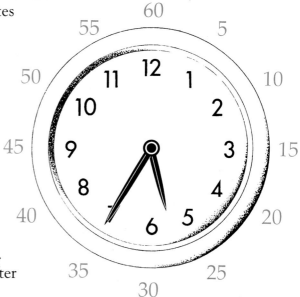

So, when the minute hand is on the 7, 35 minutes have passed since the hour. Now look at the hour hand (the short hand). It is between the 5 and the 6. That means the time is after 5 o'clock, but it is not yet 6 o'clock. It is 35 minutes after 5.

There's a short way to write 35 minutes after 5. It looks like this:

5:35

The two little dots are called a colon. The number to the left of the colon tells the hour. The number to the right of the colon tells the minutes. The quick way to say this time is just to say "five thirty-five" instead of "35 minutes after 5."

Measuring Time: Half and Quarter Hours

There are 30 minutes in half an hour. On this clock, the time is 30 minutes after 2, which is also called "half past two."

When it is more than 30 minutes past the hour, we sometimes count backward around the clock and say how many minutes it is until the next hour. For example, look at this clock:

What time does the clock show? If you count by fives, you'll see that it's 40 minutes past 5. You can also say that it's 20 minutes before 6. This makes sense because, as you know, there are 60 minutes in an hour, and 20 + 40 = 60. For 20 minutes before 6, people also say "it's 20 to 6" or "20 of 6" or "20 till 6"—they all mean the same thing.

Can you tell the time on this clock by saying how many minutes before the hour it is?

When you learned about fractions, you learned that another word for one fourth is one quarter. Fifteen minutes is one quarter of an hour. That is why when the time is 4:15, people often say that it's "quarter past 4" or "quarter after 4."

Do you remember what A.M. and P.M. mean? The A.M. hours are the hours before noon. The A.M. hours are between 12 midnight and 12 noon. Time after noon is called P.M. The P.M. hours are between 12 noon and 12 midnight.
So, in each day there are 12 A.M. hours and 12 P.M. hours. Which makes how many hours in a whole day? (12 + 12 = 24 hours in a day)
Do you go to bed closer to 9:00 A.M. or 9:00 P.M.?
Does the sun rise closer to 6:00 A.M. or 6:00 P.M.?

4:15, or quarter past 4

Here's a clock that shows 2:45, which is the same as 15 minutes before 3. You can also say 2:45 as "quarter to 3."

So, "quarter past" means 15 minutes after the hour, and "quarter to" means 15 minutes before the hour.

2:45, or quarter to 3

Measuring Time: How Much Time Has Passed?

Sometimes we need to know how much time has passed. Billy leaves his house at 2:00 to go play with Carlos. Billy's mother tells him to be back home in 3 hours. So, when does Billy have to be back home? At 5:00. From 2:00 to 5:00 is 3 hours.

At 10:00 in the morning Andrea's stomach starts to growl. She knows that she must wait until 1:00 before lunch will be served in the school cafeteria. How many hours will pass before she can eat lunch? To figure this out, you can't just subtract 10 from 1. Instead, first you think that from 10:00 to 12:00 is 2 hours, and from 12:00 to 1:00 is 1 hour. So, 1 + 2 = 3 hours before Andrea can eat lunch. Poor Andrea!

Christie gets out of school at 2:45. She goes to the library and then to soccer practice. When she gets home, it is 5:45 P.M. How many hours have passed since she got out of school? To help you figure that out, look at these two clocks:

You can see that the minutes are the same on both clocks. When the minutes are the same, the change in hours tells you how much time has gone by. Three hours passed between the time Christie left school and the time she got home.

When Christie left school.

When she got home.

Geometry

Plane Figures

You know the names of these flat shapes:

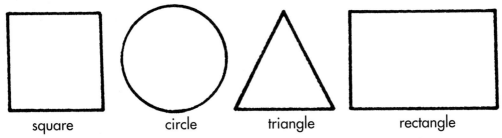

square   circle   triangle   rectangle

Flat shapes are also called *plane* shapes or plane figures. Can you answer these questions about some plane shapes?

- All rectangles and squares have the same number of sides—how many? What's the difference between a rectangle and a square? (*All rectangles and squares have four sides. All the sides of a square are the same length.*)
- How many sides does a triangle have? (*A triangle has three sides.*)
- What do we call figures that are the same size and shape? (*Figures that are the same size and shape are called "congruent."*)

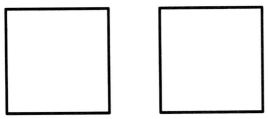

These two squares have the same shape and the same size. They are congruent.

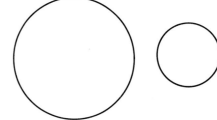

These two circles have the same shape but not the same size. The are *not* congruent.

The inside of a shape is called the interior. The outside of a shape is called the exterior.

interior

exterior

You can measure the length of the sides of a square or rectangle. When you add up the length of all four sides of a square or rectangle, you get the *perimeter*, which is the distance around a plane figure. Look at this rectangle.

Add the length of each side: $1 + 1 + 2 + 2 = 6$ inches. The perimeter is 6 inches.

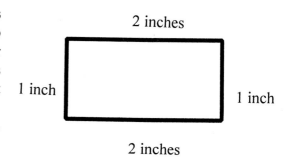

Solid Figures

Trace this pattern on a piece of paper. Cut it out, then fold at the dotted lines and tape the edges.

You have made a solid figure called a cube.

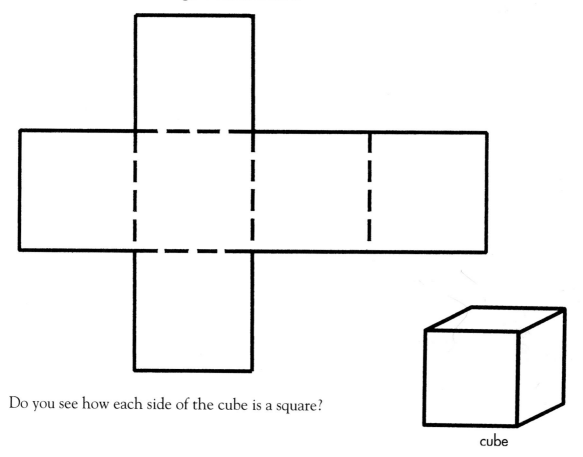

Do you see how each side of the cube is a square?

cube

Here are the names and shapes of other solid figures:

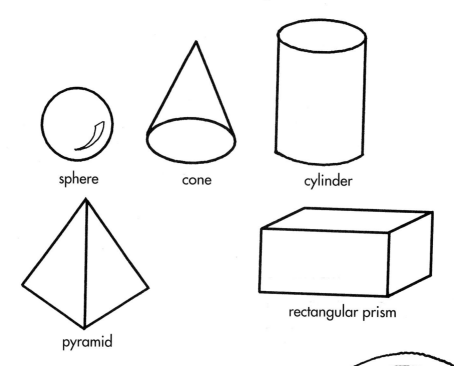

sphere   cone   cylinder

pyramid

rectangular prism

What plane shape is each side of the pyramid?
(*Each side of a pyramid is a triangle.*)

Imagine that you were to cut a sphere-shaped object, like an orange, down the middle. What plane shape would you see? (*You would see a circle.*)

Here are some things you might see at home or school. Each one has the shape of a solid figure. Can you name the solid figure for each object?

Points, Lines, and Segments

In math, a point is an exact spot. You show a point with a dot like this: •
You can give the point a name, to make sure that we can tell it from other points. In math, to name a point we use the letters of the alphabet. So, we'll call it point A, like this: •

A

If you put two points on a paper and then connect them, you will have a line. Here is a line going through point A and point B:

A   B

A line is straight and goes on forever. The arrows show that the line continues forever in both directions. The line goes through points A and B, so we call it line AB or line BA. A short way to write line AB is $\overleftrightarrow{AB}$.

A segment is a part of something. A line segment is a part of a line. A line goes on

C   D

forever, but a line segment has two endpoints.
We name a line segment by its endpoints. What do you think this line segment is called? It can be called either line segment CD or line segment DC. A short way to write line segment DC is $\overline{DC}$.

A line that goes across is called a *horizontal* line. A line that goes up and down is called a *vertical* line.

Have you ever seen the piece of equipment used by a gymnast called the parallel bars? If lines run side by side and never meet, they are called *parallel* lines. Here are some pairs of parallel lines:

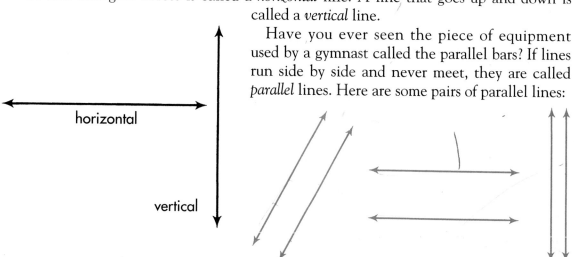

horizontal

vertical

Parallel lines always stay the same distance apart. They never cross each other.

When two lines meet and form an exact L (either a forward or backward L), then those lines are called *perpendicular*. Here are two pairs of perpendicular lines:

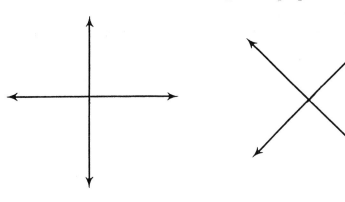

These two lines meet but they are not perpendicular:

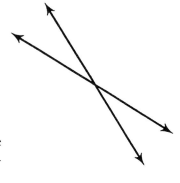

You can find perpendicular lines in any square or rectangle. Use your finger to trace the perpendicular lines in these figures:

Lines of Symmetry

Take a piece of blank paper and fold it exactly in half so the two parts match.

Now open the paper. Do you see the line down the middle, formed by the crease where you folded the paper? That is called a line of symmetry. A line of symmetry divides a shape into two parts that match.

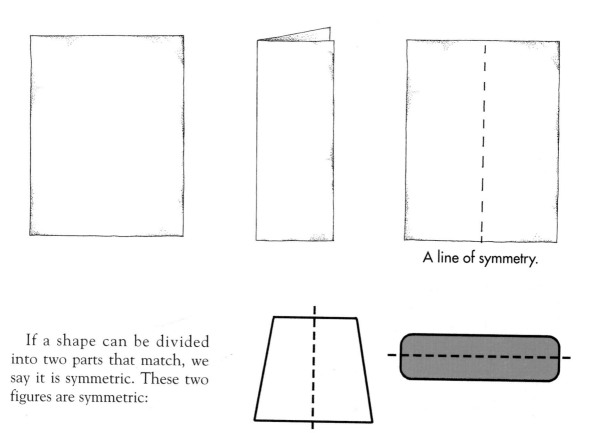

A line of symmetry.

If a shape can be divided into two parts that match, we say it is symmetric. These two figures are symmetric:

These two figures are not symmetric.

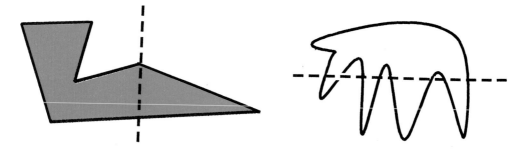

Multiplication

What Is Multiplication?

Multiplication is a quick way of adding the same number over and over again. Here's an example. There are five groups of two turtles. How many are there in all?

You could add 2 five times: $2 + 2 + 2 + 2 + 2 = 10$.

You could also say that 5 twos = 10. You can write that as a multiplication problem:

$$5 \times 2 = 10$$

We read that as "five times two equals ten." The sign $\times$ means "times," and it shows that you are multiplying. You can also write that problem as

$$\begin{array}{r} 5 \\ \times\ 2 \\ \hline 10 \end{array}$$

The numbers in a multiplication problem have special names. The numbers that are being multiplied are called *factors*. The answer is called the *product*. In $4 \times 3 = 12$, 4 and 3 are factors, and 12 is the product.

$$4 \times 3 = 12$$

factor**factor****product**

What are the factors and what is the product in this multiplication problem?

$$5 \times 2 = 10$$

Practicing Multiplication

When you are learning to multiply, it can help to practice with things you can count, such as pennies, dried beans, or buttons.

For example, to figure out 6×4, you can make 6 groups of 4, like this:

Count how many you have altogether. You should get 24. So, $6 \times 4 = 24$.

You can also practice by turning a multiplication problem into an addition problem. For example, what is 4×2? You can change that to $2 + 2 + 2 + 2$, which equals 8. So, $4 \times 2 = 8$.

What is 5×3? You can change that to $3 + 3 + 3 + 3 + 3$, which equals 15. So, $5 \times 3 = 15$.

Adding 3 over and over again is the same thing as counting by threes: 3, 6, 9, 12, 15. When you count by threes, you get the products of multiplying by 3, like this:

$$1 \times 3 = 3$$
$$2 \times 3 = 6$$
$$3 \times 3 = 9$$
$$4 \times 3 = 12$$
$$5 \times 3 = 15$$

Practice counting by twos, threes, fours, and fives. This will help you learn your multiplication tables for 2, 3, 4, and 5.

Two as a factor	*Three as a factor*	*Four as a factor*	*Five as a factor*
$2 \times 0 = 0$	$3 \times 0 = 0$	$4 \times 0 = 0$	$5 \times 0 = 0$
$2 \times 1 = 2$	$3 \times 1 = 3$	$4 \times 1 = 4$	$5 \times 1 = 5$
$2 \times 2 = 4$	$3 \times 2 = 6$	$4 \times 2 = 8$	$5 \times 2 = 10$
$2 \times 3 = 6$	$3 \times 3 = 9$	$4 \times 3 = 12$	$5 \times 3 = 15$
$2 \times 4 = 8$	$3 \times 4 = 12$	$4 \times 4 = 16$	$5 \times 4 = 20$
$2 \times 5 = 10$	$3 \times 5 = 15$	$4 \times 5 = 20$	$5 \times 5 = 25$
$2 \times 6 = 12$	$3 \times 6 = 18$	$4 \times 6 = 24$	$5 \times 6 = 30$
$2 \times 7 = 14$	$3 \times 7 = 21$	$4 \times 7 = 28$	$5 \times 7 = 35$
$2 \times 8 = 16$	$3 \times 8 = 24$	$4 \times 8 = 32$	$5 \times 8 = 40$
$2 \times 9 = 18$	$3 \times 9 = 27$	$4 \times 9 = 36$	$5 \times 9 = 45$

Practice the multiplication tables for 2, 3, 4, and 5 often. In third grade you will learn the rest of the multiplication tables.

Multiplying by 10

Here are five groups of beans, with ten beans in each group.

How many beans are there in all? To find the answer, you could add 10 five times. Or you could count by tens. Try it. Put your finger on each group of beans as you count by tens: 10, 20, 30, 40, 50. There are fifty beans in all.

So, five groups of ten equals 50. You can also say that as a multiplication problem:

$$5 \times 10 = 50$$

In the picture above, cover one group of beans with your hand. Now, how many beans are in four groups of ten? You could add 10 four times, or count by tens: 10, 20, 30, 40. Or, the quick way is to multiply.

$$10$$
$$\times\,4$$
$$\overline{40}$$

So, four groups of ten equals 40. $4 \times 10 = 40$. And, as you learned earlier, $5 \times 10 = 50$. Do you see a pattern here? Can you figure out how many are in two groups of ten? And how many are in three groups of ten?

You are learning to multiply by 10. See if you can give the products for these problems that ask you to multiply by 10. (Later, practice these problems until you know the answers quickly.)

10	10	10	10	10	10	10	10	10	10
$\times\,1$	$\times\,2$	$\times\,3$	$\times\,4$	$\times\,5$	$\times\,6$	$\times\,7$	$\times\,8$	$\times\,9$	$\times\,10$

Three Rules for Multiplication

Rule number 1. *No matter what order you multiply numbers in, the product is always the same.* For example, look at the groups of crayons in the picture. Three groups of 2 equal the same as two groups of 3.

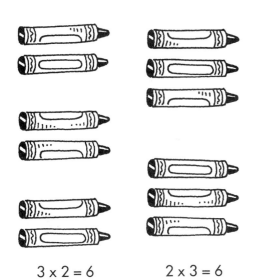

$3 \times 2 = 6$ $2 \times 3 = 6$

Rule number 2. *When you multiply a number by 1, the product is always that number.*

$$1 \times 7 = 7 \quad 5 \times 1 = 5 \quad 6 \times 1 = 6$$
$$75 \times 1 = 75$$

Rule number 3. *When you multiply a number by 0, the product is always 0.*

$$0 \times 9 = 0 \quad 6 \times 0 = 0 \quad 0 \times 3 = 0$$
$$89 \times 0 = 0$$

Word Problems and Missing Factors

You will need to use multiplication to solve some word problems, like this one. *Nine children went to the store. Each child bought 2 pencils. How many pencils did they buy in all?*

You could add 2 nine times, but it's easier to multiply. $9 \times 2 = 18$. They bought eighteen pencils in all.

Lisa has four boxes. In each box she has five bottles of orange juice. How many bottles of orange juice does she have in all?

Lisa has the same number of bottles of orange juice in each box. So, you could add 5 four times, but it's much quicker to multiply. You write: $4 \times 5 = 20$. Lisa has twenty bottles of orange juice.

Here's another word problem. The librarian asked Robert to help her move books to some new shelves across the room. Robert can carry six books at a time. He makes five trips across the room. How many books does he carry in all?

Robert carries the same number of books each time. So, you multiply: $6 \times 5 = 30$. Robert carried thirty books in all.

Here's a different kind of problem. It gives you the product, but asks you to figure out one of the factors.

Mrs. Johnson wants to buy cupcakes for her class. There are sixteen children in the class. The cupcakes come in packages of four. How many packages does she need to buy?

You can put that in the form of a multiplication problem: $4 \times \_ = 16$. Four times what equals 16? If you know your multiplication tables well, then you know the answer is 4 because $4 \times 4 = 16$. So, Mrs. Johnson needs to buy four packages of cupcakes.

You can practice your multiplication facts by solving problems with missing factors, like these:

$$3 \times \_\_ = 18 \quad 5 \times \_\_ = 35 \quad 4 \times \_\_ = 28 \quad 2 \times \_\_ = 14 \quad 3 \times \_\_ = 30$$

Another way to solve multiplication problems with missing factors is to use division—which you will learn about in third grade.

VI.

Science

INTRODUCTION

Children gain knowledge about the world around them in part from observation and experience. To understand magnetism, insect life cycles, or human body systems, children need opportunities to observe and experiment. In the words of *Benchmarks for Science Literacy* (a 1993 report from the American Association for the Advancement of Science): "From their very first day in school, students should be actively engaged in learning to view the world scientifically. That means encouraging them to ask questions about nature and to seek answers, collect things, count and measure things, make qualitative observations, organize collections and observations, discuss findings, etc."

While experience counts for much, book learning is also important, for it helps bring coherence and order to a child's scientific knowledge. Only when topics are presented systematically and clearly can children make steady and secure progress in their scientific learning. The child's development of scientific knowledge and understanding is in some ways a very disorderly and complex process, different for each child. But a systematic approach to the exploration of science, one that combines experience with book learning, can help provide essential building blocks for deeper understanding at a later time. It can also provide the kind of knowledge that one is not likely to gain from observation: consider, for example, how people long believed that the earth stood still while the sun orbited around it, a misconception that "direct experience" presented as fact.

In this section we introduce second graders to a variety of topics consistent with the early study of science in countries that have had outstanding results in teaching science at the elementary level. Below we suggest some resources to take you beyond these pages. In closing, let us repeat that while this book learning is essential, children also need imaginative help from teachers and parents in providing opportunities for observation and hands-on experience of the natural world.

Suggested Resources

The Cycle of Life and the Seasons
The Caterpillar and the Polliwog by Jack Kent (Simon & Schuster, 1982)
The Reason for a Flower by Ruth Heller (Grosset and Dunlap, 1983)

Weather: The Water Cycle and More
It's Raining Cats and Dogs: All Kinds of Weather and Why We Have It by Franklyn M. Branley (Houghton Mifflin, 1987)
Where Do Puddles Go? by Fay Robinson (Childrens Press, 1995)

Insects
Amazing Insects by Laurence Mound (Knopf, 1993)
Bugs by Nancy Winslow Parker and Joan Richards Wright (Greenwillow, 1987)

The Human Body

Cells and Tissues by Leslie Jean LeMaster (Childrens Press, 1985)

What Happens to a Hamburger by Paul Showers (HarperCollins, 1985)

Magnetism

All About Magnets by Stephen Krensky (Scholastic, 1993)

Experiments with Magnets by Helen J. Challand (Childrens Press, 1986)

Simple Machines

Simple Machines by Ann Horvatic (Dutton, 1989)

For more good resources, see *Books to Build On: A Grade-by-Grade Resource Guide for Parents and Teachers* edited by John Holdren and E. D. Hirsch, Jr. (Dell, 1996).

The Cycle of Life and the Seasons

The Life Cycle

Do you know the word "cycle," or a word with "cycle" in it? How about words like "bicycle" or "tricycle"?

Think about a bicycle's wheel: can you tell where it begins or ends? You can't really find a beginning or end, can you? It's a circle that goes around and around.

That's the way it is with cycles in nature, too. In nature, all living things are part of the cycle of life, a process that keeps going around and around. All living things are born, grow, and eventually die. To keep life going, living things need to "reproduce," which means to make young like themselves.

This kitten looks like its mother.

Imagine a farmyard with lots of chickens. A chicken lays an egg. Out of the egg hatches a little baby chick. The chick grows up to be a hen. The hen mates with a rooster, then soon the hen lays an egg. Out of the egg hatches a chick. That chick grows up and the cycle continues.

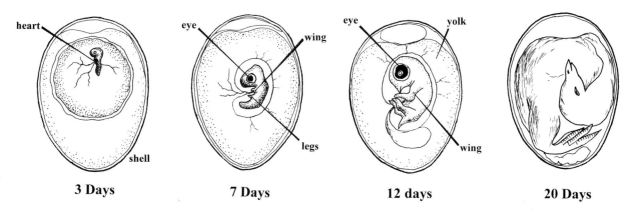

A baby chicken grows inside an egg.

Look at the picture of the life cycle of a chicken. Here's an old question that no one has ever answered: which came first, the chicken or the egg? You can't tell. It's a cycle, with no beginning or end, that keeps going around and around.

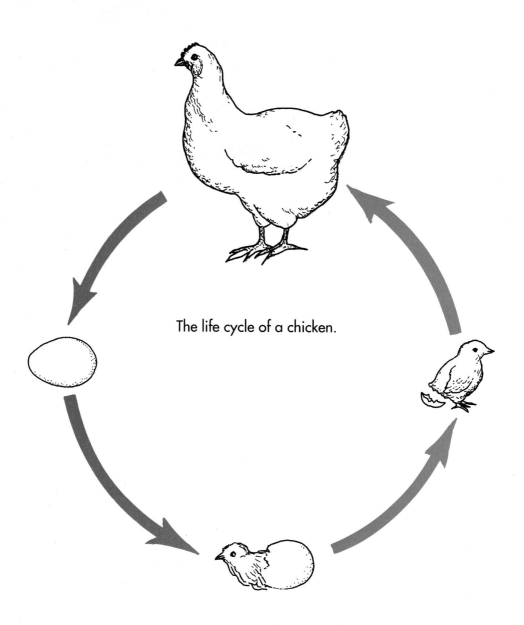

The life cycle of a chicken.

The cycle of life has four parts: birth, growth, reproduction, and death. Let's look at the life cycles of some different living things.

From Seed to Seed: A Plant's Life Cycle

When you plant a seed in the ground, what happens?* With the right combination of soil, water, and temperature, the seed sprouts and a plant starts growing. Roots grow down and leaves grow up. The plant grows bigger, until it is mature enough to make flowers.

Flowers help the plant reproduce. How? Often it happens like this. Part of the flower makes male *pollen*. Then the wind blows, or maybe a bee lands on the flower and carries the male pollen to the female part of the flower, called the *ovule*. ("Ovule" means "little egg.") When this happens, we say that the ovule has been "fertilized," and now it can grow until it becomes a seed.

Can you see the many seeds in these sunflowers?

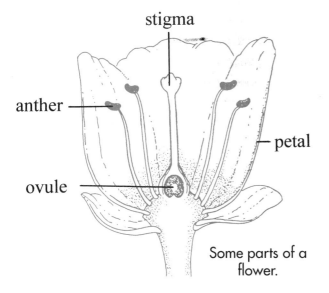

Some parts of a flower.

If you plant that seed in the ground, what happens? The seed sprouts, and a new plant grows. It makes new seeds, and the plant's life cycle goes on.

From Frog to Frog: An Amphibian's Life Cycle

Animals go through the same life cycle as plants: birth, growth, reproduction, death, and all over again. You can see this in the life cycle of a frog.

Imagine a little pond. At the edge of the pond you see something floating on the greenish-brown water. It's a bunch of frog eggs. They look like little balls of almost-clear jelly, all clumped together.

If you look closely, you see a dark speck inside each little ball. The speck grows bigger and begins to take shape. When it hatches has a broad face and a long flat tail. This baby frog is called a tadpole. It lives in water, and swims around in the pond.

* To review how plants grow, see the Science section of *What Your Kindergartner Needs to Know*.

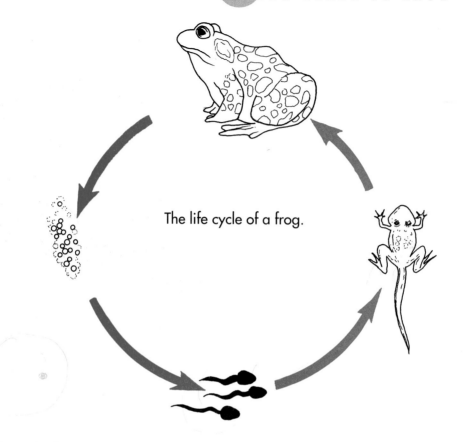

The life cycle of a frog.

As the tadpole grows, two little legs begin to sprout from the back of its body. Soon, two more little legs begin to grow in front. At the same time, the tadpole's tail shrinks and its body grows bigger. It looks more and more like a frog.

The frog grows and matures until it is ready to reproduce. A female frog lays about one thousand eggs at a time! But not many of these eggs will hatch into tadpoles because so many other creatures in the pond, such as fish, like to eat frog eggs. After the female frog lays the eggs, and a male frog fertilizes them, then the fertilized eggs float in the water like a glob of little jelly balls with dark specks inside. The specks grow bigger and begin to take shape, and the life cycle of the frog keeps on going.

The Cycle of the Seasons

You know that the life cycle has four parts: birth, growth, reproduction, and death. For many living things, the cycle of life follows the cycle of the four seasons of the year—spring, summer, fall, and winter. For example, a sunflower seed sprouts from the ground in the spring. The plant grows in the summer. The seeds of this adult plant ripen in the fall, and some of the ripe seeds fall on the ground. The plant dies in the winter. But next spring, some of the seeds that fell on the ground sprout, and new sunflower plants begin to grow. Just as the life cycle repeats itself, so the cycle of the four seasons happens over and over again every year.

Let's look at how the lives of some plants and animals in one typical region of North America change with the different seasons.

A young grizzly bear begins life in the spring.

Spring

After the cold winter, nature seems to wake up and come alive in spring. In spring, as the earth grows warmer, the seeds of plants begin to sprout. A sunflower seed sends roots down into the warm soil, while a little green seedling pushes up through the dirt to become a new sunflower plant. Maple and oak trees that were bare and leafless during winter begin to send sap up to their branches to help new leaves sprout and grow. (Sap is a sugary liquid that carries nutrients. You can eat the sap of some maple trees—it's what maple syrup comes from!)

In spring, many animals wake up from a long winter nap. Squirrels scurry about, and young bears born during the winter join their mothers to search for food. Birds that had flown south during the winter (why do you think they went south?) now return and build nests to lay their eggs in. Insect eggs that lay quietly all winter now begin to hatch. From some, out come tiny grasshoppers that feed on the just-budding leaves of the plants.

Summer

In summer, when the weather is warm and there's plenty of sunshine, many plants and animals grow larger. The little sunflower seedling grows into a mature, adult plant and begins to make seeds. Fruits like apples and vegetables like pumpkins grow bigger and begin to ripen. Trees add inches to their branches.

In summer, the baby animals that were born in the spring grow bigger and stronger. Tadpoles grow into adult frogs. Young insects like grasshoppers become adults. The

A snake snoozes in the summer sun.

These geese are migrating. They are flying south to warmer weather.

baby birds that hatched out of their eggs in the spring grow up and learn to find their own food.

Fall

In the fall (or autumn), many plants become mature, which means fully grown. On an apple tree, the apples grow heavy on the branches, and if you don't pick them, they fall to the ground. Acorns fall from the oak trees. From a vine on the ground, a pumpkin grows big and turns orange all over. In the fields, stalks of wheat turn brown and bend over, weighted down by plump heads of grain. On many trees, the leaves turn from green to red, gold, yellow, and brown, and then fall to the ground.

As the weather gets cooler in the fall, many animals prepare for the coming changes. Squirrels scurry about gathering nuts and storing them for the cold months ahead. Bears eat as much as they can to build up extra fat, and they look for a den to protect them from the cold. Some birds, like the Canada goose and the robin, take a big trip, or *migrate*. When they migrate, they fly south to warmer weather. In the oceans, big whales also migrate to warmer waters. Some gray whales swim for thousands of miles to find warmer water.

Do you remember the special names for trees that lose their leaves in the fall? They are called *deciduous* trees. Trees that keep most of their leaves all year round, such as pines and spruces, are called *evergreens*.

Winter

In winter, the world of living things grows more quiet and still. Many small green plants have shriveled up and died, leaving their seeds in the ground. The seeds will sit quietly through the winter, then be ready to sprout when warm weather arrives again. Trees that have dropped their leaves may look dead but they're alive. They're just *dormant*, not actively growing but, in a way, sleeping though the winter.

Some animals sleep through the winter, too, which is called *hibernation*. For example, chipmunks sleep in their holes through most of the winter, living off fat they built up during summer and fall. Frogs hibernate too: they burrow into the cold mud at the bottom of a pond and wait for spring to come again.

Birds that migrated south in the fall spend the winter resting and eating. They need to build up their strength for the long trip back north in the spring.

And then, as surely as the earth moves along in its orbit around the sun, spring comes again. The weather warms up, sap rises, seeds sprout, animals awake from hibernation, and the cycle of life on earth begins again.

This hibernating chipmunk is all curled up for a long winter nap.

The Water Cycle

You've been learning about different cycles in nature, such as the cycle of the seasons, and the life cycles of plants and animals. Well, here's another cycle. It's called the *water cycle*, and it has a lot to do with the weather.

Before we talk about the water cycle, let's remember what you learned about water (in the first-grade book of this series). Water can exist in the three states of matter: as a solid, liquid, or gas. The water you drink is a liquid. You know what we call water when it's a solid—ice. When you boil water on

Water can be a liquid, a solid, or a gas.

a stove, it turns to a gas called steam or water vapor. Water vapor is a gas in the air around you.

Now, as we go on to learn about the water cycle, keep in mind that ice, water, and water vapor are all water, just in different states of matter. Whether it's in the form of a solid, liquid, or gas, water is water.

Evaporation

Think of some places on the earth where you can find water. Did you think of rivers, lakes, and, most of all, oceans? There's lots of water on this planet: almost two-thirds of the surface of the earth is covered with water!

The water in rivers, lakes, and oceans is liquid. But every day, some of this liquid turns to gas. Every day, as the sun shines down, some of the water *evaporates*: it turns into water vapor and mixes with the air. Do you see the word "vapor" inside that big word "evaporation"?

Here's a question to think about: where do you think most of the water vapor in the air comes from? Hint: where is most of the water on the earth? That's right, the oceans.

You can do this evaporation experiment.

There's water vapor in the air around you. Try this. Put a few inches of water in a glass. With a piece of tape or a washable marker, mark where the water comes up to. Then put the glass where it won't be disturbed. Every day come back and check how much water is in the glass. What has happened to the water? It has evaporated. It has turned into water vapor and become part of the air around you. Maybe you're breathing it in right now!

At different times, there are different amounts of water vapor in the air. When we talk about the amount of water vapor in the air, we talk about *humidity*. A day with a lot of moisture in the air has "high humidity." A day with very little water in the air has "low humidity." On a hot, humid summer day, have you ever heard someone complain, "It's not the heat, it's the humidity"? That means that what makes us feel sticky and uncomfortable on such a day isn't so much the high temperature but instead the high amount of water vapor in the air.

Going Up, Going Down

When it rains hard, puddles of water form on the ground. When it stops raining and the sun starts to shine, what happens to the puddles? Slowly, they get smaller, and then

After it rains, what happens to the puddles?

they go away. Where does the water go? Well, some of it evaporates. It turns to water vapor and goes up into the air, just as steam rises from a pot of water that you heat on the stove. But in nature, it's the sun that heats the water and turns it to vapor.

The water that doesn't go up into the air soaks down into the earth. It becomes *groundwater,* which is the name for water found under the ground. When people drill a well, they are drilling down to find the groundwater. Once they dig deep enough to find this underground water, they can put long pipes into the hole and then pump the water up to use in their homes, schools, or other places.

Condensation and Precipitation

What happens to the water vapor in the air? Some of it mixes with the air near the ground and some of it rises high into the sky, way up where the air is cooler. In this coolness, the water vapor turns back into little droplets of liquid water. When water vapor turns from a gas back into a liquid, we say it *condenses.*

Here's a way to see condensation happen. Fill a glass with ice and water. Make sure the outside of the glass stays good and dry. Let it sit for a little while, maybe five or ten minutes. Pretty soon, the outside of the glass will develop a thin coating of water. Feel it—it's wet. Now, where did that water come from? Your glass didn't leak. No, the water came from the air. The ice water made the glass cold, which made the air around the glass cool, just like the air high up in the sky. Then the water vapor in the air condensed—it turned back into liquid—on the outside of your glass.

Up in the sky, when water vapor condenses into droplets of liquid, it forms clouds. Yes indeed, even though they may look like cotton candy, clouds are made of billions of water droplets (or sometimes, if the air is very cold, billions of tiny ice particles). In the clouds, the water droplets bump against each other. But instead of saying "excuse me" and getting

This picture shows three different types of clouds. At the top are wispy, feathery *cirrus* [SIHR-us] clouds. They form high in the sky and are made of tiny ice crystals. In the middle are big, puffy *cumulus* [KYOOM-yuh-lus] clouds. They are usually signs of fair weather. At the bottom are *stratus* clouds, which look like flat gray sheets. When a dark layer of stratus clouds covers the sky, it oftens means rain is on the way.

out of each other's way, they join and turn into bigger drops. When the drops get heavy enough, they fall from the clouds—it's raining! Or, if it's cold enough, instead of rain, snow will fall. Snow is water frozen into tiny crystals that fall as snowflakes.

On television, have you ever heard the weather reporter say something like, "Tonight will be cloudy with a chance of *precipitation*"? That means, there's a chance that water, in some form, is going to fall from the sky. Rain and snow are the most common forms of precipitation, but there are others, such as hail or sleet.

Putting It All Together: The Water Cycle

Every day water is evaporating up into the air and then condensing and falling back to the earth. We can draw all these movements of water as a great big circle, called the *water cycle*.

The water cycle.

Every day, water evaporates from the earth, especially from the oceans. As it rises into the sky, the water vapor condenses into little droplets that form clouds. When the droplets get big enough, then the water falls back to the earth as some form of precipitation. It fills rivers, lakes, and oceans, and some of it soaks into the earth's groundwater. From the rivers, lakes, and oceans, water evaporates and rises into the sky, and—well, you know what happens next. That's the never-ending water cycle: on and on it goes, over and over.

Insects

Insects Everywhere!

How many insects can you name?

Did you think of a fly that bothers you as it buzzes around the room? Or a bee that floats from flower to flower collecting nectar to make into honey? Or a mosquito that can bite you and make you itch? Or a butterfly with beautiful, colored wings?

Did you know that in the United States and Canada alone there are over one hundred thousand different kinds of insects? But that's just the beginning: around the world, there are almost a *million* kinds of insects. Most are smaller than one of your fingernails. Some are so small that you have to use a microscope to see them. But some, like the praying mantis, can grow to be four or five inches long.

Whenever a mosquito bites you, you know this fact: some insects are harmful to people. Flies carry germs that can spread diseases. Swarms of locusts can destroy a

It's lunchtime for this mosquito, who's about to bite a person's arm.

A ladybug munches on an aphid.

farmer's crops. Tiny aphids can damage or kill plants. Horseflies can give you a bad sting.

But other insects can be very helpful to people. Ladybugs help us because they eat aphids and other insects that harm crops. Bees make honey. Bees and butterflies help flowers grow when they carry pollen from one flower to another.

What Makes an Insect an Insect?

Hi there! I'm Edward Ant. You can call me Eddie. They've asked me to tell you what makes me an insect. That's simple. Like all insects, I'm smart, handsome, a great dancer, and . . . What's that? Oh, you want to know the *scientific* facts? Okay, no problem.

I'm an ant, right? And a cricket's a cricket, and a bee's a bee. But we're all insects. Along with butterflies, grasshoppers, and, yes, even cockroaches. We're all different in many ways, but here's what we have in common (though I just *hate* to think about having anything in common with a cockroach—ugh!).

Let's start with the legs. How many do you have? Only two? How in the world do you manage with only two legs? You poor creatures. Well, take a look at us insects. Every insect has *six* legs, three on each side of its body. Count them and see.

Now let's take a closer look at an insect body. A really strong, handsome body—like mine, for example. Every insect, whether it's in your backyard or in a jungle halfway around the world, has three main body sections: the *head*, the *thorax*, and the *abdomen*.

An insect's head is kind of like yours, just not so hairy. Like you, we have eyes and a mouth. And most of us have antennae, or feelers. We use these to feel, taste, and smell things.

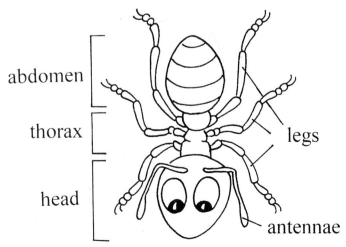

abdomen

thorax

head

legs

antennae

The middle part of an insect's body is called the *thorax*. That word comes from a Greek word for "chest." (How do I know Greek? Hey, I studied hard in school!) On the thorax most insects have wings. I don't, but some of my fellow ants do.

From the head and the thorax, we move back to the hind part of an insect, called the *abdomen*. You may already know that word because sometimes people use it to refer to their belly. For us insects, the abdomen is usually the largest of our body sections. I tell you, I've tried all sorts of diets, but nothing seems to help.

Where's your skeleton? It's inside your body, of course! Well, we insects have skeletons too, but our skeletons are *outside* our bodies. Every insect has an *exoskeleton*—which means an "outside skeleton." Your skeleton is made of bones, but not mine. My

This picture shows a fly's eyes, shown *many* times larger than their actual size. A fly has eyes made up of many parts. These eyes, called compound eyes, let the fly see all around. Maybe that's why it's so hard to swat a fly!

exoskeleton is made of a material called *chitin* [KITE-un]. It's the hardest part of my body. It's like a suit of armor on a knight.

Inside the chitin, insect bodies are soft. Maybe you've noticed that if you've ever swatted a fly. But yuck, I don't want to think about that.

Say—you're not one of those kids who goes around stepping on ants, are you? Good, I didn't think so.

So, let's review. If it's an insect, you can be sure it has

- **six legs**
- **three main body sections (head, thorax, and abdomen)**
- **and a hard exoskeleton.**

Hey, it's been nice talking with you. Maybe I'll see you at your next picnic!

Are They Insects?

Now you know some characteristics that every insect shares: six legs, three body sections, and an exoskeleton. You might think certain creatures are insects, but that's not how scientists classify them. Here are some creatures that might look like insects but they're not. Can you see why? (Hint: Look closely at their bodies. Count their legs.)

At first you might think that caterpillars are not insects because they appear to have more than six legs. But only the first three pairs of legs are true legs. Further back on their bodies, caterpillars have stubby little bumps called "prolegs," which help them hold up and move their hind parts. So, caterpillars really are insects.

Ticks, spiders, and centipedes are *not* insects!

abdomen thorax head true legs prolegs

This caterpillar *is* an insect.

Insect Life Cycles

Nature does some amazing things. For example, who would think that from that a little crawling caterpillar would come a beautiful butterfly?

That's a very big change! And there's a very big word to describe this kind of change. The word is *metamorphosis* [MET-uh-MORE-foh-sis]. It comes from a Greek word for "changing shape."

Let's take a closer look at the big change from a caterpillar to a butterfly.

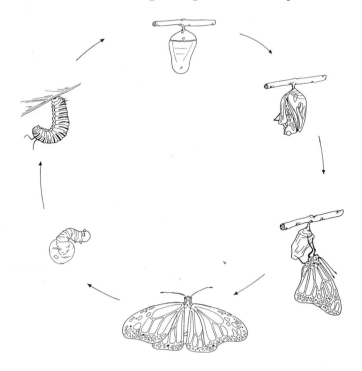

A female butterfly lays eggs. They look like tiny beads attached to the bark of a tree or the underside of a leaf. When the eggs hatch, out comes—no, not a butterfly, not yet—but a caterpillar. The caterpillar is the *larva* [LAHR-vuh], or the baby insect.

The caterpillar crawls up and down the stalks of plants, finding fresh green leaves to chew on. The caterpillar eats and eats—it's like a little eating machine!—and it grows longer and fatter. When the caterpillar matures, it attaches itself to a leaf or twig. It makes a tough, shiny covering, called a cocoon, and wraps itself completely inside the cocoon. Now the larva has become a *pupa* [PYOO-puh].

From the outside, the pupa looks asleep. It looks as if nothing is happening. But inside, the insect is still growing, and big changes are happening. When the pupa finally opens, the adult insect comes out, but it doesn't look like a caterpillar anymore! Now you can tell it's a butterfly. When it first comes out, the butterfly is weak, damp, and crumpled. Then slowly it spreads its wings. When the wings have dried, the butterfly is ready to fly away and flutter from flower to flower to look for food.

So, in growing up, the butterfly has gone through these stages in its life:

$$\text{egg} \rightarrow \text{larva} \rightarrow \text{pupa} \rightarrow \text{adult}$$

A Simpler Kind of Metamorphosis

Different insects go through different kinds of metamorphosis. For some insects, like butterflies and ants, when the baby is born it doesn't look anything like the adult. As it grows it goes through a complete change of shape. But for other insects, the baby can look like a little adult. These insects start small and get bigger, but they don't completely change shape. For example, when baby grasshoppers hatch from eggs, you can tell they're grasshoppers. They just look smaller than the adults. Each baby grasshopper has a rounded head, straight wings, and long back legs. It eats whatever leaves and grass it can find, until it's about to burst.

And in a way, that's what it does. The grasshopper eats and grows until it gets so big that its old exoskeleton splits open and drops off, just like an old coat that doesn't fit anymore. Out climbs a bigger grasshopper. When this happens, we say the grasshopper has *molted*, which means that it has shed an old exoskeleton and is developing a new one. Grasshoppers molt about five times as they grow from newborn babies to adults.

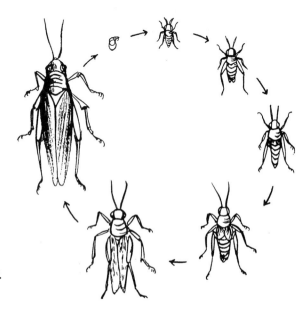

The life cycle of a grasshopper.

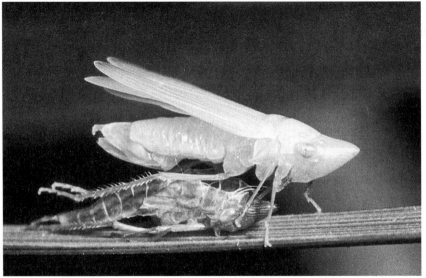

This picture does not show two insects, but just one leafhopper molting!

Social Insects

Have you ever seen an ant hill? Then you know that ants don't live alone: they live and work together with other ants. Ants live in groups and they depend on each other to survive. We call ants "social insects." Other social insects include honeybees, termites, and wasps.

The word "social" comes from the word "society." A society is a group of beings that live together and generally cooperate with each other to get things done. What other animals do you know that live in a society? Human beings do! We cooperate with each other in all sorts of ways—growing food, building houses, making clothes, teaching each other. We are able to cooperate because we use language to communicate. Do ants speak? No, but they can communicate, as you'll see.

An Ant Colony

A group of ants living and working together is called an ant colony. If you find a few ants in your house or at school, then there must be an ant colony somewhere close by. If you find ants at home or at school, put a drop of syrup near the ants. You may have to wait an hour, or even a day, but after a while, you will see a parade of ants walking to the drop, like soldiers marching in single file. And another line of ants will be walking away from the drop, back to the colony, each one carrying a tiny droplet of syrup.

How do the ants tell each other where the syrup is? They don't use language like we do, but their bodies communicate with chemicals. When the first ant found the syrup, it got very excited. That excitement made its body lay down a tiny chemical trail to the food. Other ants sensed that chemical signal, and they followed the trail to the syrup.

Ants cooperate in many other ways, too. They build complicated nests. They share the work of taking care of the babies and young ants. When a special ant, called the queen, lays the eggs, other ants called workers dig tunnels and help keep the eggs clean and warm. When the eggs hatch, the worker ants gather food and help feed the larvae [LAHR-vee; it means "more than one larva"]. Later, they help the growing ants break out of their cocoons. In some colonies, other ants, called soldiers, protect the colony against insect enemies.

In a Beehive

Have you ever tasted sweet, golden honey? Do you know where honey comes from? From the nests of honeybees!

Where do the honeybees get the honey? They make it from the sweet liquid, called nectar, that they gather from hundreds of flowers. In their home, called a beehive, the bees feed the sweet honey to the young larvae.

Like ants, honeybees can communicate with each other by giving off a chemical scent. But honeybees can communicate in another way, too. When a honeybee finds a field of flowers with lots of nectar, she can tell the other bees in her hive where to find those flowers. How? By doing a "waggle dance"!

She turns from side to side, flaps her wing, and buzzes. Her dancing imitates how she flew to the flowers. The other

People who work as beekeepers make special beehives so they can carefully remove some honey to put in jars for people to eat. Beekeepers always leave some honey behind, because they know the bees need the honey to feed the larvae so they will grow into adult honeybees. Do you see the beekeeper's protective clothing?

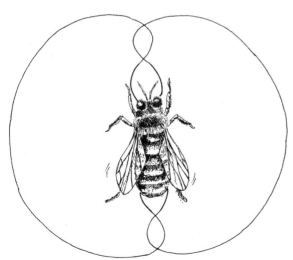

The lines show the pattern of a bee's "waggle dance."

Honeybees are social insects. There are many other kinds of bees, and most of them live alone: they are not social insects.

When bees gather nectar from flowers, they also gather a substance called pollen. You can see a clump of pollen on this bee's hind leg. One of the most important things that bees do is to take pollen from one flower and put it on another so that flower can make seeds.

bees understand her message and they fly to the flowers.

In a honeybee hive, there are three different kinds of bees. Each hive has one *queen bee*. She is female, and she grows bigger than the rest. Her job is to lay all the eggs in the beehive. She is the mother of every bee in the hive. In the spring and summer, she can lay as many as hundreds or even thousands of eggs in a single day!

In a hive, the queen is surrounded by many bees who are constantly feeding her and cleaning her. These are the *worker bees*. Most of the bees in a hive are worker bees. They are female, but they do not lay eggs (only the queen does that). The workers do a lot more than take care of the queen. From their own bodies they make a special wax that they use to build

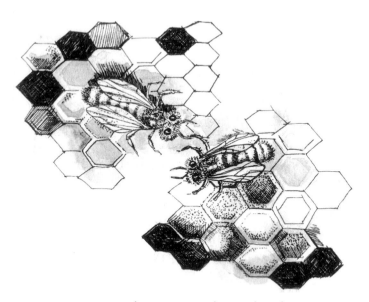

Bees produce a special wax that they use to build honeycombs.

the honeycombs. These amazing structures have thousands of little six-sided compartments in which the honey is stored. The honey is food for each baby bee growing in

WORKER | QUEEN | DRONE

one of the little compartments! The workers help take care of the larvae. They fly out from the hive and find flowers with sweet nectar, so they can make honey.

Besides the one queen bee and the many worker bees, a honeybee hive has many *drone bees*. The drones are male. Compared to the female worker bees, drones seem pretty lazy. They do not gather nectar or make honey or help build the hive. Their only job is to mate with the queen to help her make more bees. They are the fathers of every bee in the hive.

How do honeybees start a new colony? First they make a new queen. They pick a baby bee and feed it only special food called "royal jelly," made from pollen, honey, and bee saliva. When the baby queen grows up, she flies away and many bees follow her. When they find a good place with lots of flowers, they start building a new hive.

"Royal jelly! Yummy!"

Have you ever been stung by a bee? Ouch! Honeybees only sting to defend themselves if they think you are trying to hurt them or steal their honey. In fact, if a honeybee stings you, it dies soon afterward, because it leaves its stinger and part of its body behind.

The Human Body

Cells: The Building Blocks of Living Things

If you have a magnifying glass, look at the back of your hand through it. The hairs look thicker and your skin looks like it has little hills and valleys. Now imagine that you have a super-powerful magnifying glass, and you use it to look at just one hair on your body. It makes the hair look almost like a telephone pole sticking up out of the ground. And when you look even closer, you see that the hair is made up of many, many little pieces. Each one of those little pieces is called a *cell.*

All living things are made up of cells. Cells are the building blocks of all plants and animals. Every living thing—a flower petal, a maple leaf, a blade of grass, a worm, your body—is made up of cells.

Through your imaginary super-powerful magnifying glass, you would be able to see that all living things are made up of cells. Well, scientists actually have super-powerful magnifying glasses called *microscopes.* Microscopes help us see things that are much too small to see just with our eyes. Thanks to microscopes, we understand a lot about cells.

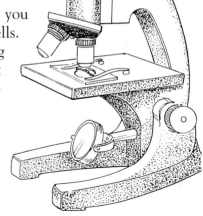

To find out about one of the first scientists to learn a lot with microscopes, turn to page 334 and read about Anton van Leeuwenhoek.

With a very powerful microscope, you can see what some cells look like:

A microscope.

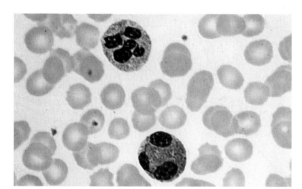

These are blood cells from a person.

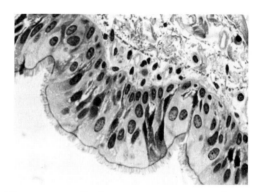

These are cells from a person's windpipe.

Cells and Tissues, Organs and Systems

Cells develop into different shapes, depending on what part of a living thing they make up and what job they perform. In your body, there are many different kinds of cells. Your brain cells are very different from the cells that make up your lungs, and both are different from your skin cells or bone cells.

A lot of cells of the same kind join together to form a tissue. No, this isn't the kind of tissue you blow your nose in! This kind of tissue is a group of the same kinds of cells that work together. These different tissues work together to form organs. Some of the most important organs in your body are your brain, your heart, and your lungs.

Some tissues and organs in your body work together like the members of a team. The parts that work together are called a *system*. For example, your mouth, teeth, tongue, stomach, and intestines all work together to help you chew and digest your food. They're all important players on the team called the digestive system.

In the first-grade book in this series, you learned about some of the most important body systems: the skeletal system, the muscular system, the circulatory system, the nervous system, and the digestive system. Now we're going to learn more about the digestive system.

What Happens to the Food You Eat?

Have you heard the saying "An apple a day keeps the doctor away"? Eating apples and other healthy foods helps you grow stronger. But how?

In order for your body to get what it needs from an apple, it needs to *digest* it. Digesting means breaking food down into little pieces—so little you can't see them with just your eyes—so that your body can take those pieces and use them for energy and for building its own cells, tissues, and organs.

Pretend you're holding a big, crisp, juicy red apple. The digestive process begins even before you take a bite. Your eyes, your nose, and your fingertips send signals to your brain, and your brain sends a message to your mouth and stomach: *"Get ready, food is coming!"*

When you take a bite of the apple, your tongue tastes the sweetness and tells your brain, "Mmm, here's something good and sweet." Then your brain sends an order to the parts of your mouth called the salivary [SAL-ih-vary] glands: "Get to work!" And they hop to it by making a watery liquid called saliva [suh-LIE-vuh]. You may just call it "spit," but saliva is an important team player in your digestive process. It helps make the food you eat wet and soft, and it has chemicals that help you digest your food.

When you bite the apple, the piece in your mouth is still too big to swallow. So you chew it up. Your teeth are important players on the digestive team as well. They cut, munch, and crunch the food into smaller and smaller pieces. Your front eight teeth, four on the top and four on the bottom, are called your incisors. To incise means to cut. Growing right next to your incisors are four pointy teeth called your canines [KAY-nines]. They tear the food into pieces. By the way, "canine" is an old Latin word for "dog"! Why do you think your sharp, pointy teeth are called "canines"?

After your incisors and canines bite and tear the apple, your tongue pushes the pieces of food to the teeth in the back of your mouth. Your bicuspids have two bumps on them that help crush the apple pieces. Your molars have flat tops for grinding the food into pieces small enough to swallow.

> On the surface of your tongue there are many tiny *taste buds*. Different buds taste different flavors: sweet, salty, sour, and bitter. The taste buds send messages to your brain, like "Yum, this apple is sweet and delicious," or, "This pretzel is salty," or, "What a sour lemon!" or "Ugh, this is too bitter—spit it out!"

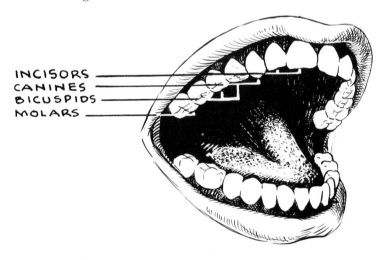

INCISORS
CANINES
BICUSPIDS
MOLARS

Wash your hands with soap and water, then look in a mirror and try to point to and identify your different teeth.

Now that you've chewed enough, the apple pieces are small enough to swallow. Gulp!—down they go. Go where? Down your throat, though a tube called the esophagus [e-SOF-ah-gus], and into your stomach.

Do you know where your stomach is? Put your right hand to the left of the center of your body. Feel your ribs. Your stomach is inside there. Your stomach is a big muscle designed to stir up the food you eat. As it stirs, it adds liquids and chemicals to help digest the food. In your stomach, the bite of apple you took no longer looks anything like an apple. All the grinding, stirring, and chemicals make it look like soup.

Now the food is almost small enough for your body to use. From your stomach the soupy stuff moves to the intestines. Your intestines are a long, coiled-up tube that winds around inside your belly. If you stretched them out, they would measure much

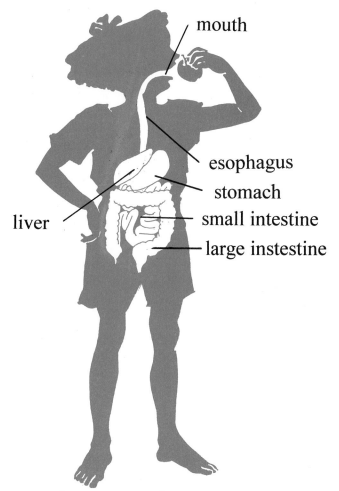

mouth

esophagus

stomach

small intestine

large instestine

liver

These are some of the major organs in
your digestive system.

Maybe someone you know has had an operation
to take out the *appendix.* The appendix is a little
tube that grows where the small intestine joins the
large intestine. Even though it's there, it doesn't really have a job. Usually it doesn't bother anyone,
but sometimes the appendix can get swollen and
infected. When that happens, a person has to have
an operation to have the appendix removed. But
it's okay to take it out because you don't really
need it.

longer than you are tall. An
adult's intestines are almost
twenty-seven feet long! Most of
the intestine is like a narrow
rope. This is called the small intestine. The last part of the tube
is bigger. This is called the large
intestine.

In your small intestine, the
soupy food is mixed with more
liquids and chemicals that break
down the food into bits too small
to see. The good particles, called
the nutrients [NOO-tree-ents],
are then absorbed into your
blood. Your blood carries the nutrients to all the cells of your
body.

As your blood passes through
your body, it goes through another organ in the digestive system, the liver. Take your left
hand and feel the lowest rib on
the right side of your body. Your
liver is just under there, and it's
about as big as your shoe. One
job of the liver is to clean your
blood. It also sends liquids and
chemicals to the small intestine
to help digest what you eat.

But some of the food you eat is
left over in your small intestine
and cannot be digested. What
happens to it? It gets passed on
to the large intestine. Here, water is absorbed into your blood.
The solid waste that is left behind goes out of your body
through the little hole called the
anus when you use the toilet.

When you go to the bathroom, you don't just get rid of solid waste. You also get rid of liquid your body can't use. How does this happen? It starts with your blood. Your blood carries good, healthy nutrients all through your body. But your blood also carries waste away from the cells of your body. As your blood flows, it goes through two organs called the kidneys. The kidneys help clean your blood by separating the blood from the watery liquid waste you can't use, called urine. The urine then goes out of your kidneys and into a little bag in your body called the bladder. When you go to the bathroom, you push the urine out of the bladder through a little tube called the urethra [yoo-REE-thra].

You're Mostly Made of Water!

Your body needs a lot of liquid. It's good to drink about eight glasses of water a day. Your blood is mostly water. Water plays an important part in digestion, helping to break food down, make it soupy, and pass it through the body. In fact, about three-fourths of your body is water!

That may seem hard to believe since your body feels solid. But think about a wet sponge. It feels solid even when it's holding a lot of water. Your body holds water inside every one of its millions and millions of cells.

A Healthy Diet: The Food Pyramid

Your digestive system breaks down food so that your body can use the nutrients to keep you strong and healthy. But for your digestive system to do a good job, you need to give it good food to work with.

To be sure you're eating enough of the food that's good for you, take a look at this picture, called the food pyramid.

A pyramid is big at the bottom and small at the top. The food pyramid is divided into four sections with different kinds of foods in each section: the bigger the section, the more of that kind of food you should be eating.

Most of all you need to eat grains, like bread, cereal, rice, and pasta. You also need to eat plenty of fruits and vegetables. And you need to eat foods

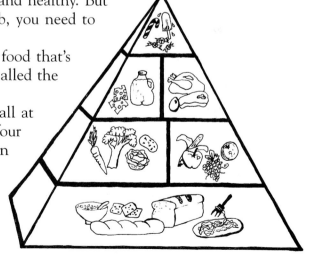

The food pyramid.

that give you proteins. These foods include dairy products, like milk, cheese, and yogurt. You also get protein from meat, fish, eggs, and nuts.

See how much smaller the section at the top of the pyramid is compared with all the other sections? This smallest section includes fats, oils, and sweets, which means we need very little of these. In fact, if you are eating the foods shown in the bigger sections of the food pyramid, you are already getting some fats and sugars. For example, if you eat a hamburger, you're getting some protein, but you're also eating a lot of fat, too. If you eat fried foods like french fries and fried chicken, you are eating a lot of fat along with the potatoes or the chicken. That's why the food pyramid says you should eat very few extra fats and sweets. Fats and oils include things like mayonnaise, salad dressing, and butter. Your body needs some fats or oils, but just a little bit. Too much fat can do bad things, such as damage your heart.

Does anybody *not* like sweets? They taste so good it's hard to resist them. But be careful not to eat too many sweets, like soda pop, candy, cookies, cakes, and ice cream. These foods are all made with sugar. Your body does need sugar for energy. But many of the good foods in the food pyramid, such as fruit and bread, already give your body good natural sugar. To keep your body strong and healthy, it's best not to eat many sweets or drink a lot of soda pop.

Vitamins and Minerals

You can't see them, but *vitamins and minerals* are some of the important nutrients that come to you in good foods, especially in vegetables and fruits. To be as healthy as you can be, your body needs the right combination of vitamins and minerals every day. Without enough vitamins and minerals, you could get very sick.

Vitamins are named with letters of the alphabet, and there are at least thirteen that our bodies need. Here are some of them.

- Vitamin A helps the skin, tissues, and eyes grow strong. You can get plenty of vitamin A by eating carrots, sweet potatoes, and other orange vegetables, and by drinking milk.
- There are eight different vitamins called vitamin B, each with its own role in keeping your body healthy. Most come in meat, and many come in vegetables as well.
- Vitamin C helps cells grow strong, and it helps your body fight against disease. You get plenty of vitamin C by eating oranges, tomatoes, and broccoli.
- Vitamin D is important because it helps your teeth and bones grow strong. Your skin absorbs some vitamin D from sunshine, and you also get vitamin D from tuna, egg yolks, and milk.

Besides vitamins, your body also needs minerals. Does that mean you have to eat rocks? No, but the minerals your body needs are actually tiny amounts of the same

Vegetables and fruit provide many important
vitamins and minerals.

minerals that can be found in the earth. Your body only needs small amounts of these minerals, which you can get from the right foods.

Your body needs iron to build blood cells. When people don't have enough iron in their blood, they feel tired and sick. Foods with plenty of iron include meat, green leafy vegetables, whole grain cereals, raisins, and dried beans.

Calcium is a mineral that helps make your bones and teeth strong, and helps your muscles work hard. When people don't have enough calcium, their bones sometimes break easily. Foods with lots of calcium include milk, yogurt, dried beans, and green leafy vegetables like lettuce.

Magnetism

That Special Magnetic Attraction

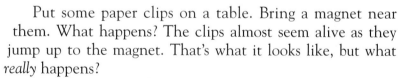

Put some paper clips on a table. Bring a magnet near them. What happens? The clips almost seem alive as they jump up to the magnet. That's what it looks like, but what *really* happens?

What happens is that the magnet exerts a *force of attraction* on the paper clips. You can't see the force, but it's there, and it's strong enough to pull the clips up off the table once the magnet moves close enough to them.

Will the magnet attract everything? For example, will it pull a shoelace or tissue or plastic comb toward it?

No. The shoelace, tissue, and comb are not made of iron. But the paper clip is made of a metal that has iron in it. Magnets attract things made of iron. But magnets won't attract copper or aluminum. Bring a magnet close to a copper penny or an aluminum soda can and you'll see.

Many magnets that we use today have been manufactured out of metals containing iron. People make some magnets, but others occur in nature. They can be found in

Magnets come in many shapes and sizes. Here you can see a horseshoe magnet, a round magnet, and a bar magnet.

stones in the earth called *lodestones*. Lodestones are special pieces of iron ore that act just like the magnets we make. Lodestones are the first magnets that were ever found.

Magnetism is a force all around us. You can't see it, but you can see the way it acts in the world. People use magnetic force every day, whether it's to attach a note to the refrigerator or lift an old wrecked car at a junkyard. Magnets work around the home in doorbells, television sets, and electric can openers.

Have you ever used a computer? Maybe you've put a floppy disk into a computer. The disk uses magnetic material to store information. That's why you should *never put a magnet near a floppy disk*, because it could mess up the information stored on the disk.

Magnetic Poles

Here's an experiment you can do with two bar magnets.

Put the two bar magnets on a table. Bring an end of one of the magnets toward an end of the other. What happens? Do they pull together or push apart?

Now turn *just one* of the magnets around, and bring the ends together. What happens now? If your magnets pulled together the first time, then this time they will push apart. If your magnets pushed apart the first time, then this time they will pull together.

Why? To find out, let's look at a picture of a bar magnet. Even though you can't see the forces coming from that magnet, we will use little lines to show them in this picture. The lines show what's called the *magnetic field*. The magnetic field is present in the space around the magnet in which the magnetic force can be felt. If you put a paper clip inside the magnetic field, the magnet will attract the clip.

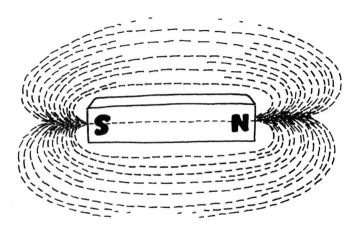

The dotted lines show the magnetic field.

In the picture, can you see where the magnetic force is strongest? It's strongest at the two ends of the magnet. We call those two ends where the magnetic force is strongest the *magnetic poles*.

Even though the poles of a magnet may look the same, they are different. We need names for these two poles so we can tell them apart. We call one pole north and the other south.

Why are the poles called north and south? For the answer, try this. Take a bar magnet and tie a string around its middle so it balances when you hold it by the string. Tie the other end of the string so that the magnet can hang and move freely. Watch what it does when you let it go.

The bar magnet will turn around until it settles in one direction. Notice something in the room that one pole (one end of the magnet) is pointing to, for example, a nearby lamp or picture. Put a little sticker on the end pointing to the lamp or whatever you've chosen. Then gently twirl the magnet. When it stops again, what happens? The pole with the sticker is pointing in exactly the same direction, isn't it?

If you kept doing this experiment with every bar magnet you could find, every one of them would point to the same direction. That's because your magnets are finding the forces of magnetic attraction that exist in

You can try this experiment with a bar magnet.

nature. They are being pulled by great fields of magnetic attraction that surround the earth.

That's right, the earth is like a great big magnet! The magnetic fields surrounding the earth are strongest very near the North Pole and the South Pole. So, one end of your magnet is pointing north and the other is pointing south. And that's why the poles of your magnet are called north and south.

Ask an adult to help you figure out if the sticker end of your magnet is pointing north or south. Once you know that, you can label one end of your magnet *north* and the other end *south*.

Now that you know that magnets have different poles, let's go back and think about what happened when you brought the ends of two bar magnets together. Once they pulled toward each other, but once they pushed apart. They were following a rule of magnetic force that says

unlike poles attract but like poles repel.

"Repel" means "push away." The north pole of a magnet pulls or attracts the south pole of another magnet. But if you bring two north poles together, or two south poles together, they repel each other—they push apart. Try it!

Using a Compass

You know that we use magnets in many ways. One of the most useful things a magnet can do is tell us what direction we're going—north, south, east, or west. When a magnet is used in this way, we call it a compass.

Compasses help sailors find their way at sea. They help hikers find their way through forests. They can help you find your way.

If you did the experiment of tying a bar magnet to a string, you made a kind of compass. Most compasses have a small magnet in the shape of an arrow, called a needle. This magnetized needle can spin around. When it stops spinning, the needle always points north.

Take a compass and turn it around. You'll see that the needle always points the same way—north. But what if you want to go *east?* How would you use the compass to do that?

First, face in the direction of the needle—north. So, what direction is behind you? That's right, south. Which way is east? Is it to your right or your left? East is to your right, and west is to your left.

That's the way maps work, remember? The top is north, the bottom is south, the right is east, the left is west. ("Left—west." They sound alike, remember?)

So, if you need to go east, what do you do? Your compass needle points north. East is to the right of where the needle points. So, you can go east by turning yourself until the needle is pointing to your left. Then you march straight ahead, always keeping the needle pointed to your left.

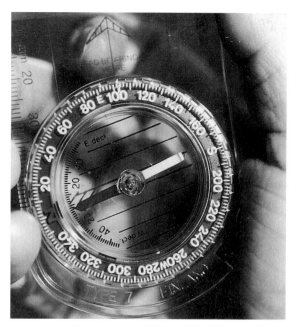

A compass. The needle is pointing north, and the arrow is pointing east.

Simple Machines

Tools and Machines

The world we live in today depends on many tools. With tools, we build and dig, we lift and cut, we grip and carry. What tools can you name? Did you think of a hammer, screwdriver, or pliers? What's a hammer for? To pound in a nail. What's a screwdriver for? To twist a screw. What are pliers for? To grip and pull. With the right tool, you can do a lot more than you can with just your hands alone.

We use tools to help us do things; we also use machines. When you hear the word "machine," you may think of something like a sewing machine, or a washing machine, or a bulldozer. Those are one kind of machine, but there's another. We call this other kind *simple machines*. They make a lot of work easier for us to do. Let's learn about some of the simple machines that help people every day.

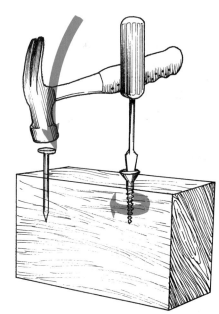

A hammer and a screwdriver.

Levers

The simple machine called a *lever* is so simple you might not even think it's a machine. But like other machines, levers help us do work. You use a lever when you pry open the lid of a can of paint. You use a lever when you use the claw of a hammer to pull a nail out of a board.

Levers can help you lift things. Try this. Put a stack of three or four books on a table. Line up the books with the edge of the table. Now slide one end of a ruler under the bottom of the books. Push down on the other end of the ruler. What happens? The ruler acts as a lever and helps you lift the books.

A screwdriver acts as a lever when you use it to pry open a paint can.

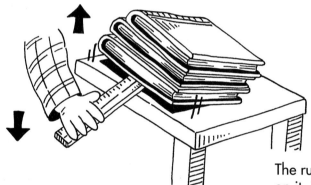

The ruler acts as a lever. When you push down on it, it lifts up the books.

Take a look at the picture here. This girl was taking a walk and she found a big rock. She wanted to see what was under it, but it was much too big and heavy for her to lift. So she found a strong stick and a little rock nearby. She pushed one end of the stick under the big rock. Then she supported the stick on the little rock. Smart! She's using the stick as a lever. When she pushes down, then the big rock moves up. With a lever, she can lift something that she could not lift just with her hands.

The big stick acts as a lever, and helps the girl lift the rock.

Wheels

There's something missing in this picture.

You'd have a very hard time pulling your friends in this wagon, because the *wheels* are missing!

The wheel is a simple machine that makes work easier. Wheels turn, and they help us move things. If you have a wagon or a toy car or truck, you can see that wheels turn around on something. A wheel turns around on an *axle*, which is like a stick stuck through the middle of a wheel. An axle can join two wheels together. If you have a wagon or toy car, look at how the axle joins the wheels.

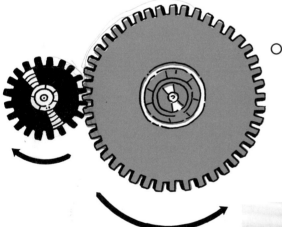

One gear turns another.

A *gear* is a wheel with teeth. The teeth on gears fit together so that one gear can turn another. You can find gears in many machines, such as clocks and bicycles.

The gears on a bicycle are connected by a chain. When you pedal, you turn the big gear by moving your feet, which makes the chain move, which makes the gears behind go around, which makes the bicycle start moving.

Friction

Imagine that you're riding a bike. You're pedaling hard and the wheels are turning fast. You see a STOP sign ahead, so you put on the brakes. The brakes press against the wheels and stop them from turning.

When the brakes press against the wheels, they cause *friction*. When two surfaces rub against each other, you get friction. You can feel friction. Quickly rub the palms of your hands together, back and forth. Keep rubbing and what do you feel? Heat! This heat is produced by the friction caused when the surfaces of your hands rubbed against each other.

Sometimes friction can be a good thing, such as when you use your brakes to stop a bike, or when you rub an eraser on paper to take away a mistake. But sometimes you don't want friction. For example, have you ever started riding a bike and heard a squeaking sound? That squeaking can happen when there's too much friction. What do you do then? You can put a few drops of oil between the wheel and axle. The oil is slippery and slidy. The oil *lubricates* the surfaces: it cuts down the friction between them.

You can feel how lubrication works. First, rub your hands together. Now, put a few drops of liquid soap or vegetable oil in your hands, then rub them together again. Do you feel how the soap or oil lubricated your hands and cut down the friction between them?

Pulleys

With wheels and ropes you can make another simple machine called a *pulley*. The name, pulley, says what it helps you do—pull. If you've ever pulled on a cord to raise some blinds on a window, then you've used a pulley. When you pulled the cord down, the blind went up—that's because a pulley changes the direction of a pull.

If there is a flagpole at your school, take a close look at it: does it use pulleys to help you raise and lower the flag?

A pulley helps you lift.

With pulleys, you can lift some very heavy things. Pulleys work for us every day. Tow trucks use pulleys when they lift cars. Cranes use pulleys to lift huge beams to build a city's skyscrapers. Elevators use pulleys to lift people up and down.

Inclined Planes

Imagine you're pulling a heavy load in a wagon—maybe your brother or sister, or a pile of rocks you've collected. You come to a curb, and you can see that it's going to be hard to pull your loaded wagon up that curb. How can you get the wagon easily up the curb? Luckily, you see two boards nearby. You place them so that your wagon can roll right up the boards and over the curb. There, that was easy!

When you used those boards, you made a simple machine called an *inclined plane*. "Inclined" means slanted or leaning. A plane is a flat surface. When you pulled your wagon up the boards, the boards helped spread out the work of lifting the loaded wagon.

People in wheelchairs also use inclined planes—ramps. Ramps make it possible for people in wheelchairs to get in and out of buildings, and to roll smoothly on or off a sidewalk. Look for these inclined planes at the buildings in your town.

Wedges

Have you ever used a V-shaped simple machine called a *wedge* [wej]? You can use a wedge to hold something tight. If you slide a wedge under a door, it will hold the door tightly in place.

A wedge can also be used to split things apart. To split a log, you can use a wedge made of metal. You hammer the wedge into the end of the log until the log splits apart.

Take a look at the picture: as you hammer the wedge in from the top, it splits apart the wood from side to side.

This wedge holds the door in place.

This wedge helps split the log.

What's the name of the tool that has a sharp metal wedge attached to a handle? It's an ax, or a hatchet. Thousands of years ago, people made hatchets with sticks for handles and stones for blades. Today, we make the blades out of steel. Whether it's an ancient hatchet made of stone or a brand-new ax made of steel, the basic tool is the same: a wedge on a handle.

Father, I cannot tell a lie. I chopped it down with my little wedge on a handle.

Screws

The last simple machine we're going to learn about is the *screw*. Take a look at the kind of screw you can use to hold pieces of wood together. Do you see the slanted ridges going up and down it? Those ridges, which are called the "threads," are really one long inclined plane.

To see how a screw is an inclined plane, try this. On a sheet of paper, draw a triangle like the one below. Make the bottom about six inches long, and the short side about three inches high. Use a colored pencil or marker to draw the long slanted side.

You have drawn an inclined plane. Now, cut it out and wrap it around a pencil. Do you see how the colored line you drew looks like the threads of a screw? This shows how an inclined plane curves up and up on a screw.

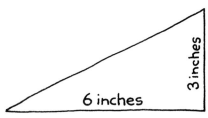

6 inches · 3 inches

A wood screw.

This big earth auger works as a screw. You can use it to dig holes in the ground. As you twist it down into the earth, it pulls dirt up and makes a hole.

Stories About Scientists

Anton van Leeuwenhoek

Anton van Leeuwenhoek.

Cells, bacteria, plankton—these are just a few of the things that you learn about in science but that you can't see. Even though we can't see these things, we know they exist. Why? Because scientists have seen them—not with their eyes alone, but through a microscope.

Have you ever looked through a microscope? If you haven't, maybe you've looked through a magnifying glass. Most microscopes use specially made pieces of glass, called lenses, to magnify things. Do you know what it mean to "magnify"? It means to make something appear bigger.

One of the first people to explore the world of tiny things we can't see with our eyes alone was Anton van Leeuwenhoek [LAY-wun-hook]. He was born in Holland in 1632. (Can you find Holland, in Europe, on a map or globe? It's also called The Netherlands.) He made his living as a merchant, buying and selling cloth. He was a curious and inventive man. He made his own magnifying lenses and looked through them just to see what he could find.

He put a drop of dirty lake water under a lens. What do you think he saw? He saw a bunch of tiny, squirming, squiggly shapes. There were living creatures in the water! He scraped some brown stain from his own teeth and put it under a lens, and he saw more squirmy, squiggling shapes. There were tiny creatures living in his own mouth!

Leeuwenhoek called these little creatures "animalcules." Scientists today would call them microorganisms. ("Micro" means small, and an organism is a living thing, so a microorganism is a small living thing—not small like a bug or kitten, but *really* small, too small to see with your eyes alone.)

Leeuwenhoek built more and more microscopes—more than two hundred of them. Word got around about the amazing things you could see through the microscope. Even the queen of England and the czar of Russia came to look through his lenses.

Here's a poem about Leeuwenhoek and his microscopes.

"The Microscope"
by Maxine Kumin

Anton Leeuwenhoek was Dutch.
He sold pincushions, cloth, and such.
The waiting townsfolk fumed and fussed,
as Anton's dry goods gathered dust.
He worked, instead of tending store,
at grinding special lenses for
a microscope.

Some of the things he looked at were:
mosquitoes' wings, the hairs of sheep, the legs of lice,
the skin of people, dogs, and mice;
ox eyes, spiders' spinning gear,
fishes' scales, a little smear
of his own blood,
and best of all,
the unknown, busy, very small
bugs that swim and bump and hop
inside a simple water drop.

Impossible! most Dutchmen said.
This Anton's crazy in the head.
He says he's seen a horsefly's brain.
We ought to ship him off to Spain.
He says the water that we drink
is full of bugs. He's mad, we think!
They called him domkop, which means dope.

That's how we got the microscope.

Florence Nightingale

Florence Nightingale.

Florence Nightingale was born in 1820 into a wealthy English family. So it was clear what she was expected to do when she grew up. She should marry a rich gentleman and raise a wealthy English family.

But Florence had different plans. She loved to use her mind. She was fascinated by mathematics. When a young man asked her to marry him, she thought long and hard, and then said no. She believed that she was destined to lead another sort of life.

When she told her family that she wanted to work as a nurse in a hospital, they were shocked. In those days, hospitals were dirty, dreary places. Wealthy people paid doctors to come to their homes to take care of anyone who got sick. Only people with little money stayed in hospitals. And that often made things worse, since most hospitals were so filthy that diseases spread faster there than anywhere else.

But Florence Nightingale understood that hospitals could, and should, be kept clean. She had visited a hospital in Germany where women took excellent care of patients. The place was clean and people often got well there. She decided to devote her life to improving medical care in England.

In 1854, England entered into war in a part of Asia called the Crimea (which is now part of the country called Ukraine). The English government asked Florence Nightingale to go with forty other nurses and run the hospital for British soldiers. She found the hospital dirty and full of disease, and the soldiers cold, starving, and badly wounded.

Florence Nightingale worked as hard as she could to keep British soldiers from dying. She was called "the lady with the lamp," because she worked through the night, carrying a lamp to light her way. She became famous around the world for the good work she was doing.

After the war, Florence Nightingale wrote many reports with careful facts and figures to show that fewer people would die if hospitals were cleaner. The hospitals began to do what she said they should. She also helped start a nursing school in London. She spoke out for the poor, saying that they deserved good, clean medical care. Thanks to her work and ideas, nursing is a respected profession today.

Daniel Hale Williams

When Daniel Hale Williams was born in 1856, some African Americans still worked as slaves. His father and mother had never been slaves, though. They lived in their own big family house in Pennsylvania, where Daniel's father ran a barbershop. Daniel loved to sit and watch his father trim men's hair and shave their beards. His customers were black, and they talked about the day when the slaves would be free and when black and white people might live equally together.

Daniel's father died when the boy was only eleven. But in those days, that wasn't too young to start learning a job. So, by himself, Daniel went to Baltimore and learned shoemaking. As he drew the needle through tough shoe leather, he longed for home, and for work more like his father's. Finally he went back home to Pennsylvania, and he did find work in barbershops.

Daniel Hale Williams.

Daniel wanted to go to school. He read every book he could get his hands on. He saved his money and paid his way through private school. He graduated from high school at the age of twenty-one. He still wanted to learn more. He convinced the town doctor to hire him as an assistant, and started reading medical books to learn even more. Two years later, he entered Chicago Medical College, and in three years he received his M.D. degree. That meant he was a real doctor, and now he could practice medicine.

As far as Dr. Williams was concerned, it did not matter whether his patients were black or white. But for some people then, it still mattered. Like other black doctors, he was not allowed to work in a hospital. He served as a doctor at an orphanage and as a surgeon for the railway company. He taught medicine at the college he had attended. He got upset when he saw that black patients did not receive the same medical care as whites, and when he saw that the smart young African American women could not study to be nurses, just because of the color of their skin. To right these wrongs, he built Provident Hospital in Chicago in 1891, the first hospital in the United States where black and white nurses and doctors cared for black and white patients, all together.

Provident Hospital was an important achievement, but one operation made Daniel Hale Williams famous in medical history. In 1893, Dr. Williams examined a man who had been stabbed in the chest with a knife. He could not see what was wrong inside the man, since there were no X-ray machines back then to let doctors look inside patients. All he could do, he thought, was open the wound and look right into the man's chest. Yes, it was dangerous, but unless he took the chance, the man might die. Six other doctors watched and assisted as Dr. Williams opened the man's chest, then opened it even more. Dr. Williams found the problem: he repaired a torn blood vessel, and then stitched the tissue around the man's heart. "SEWED UP HIS HEART!" read newspaper headlines around the world. Dr. Williams had successfully performed the world's first heart surgery.

Daniel Hale Williams was brave enough to try new surgical techniques, and careful enough that he succeeded in them. And he never stopped believing that everyone deserved quality health care and education.

Elijah McCoy

Have you ever heard someone say, "That's the real McCoy"? It's a phrase that means, "That's the real thing, the genuine item." Some people say that the phrase got started thanks to the work of a man who designed machines over one hundred years ago.

Elijah McCoy was born in Canada in 1844. His parents were black Americans who had escaped a life of slavery. Remember Harriet Tubman, who helped organize the Underground Railroad as a way for slaves to escape? Elijah McCoy's parents were among the people who made their way to freedom on the Underground Railroad. Soon after Elijah was born, his parents felt safe enough to return to a farm in Michigan.

As a boy, young Elijah was fascinated by engines. His parents sent him to Scotland at the age of fifteen to study how engines operated. When he returned to the United States, he knew a lot about mechanics and engineering. He looked for a job to apply his skills. But in those days, many people held the mistaken belief that a black man couldn't understand much about engines. So, when a train company in Michigan hired Elijah McCoy, it gave him the job of shoveling coal into the train's engines and oiling the machinery.

Elijah McCoy.

In the 1860s, locomotives ran by steam power. Big furnaces burned wood or coal to heat water into steam. The pressure of hot steam pushed on iron rods and got gears moving. All that hot metal moving together caused a great deal of friction. Men had to stop the trains often and climb all over the huge locomotives to oil them. But all this stopping slowed down the trains.

The problem got Elijah McCoy thinking. Maybe, he thought, someone could design a machine that would squirt oil into the locomotive's moving parts even while the train kept moving. Maybe, he thought, I'll just do it myself!

After two years of experiments, Elijah McCoy did it. He perfected his first automatic lubricator. In only a few years, most locomotives, factory machines, and steam-powered ships in the United States and Europe were using McCoy's automatic lubricators. Often Elijah McCoy himself would install the lubricator and explain to engineers how to use it. As the years passed, when people took a close look at a machine and its parts, they began to ask, "Is it the real McCoy?" They wanted to make sure that the machinery included automatic lubricators designed by Elijah McCoy, because they wanted their machines to run smoothly.

Elijah McCoy started the McCoy Manufacturing Company and invented over fifty new devices and machines. He was well known in his home of Detroit, Michigan, not only for his inventions but also for encouraging young people to apply their energy and imagination. "If you do this," he would tell them, "you can accomplish anything." Remember his advice—it's the real McCoy!

Illustration and Photo Credits

Henri Rousseau, *Forest Landscape with Setting Sun*. 1910. 114 cm × 162.5 cm. Oil on canvas. Used with permission from Oeffentliche Kunstsammlung Basel, Kunstmuseum. Photograph from Oeffentliche Kunstsammlung Basel, Martin Bühler: 191(b)

Schomburg Center for Research in Black Culture, The New York Public Library: 337, 339

Steele Savage, illustrations from *Mythology* by Edith Hamilton. Copyright © 1942 by Edith Hamilton; © renewed 1969 by Dorian Fielding Reid and Doris Fielding Reid. By permission of Little, Brown and Company: 56, 63, 64

Nic Siler: 167(a), 327(a)

Jeanne Nicholson Siler: 329(c)

Smith College, suffrage parade along Fifth Avenue, New York City, May 6, 1912. Photo by the Pictorial News Co., 138 West 42nd Street, New York, NY. From the Sophia Smith Collection, used with permission: 170

The Smithsonian Institution, National Numismatic Collection: 129(a)

Southwest Strings, Tucson, Arizona. Photo of Peter and Michael Ronstadt, and Evelyn Craft, used with permission: 212(a)

James T. Taylor, *Major Stephen D. Ramseur and Battle of Cedar Creek*, from the James T. Taylor sketchbook, used with permission of The Western Reserve Historical Society, Cleveland, Ohio: 162

Jerome Tiger, *The Endless Trail*. 1966. Detail reprinted with permission of The Philbrook Museum of Art, Tulsa, Oklahoma: 154(a)

Thomas Jefferson Memorial Foundation, Inc. Photograph by R. Lautman/Monticello: 199(a)

Audrey Topping: 107

United States Department of Justice, Immigration and Naturalization Service, 1996. Photo by Bert Goulait: 168

United States Department of the Navy: 134

University of Virginia School of Medicine: 317(c)

Vincent van Gogh, *The Starry Night*. Oil on canvas. Used with permission from The Museum of Modern Art, New York. Acquired through the Lillie P. Bliss Bequest. Photograph © 1997 The Museum of Modern Art, New York: 192

The *Washington Post*, photo copyright © 1963. Reprinted with permission: 174

White House Collection, photo copyright the White House Historical Association. 136

Garth Williams. From "Before Breakfast," Chapter One of *Charlotte's Web*, by E. B. White. Copyright © 1952 by E. B. White. Illustrations copyright © renewed 1980 by Garth Williams. Selections reprinted by permission of HarperCollins Publishers: 33, 35

Frank Lloyd Wright, interior and exterior of the Solomon R. Guggenheim Museum, New York. Photograph by David Heald © The Solomon R. Guggenheim Foundation, New York: 201(a,b)

While every care has been taken to trace and acknowledge copyright, the editors tender their apologies for any accidental infringement where copyright has proved untraceable. They would be pleased to insert the appropriate acknowledgment in any subsequent edition of this publication

Text Credits and Sources

POEMS

"Buffalo Dusk," from *Smoke and Steel* by Carl Sandburg. Copyright 1920 by Harcourt Brace & Company. Copyright renewed 1948 by Carl Sandburg. Reprinted by permission of the publisher.

"Caterpillars," by Aileen Fisher. Reprinted by the permission the author.

"Discovery," from *Crickets and Bullfrogs and Whispers of Thunder* by Harry Behn. Edited by Lee Bennett Hopkins. Copyright 1949, 1953. Copyright © renewed 1956, 1957, 1966, 1968, by Harry Behn. Copyright © renewed 1977, 1981 by Alice Behn Goebel, Pamela Behn Adam, Prescott Behn, and Peter Behn. Reprinted by permission.

STORIES AND MYTHS

Index

ABOUT THE AUTHOR

E. D. Hirsch, Jr., is a professor at the University of Virginia and the author of *The Schools We Need* and the bestselling *Cultural Literacy* and *The Dictionary of Cultural Literacy*. He and his wife, Polly, live in Charlottesville, Virginia, where they raised their three children.

"The best year of teaching I ever had. This year has
been so much fun: fun to learn, fun to teach."
Joanne Anderson, Teacher,
Three Oaks Elementary School
Fort Myers, Florida

Collect the entire Core Knowledge series

ISBN	TITLE	PRICE
48117-9	What Your Kindergartner Needs to Know	$24.95/34.95 Can
48119-5	What Your First Grader Needs to Know (Revised Edition)	$24.95/34.95 Can
41116-2	What Your Second Grader Needs to Know (Revised Edition)	$24.95/34.95 Can
41117-0	What Your Third Grader Needs to Know	$22.50/28.50 Can
41118-9	What Your Fourth Grader Needs to Know	$22.50/28.00 Can
41119-7	What Your Fifth Grader Needs to Know	$22.50/28.00 Can
41120-0	What Your Sixth Grader Needs to Know	$22.50/28.00 Can

READERS:

The titles listed above are available in your local bookstore. If you are interested in mail ordering any of the Core Knowledge books listed above, please send a check or money order only to the address below (no C.O.D.s or cash) and indicate the title and ISBN book number with your order. Make check payable to Doubleday Consumer Services (include $2.50 for postage and handling). Allow 4–6 weeks for delivery. Prices and availability subject to change without notice.

Please mail your order and check to:

Doubleday Consumer Services, Dept. CK
2451 South Wolf Road
Des Plaines, IL 60018

SCHOOL DISCOUNTS FOR BULK ORDERS:

For bulk orders of quantities of 100 or more books in the Core Knowledge Series (*What Your Kindergartner–Sixth Grader Needs to Know*), schools receive a discount on orders placed through the Core Knowledge Foundation. Call 1-800-238-3233 for information or to place an order.

FOR MORE INFORMATION ABOUT CORE KNOWLEDGE:

Call the Core Knowledge Foundation at 1-800-238-3233.